An Odd Cross to Bear

LIBRARY OF RELIGIOUS BIOGRAPHY

Mark A. Noll, Kathryn Gin Lum, and Heath W. Carter, series editors

Long overlooked by historians, religion has emerged in recent years as a key factor in understanding the past. From politics to popular culture, from social struggles to the rhythms of family life, religion shapes every story. Religious biographies open a window to the sometimes surprising influence of religion on the lives of influential people and the worlds they inhabited.

The Library of Religious Biography is a series that brings to life important figures in United States history and beyond. Grounded in careful research, these volumes link the lives of their subjects to the broader cultural contexts and religious issues that surrounded them. The authors are respected historians and recognized authorities in the historical period in which their subject lived and worked.

Marked by careful scholarship yet free of academic jargon, the books in this series are well-written narratives meant to be read and enjoyed as well as studied.

Titles include:

*One Soul at a Time: The Story of **Billy Graham***
by Grant Wacker

*The Miracle Lady: **Katherine Kuhlman** and the Transformation
of Charismatic Christianity*
by Amy Collier Artman

***Aimee Semple McPherson**: Everybody's Sister*
by Edith L. Blumhofer

*Mother of Modern Evangelicalism: The Life and Legacy of **Henrietta Mears***
by Arlin Migliazzo

Harriet Beecher Stowe: A Spiritual Life
by Nancy Koester

For a complete list of published volumes, see the back of this volume.

An Odd Cross to Bear

A Biography of Ruth Bell Graham

—◇—

Anne Blue Wills

WILLIAM B. EERDMANS PUBLISHING COMPANY
GRAND RAPIDS, MICHIGAN

Wm. B. Eerdmans Publishing Co.
4035 Park East Court SE, Grand Rapids, Michigan 49546
www.eerdmans.com

28 27 26 25 24 23 22   1 2 3 4 5 6 7

ISBN 978-0-8028-7581-5

Library of Congress Cataloging-in-Publication Data

A catalog record for this book is available from the Library of Congress.
Excerpts from works by Ruth Bell Graham, copyright The Ruth Bell Graham
    Literary Trust, are used by permission.
Excerpts taken from *Footprints of a Pilgrim: A Journey of Love* by Ruth Bell
    Graham, copyright 2001 by Ruth Bell Graham, are used by permission of
    HarperCollins Christian Publishing. www.harpercollinschristian.com.

Dedicated to the memory of

William Alonzo Blue
(1923–2004)
who introduced me to Montreat

and

Frances Golden Blue
(1926–2020)
my best and favorite reader

My wife Ruth was the person to whom I would go for spiritual guidance. She was the only one in whom I completely confided. She was a great student of the Word of God. Her life was ruled by the Bible more than any individual I have ever known. When it comes to spiritual things, my wife has had the greatest influence on my ministry — she was the greatest Christian I ever knew.

— Billy Graham in 2007

There will be narratives of female lives
only when women no longer live their lives
isolated in the houses and the stories of men.

— Carolyn Heilbrun,
Writing a Woman's Life (1988)

But that's what life offered me in the way of being a woman and I took it.

— Rose Maxson,
in *Fences*, by August Wilson (1985)

Contents

◇

CONTENTS

Acknowledgments

—◇—

I have taken more than ten years to complete this project. The word "acknowledgment," therefore, seems too slight to describe my deep gratitude to the many generous people and institutions who supported my work. Many caring folks who asked (with increasing trepidation) about "the book" may have given up hope for its publication. Well, here we are. I have learned a lot about Ruth Bell Graham and her world, but I have also learned a lot about how I need to work, how to lean on colleagues and friends for help, and how writing is not a magical process (except when it is). Having finally learned the habit of being at my desk to write every day, no excuses, I may finish the next book in "only" five years.

I am grateful every day to Grant Wacker for getting me into this subject in the first place — not only the topic of Ruth Bell Graham but the field of US religious history. With his spouse, Katherine, Grant has created and shepherded a generation of scholars in the field. I am honored to be a part of this intellectual tribe, which has shaped my career and enriched my life.

Grant's work on Billy Graham brought me into the ambit of others who have made an impact on my research. In gatherings small and large, at Wheaton College in Illinois, in Maine, Vermont, and Montreat, and in countless emails back and forth over the years, the guidance, questions, and collegiality of Edith and Edwin Blumhofer, Andrew and Ingrid Finstuen, and Larry Eskridge kept me going during various stages. Edith applied for and won the funding from the Lilly Endowment Inc. that underwrote the Worlds of Billy Graham project at Wheaton's Institute for the Study of American Evangelicals. This book represents only one outcome of the endowment's generosity. I deeply regret that Edith died before I finished writing it. She gave me critical guidance at the beginning and all along the way. She continues to inspire me by her example of clear-eyed, creative persistence.

Other colleagues in American religion have offered indispensable help, reading drafts, suggesting fruitful research avenues, giving feedback and encouragement. Thanks to Uta Balbier, Peggy Bendroth, Kate Bowler, James Bratt, Elesha Coffman, Curtis Evans, Tommy Kidd, Jennifer Woodruff Tait, and all of the participants in the colloquia that resulted in the collection of original scholarship on Graham that Andrew Finstuen, Grant Wacker, and I coedited, *Billy Graham: American Pilgrim*, published by Oxford University Press in 2017.

At the beginning of my research, I received a series of Faculty Study & Research grants from Davidson College, which allowed me to hire several excellent student researchers. I am deeply grateful to Julia Capalino, Amy Colombo, Katie Kalivoda, and Laura Spencer, who helped establish the character of Ruth's childhood in China, pored through piles of photocopied news clippings, examined Ruth's poetry, and helped me figure out how to approach the task of telling Ruth's story. At a crucial point, Davidson sponsored my participation in the National Center for Faculty Development and Diversity's Faculty Success Program. My coaching cohort — Lara Deruisseau, Grace Kao, and Urmimala Sarkar — were godsends of support and accountability.

Over the decade of my work on this topic, opportunities to talk and teach about Ruth have shaped my approach to telling her life story. Audiences at Wheaton College filled in bare spots, expressed excitement about my attention to clergy wives, and generally welcomed a fresh look at Ruth. I am also grateful to Ronald Vinson at the Presbyterian Heritage Center in Montreat, North Carolina; Elesha Coffman and Tommy Kidd at the Baylor University Institute for Studies of Religion; and Martin Dotterweich and Whit and Maria Whitaker at King University, Bristol, Tennessee. At a critical moment in my writing, filmmaker Sarah Colt, director of the PBS American Experience film *Billy Graham*, asked excellent questions about Ruth's contributions to Billy's work. Teacher, mentor, and colleague Tony Abbott invited me several times to present my research to the Covenant Class Sunday school at Davidson College Presbyterian Church. The class, which he founded and convened, is one of the best audiences around. Tony died in 2020, but I remain grateful for him and his spouse, Susan, for their encouragement and advice.

Davidson College and the town that it gave rise to are rich settings in which to do knowledge work. I owe debts of gratitude to those whose personal experiences or professional expertise proved essential. Early on, Lacy Dick and Bill Strong shared personal stories and helped me make connections to Presbyterian missionaries from the Bells' era. Fuji Lozada and Shelley Rigger gave their translations of Chinese characters and terms. Several cohorts of students who took my course "Women in American Religion" listened to me try to explain why Ruth was both interesting and important. Among these students, Caroline Brooks, now a friend, read and commented on this project at several stages along the way, never wavering in her enthusiasm. Jay Pfeifer was always eager to get the word out about my work on Ruth. The amazing staff of Davidson College's E. H. Little Library — especially Cara Evanson, Joe Gutekanst, and Jayme Sponsel — located many of the resources that fleshed out this story. As the project neared completion, colleagues Alison Bory, Dave Robb, and Yurika Tamura provided daily writing solidarity.

Many other wise hands contributed vital assistance: my brother Bill Blue, an architect steeped in the history of design, gathered sources and mused with me about the significance of Ruth's log cabin; Robert Shuster, archivist at the Wheaton College Billy Graham Center Archives, directed me to the richest lodes of the collection on Ruth and Billy. David Bruce, Billy Graham's executive assistant, answered every phone call and email with kindness, encouragement, and a determination to help. George Marsden offered suggestions and encouragement. Heath Carter and Mark Noll gave energetic, deeply thoughtful comments on the full draft, improving it in every way. David Bratt has never flagged in his support of this project, even though my dilatory pace gave him every reason to. Tom Raabe read the manuscript with care, adding his polish. Jenny Hoffman at Eerdmans expertly saw the project through to publication.

Of course, my family — Trey, Maisie, and Al — have become experts at balancing their interest in this story with their impatience at my progress in writing it down. They are the best people I know. I love them and am grateful for their presence in my life. I dedicate this book to my parents, who shared with Ruth's generation of Southern Presbyterians connections to a landscape, commitments to the church, and love of the written word.

Introduction

What Language Shall I Borrow?

—◇—

Over the past decade of my work on Ruth Bell Graham, I have met with two distinct reactions: puzzled stares or platitudes. On the one hand, some have asked, "Why would you write about *her*?" What could there possibly be to say? Was she not just his wife? On the other hand, others — sometimes friends or relatives of the Grahams — have declared confidently, "Billy could not have been 'Billy' without Ruth," but explain by citing her care for their five children or her sense of humor.

This book attempts to take on these distinct reactions — the dismissive and the reverent. In contrast to the women I often teach my students about — Harriet Beecher Stowe or Ida B. Wells, Pauli Murray or Tammy Faye Bakker — Ruth did not go in for public campaigns. She did not promote desegregation or women's suffrage, women's ordination or gay liberation, or, for that matter, any other movement for social justice that transformed the twentieth century. She lived as a pretty ordinary white woman in the South, focused on the personal work of staying rooted in the study of Scripture, love of neighbor, and care for family. In some sense — and Ruth would have likely agreed — there really is not that much to say about her.

Yet she was hardly ordinary.

Born in China to American medical missionaries for the Southern Presbyterian Church, Ruth spent the first decade-plus of her life on a compound that housed a first-rate hospital and the community of Americans who worked there. At the end of her life, she still claimed China as her true home. Indeed, she never stopped talking about her girlhood ambition to be a solitary missionary to Tibet, even as she later looked back to dismiss such a dream as doomed from the start. Ruth devoted herself to learning everything she could about the Bible, majoring in the subject at Wheaton College and continuing to read broadly in the classics of the Protestant evangelical tradition. With missionary poet Amy Carmichael as a role model, she wrote hundreds of poems and eventually published most of them in several collections. She planted her family in Montreat, North Carolina, overseeing the construction of a log home built from and furnished with salvaged materials. She presided over a family that included five children, a shifting cast of animal companions, and a stalwart group of household support staff that did everything from cooking and child care to driving and taking dictation.

Perhaps it was less what Ruth did than the public horizon on which she did it. Being married in the postwar years put her in the position of millions of other white Protestant women — establishing and keeping a home, supporting a husband's career, rearing children who could be, like all children, at turns angelic and infernal. At Wheaton, though, she fell in love with and chose to marry a young man who became the most significant Christian evangelist of the twentieth century. Being married to Bill, as she always called him, put her in a unique position that supercharged her responsibilities and her visibility.

Nevertheless, my focus stays on Ruth. I aim to tell her story, not Billy's, and not hers through Billy. We can observe her in a variety of contexts. If viewed as a midcentury white married woman, Ruth Graham was entirely typical. If viewed as Billy Graham's wife, she emerges as something like a "political wife" or the less frequently explored but no less significant "clergy wife." If we hew closely to her individual path, what made her distinctive rises to the surface.

Human beings bear the marks, for good and ill, of their times and their ties, even when those ties are tested. Billy Graham was not Ruth's only influence, her only tie. The story I tell begins prior to her encounter with him: her family of origin, their work, and their feelings about her; the interests, ambitions, and fears of girlhood and adolescence; war years spent in college, testing out relationships and vocational paths; midcentury US marriage, child rearing, and homemaking; antifeminist evangelical womanhood and conservative US politics; and the vicissitudes of dynastic succession, especially when the dynasty that had been governed by genteel complementarianism lands in the hands of reactionary patriarchy.

I have tried to resist the temptation to remake Ruth Graham in my own image. While I am a feminist, Ruth did not identify herself as one. Indeed, she rejected and recast the midcentury notion of "women's liberation," insisting that her liberation grew from God's promises, fulfilled through Jesus. Nevertheless, Ruth's life calls for a telling that brings her out of "the houses and stories of men," to echo Carolyn Heilbrun. The tools of feminist biography offer some direction on how to tell her story, although at a certain point those tools lose their usefulness. Ruth's conventionality — her Christian faith, her commitment to domestic-focused wifehood and motherhood, her acknowledgment (even in the breach) of her husband's priority in work and home decisions — does not obliterate my interest in her as a biographical subject.

And yet, how to capture that interest, that complexity, when Ruth is known primarily — if at all — through her husband? Biographies (and fictional narratives) of women that are not shaped by feminist sensibilities have followed what Linda Wagner-Martin dubs the "marriage plot" to a happy ending, wherein the heroine finds an enduring marriage, children and motherhood, and domestic security, all of which mark the end (not necessarily chronologically but teleologically) of her story. Indeed, after Ruth married Bill in 1943, her life largely followed a conventional path through the terrain of homemaking, supporting her husband's two-person career,

3

and childbearing, child rearing, and child launching from the mid-1940s through the early 1970s. What else is there to tell?

—◇—

The British biographer Victoria Glendinning has asked, "Is the story of your life what happens to you, or what you feel happens to you, or what observers see happening to you?" The first option — telling a life story by telling a life's events — constitutes one somewhat accessible part of Ruth's story, thanks to exhaustive documentation of Billy's movements in records kept by his organization and the narration of his life in many biographies and his own autobiography. Some of the Graham children have contributed their own accounts of Ruth, as have numerous admiring friends (including crime novelist Patricia Cornwell, whose first book, a biography of Ruth, came out in 1983). The third option Glendinning posits may be the most easily available part of Ruth's story, but the least satisfying for those of us who want to understand her life beyond the glare of Billy Graham's fame. The realities of obtaining access to source material have required me to rely heavily on those observers' accounts.

The trickiest part of Ruth's story to discern — and the part that interests me most — is Glendinning's middle option: How did Ruth feel about her own life? She recorded private impressions in letters and diaries her whole life long. I had access to a very few childhood letters stored with Nelson Bell's papers at Wheaton College, and will be quoting them, and Nelson's as well, as they were written, with misspellings intact. Sadly, since Ruth's death in 2007, the two thousand pages of her letters and journals have not been available to researchers; Ruth herself gave Cornwell, her longtime friend, access. Consequently, I have used Ruth's published work — poems and recollections — in addition to accounts of "what others saw happening to her" as sources for this story. Biographers never have total access to a subject. I have tried to be accountable to my sources, and to use them in fashioning a portrait of Ruth Graham that she would recognize.

—◇—

In addition to the interest intrinsic to Ruth's distinctive story, her experiences also shed light on the lives of twentieth-century women married to male clergy. Kate Bowler's recent excellent book, *The Pastor's Wife*, provides an important update to this thread of the US religious historical narrative. Since the 1980s, memoirs and chipper advice books to ministers' wives have abounded. Bowler brings a fresh scholarly eye to this territory but attends primarily to flashier copastoring wives, a position that Ruth eschewed. Ruth's own sorely needed, mordant addition to the clergy-wife advice genre, never published, was reportedly titled *How to Marry a Preacher and Remain a Christian*. What challenges did such a title aim to grapple honestly with? The historian's impulse to measure clergymen's wives against the standards of second-wave feminism has largely limited the narrative possibilities for those women. Ruth's life invites us to revise those standards, even though her experience as the wife of an evangelist differed somewhat from that of a woman married to a man in congregational ministry. Her depiction in news stories revealed that she was held to the same standards as her contemporaries who were ministers' wives. If Billy Graham was "America's Pastor," then Ruth was responsible to the whole country for upholding its expectations that she be attractive, smart, penny-wise, tactful, modest, and uncomplainingly hospitable.

In the mid-1970s, sociologists Mary Taylor and Shirley Foster Hartley declared ordained ministry the "classic example" of a two-person career. In doing so, they set congregational ministry alongside men's careers in academia, the military, and as executives in large corporations. Women married to such men made critical (that is, nonoptional) contributions to their husbands' success. For clergymen's wives, a vast advice literature existed, stretching back to the late eighteenth century. Advice manuals and women's own accounts indicate that the expectations for women married to clergymen had changed very little over two centuries, from the time of Sarah Edwards to Catherine Marshall's day. Indeed, Ruth herself penned a brief foreword for such a book in 1957. Lora Lee Parrott's book *How to Be a Preacher's Wife and Like It* acknowledged the extreme demands made of clergymen's wives. While the tasks for clergy husband and wife differed, the seriousness of the flock's expectations did not.

Between Parrott's advice in 1957 and Taylor and Foster Hartley's study roughly twenty years later, many women in the United States experienced major shifts in their own self-understandings and in the opportunities open to them. One finding the sociologists documented was that clergymen's wives with more education found time both to work outside the home and to keep up with the traditional expectations of their husbands' congregations. Ruth bucked this trend, and in so doing followed the example of the prior generation. This pattern — hewing to the mores of her parents' generation — characterized Ruth throughout her life. She was not a reactionary, but she was a conservative.

Elsewhere, I have called the clergy-wife role an "unofficially official" one. Taylor and Foster Hartley called the work a minister's wife performed "informally required" and characterized her accomplishments in such an arrangement as vicarious. Her success happened through her husband's. Assisting in the tasks of "status maintenance, intellectual contributions, and public performances," a clergyman's wife who "fail[ed] to participate in the expected manner . . . jeopardize[d] the career." Yet these wives received neither payment nor regular public recognition. For a clergyman's wife to request, much less demand, remuneration or recognition would run contrary to the understanding (on her and her husband's part, as well as on the congregation's) of church service as a higher calling from God, its own reward if performed faithfully.

The press (including the religious press) presented Billy Graham's work and family life according to this historic clergy-family pattern. He appeared as clergyman-*pater*, guide of an ever-expanding flock and the protector of hearth, supported by his godly helpmeet. Ruth never rejected that role. Indeed, she committed herself to it as a very young woman and lived it out through more than sixty years of marriage. But she did so in her own way. Hers is not a story of "liberation," at least as second-wave feminism used the word. On a 1979 broadcast of the *Phil Donahue Show*, she announced that she was "liberated from having to earn a living" so that she could devote her time to her family and home. Yet she also described her life in private as "an odd kind of cross to bear." The lack of public recognition that went with the clergy-wife role did not chafe Ruth. Her "odd cross" required her adjustment (a favorite word) and fierce allegiance to Bill's call to preach the gospel. She loved him and she loved the Lord who called him. Her life thrust her into circumstances that she would not have chosen for herself. That she recognized that fact betokened an independent, discerning vision. This book aims to track that vision through the almost nine decades of Ruth Bell Graham's life.

—◇—

If we again expand our attention and look beyond Ruth's role as a clergyman's wife, we can see in her story new angles of white Christian womanhood. Historians Phyllis Mack and Quincy Newell have written instructively about religious women (eighteenth-century Quakers and nineteenth-century Mormons, respectively) who submitted to what Mack described as "the dominant male order" yet did so not as benighted automatons but rather as people with their own coherent views about life, work, agency, faith, and justice. Ruth rejected second-wave feminism as she understood it but did so even as she became a more public figure. Still, she did not campaign publicly for "traditional values" as Anita Bryant or Beverly LaHaye did. Emily Suzanne Johnson has written about such "women's leadership in the New Christian Right." But this work was not for Ruth. Like so many women of her era, Ruth occupied a space apart from the fiery public arguments for and against women's rights. Occasionally, she expressed her disapproval of the movement and other social protests. Ruth more consistently pursued a politics of personal servanthood that reflected both the gender conventions and Christian vocation of an earlier day. Evangelical Christian feminists like Letha Scanzoni and Nancy Hardesty worried that many women's understanding of "Christian vocation" was captive to patriarchy and therefore a distortion of Christ's message. But Ruth, like many white women of her generation, understood Christian womanhood as mostly quiet, private work — and work of their own choosing and design.

In telling Ruth's story, I want to join historian Marie Griffith in insisting that "surely there is adequate space within a feminist agenda for careful, empathic reconsideration of what might actually be at stake for those women who, for religious reasons and perhaps other reasons, as well, persistently repudiate what they take to be established feminism."

Ruth devised her own ethic of Christian womanhood, characterized by "adjusting" to Bill. In so doing, she helped bring his preaching to the world. She also lived richly, thought deeply, and left a legacy distinctively her own. This book represents my attempt to make "adequate space" for Ruth Bell Graham as a woman worth knowing.

Chapter 1

Missionary Daughter

—◇—

1920–1937

At the end of June 1916, in Waynesboro, Virginia, a newly minted surgeon named Lemuel Nelson Bell married Virginia Leftwich, a registered nurse. The wedding ceremony marked the culmination of their years-long engagement after having grown up together in this Shenandoah Valley town. Nelson had considered entering the mission field under aegis of the Presbyterian Church US (the Southern Presbyterians) but opted for a career in law since he did not feel a call to ordained ministry; Virginia, who grew up Baptist, also had missionary aspirations but let that dream fade after their engagement. He captained the championship high school baseball team and continued to play in college; Virginia played organ and piano at the First Baptist Church and served as the first librarian of the town's Carnegie Library. Through the intervention of a classmate at Washington and Lee who led the Student Volunteer chapter there, Nelson realized that he could indeed serve as a missionary, not as a minister but instead as a physician. The realization delighted Virginia, if not her mother, who told Nelson, "I've been praying for years for missions and missionaries, but I didn't expect that I'd have to give my own daughter."

In Richmond, both prepared for work in China under Southern Presbyterian auspices; Virginia joined the Presbyterians when she married Nelson.

The Executive Committee of Foreign Missions for the Presbyterian Church US insisted that while it did not want to be in the business of building "large hospitals," it did intend the denomination's medical work to open a gospel field through excellent medical care. Southern Presbyterian mission doctors therefore typically attended (mostly southern) institutions with excellent reputations, including Nelson, whose medical degree came from the Medical College of Virginia. He played semiprofessional baseball during the summers, while his fiancée studied nursing and techniques for evangelizing among women. Nelson passed his board exams in early summer 1916, as the couple married.

After working for a few months in West Virginia mining country, Nelson and Virginia departed for China in late November 1916, arriving in the bustling port city of Shanghai after a nineteen-day sail from Seattle. Virginia was a woman of slight build. The missionaries who welcomed the Bells lamented, "Poor little Virginia Bell! She won't last a year!" To the contrary, she and her husband constituted an estimable pair of workers and stayed until 1941, building a house, creating a home, and rearing four children, the first of whom, Rosa Wertenbaker (born in 1918), was soon joined by Ruth McCue (1920). The local Chinese had not thought much of Rosa because she was a girl. When Ruth arrived, their pity intensified for Dr. Bell, whom they called "Chong Ai Hua" — the Bell who loves the Chinese people — because now he had not one but "two little nuisances." For millennia, Chinese tradition had valued boy children more than girls because the former would carry out filial duties of elder care and commemorative pieties, all bound up with the family's legacy. Girls, on the other hand, required dowries that ate up family wealth — effectively consuming part of that legacy. Infanticide of girl babies posed enough of a problem by the late 1920s that the Nationalist government moved to forbid drowning specifically. The Bells' burden, in the view of their Chinese patients, only increased with the birth of Virginia (nicknamed "Mai-Mai") in 1927. Clayton Bell arrived in 1932. An earlier baby boy, Nelson Jr., was born in late 1924 but died of dysentery at ten months of age.

Nelson and Virginia enjoyed the benefits of living and working at the increasingly prestigious mission compound hospital. They also enjoyed Tsingkiangpu's relative isolation, which allowed them to act with some independence from denominational authorities Stateside. Nelson and Virginia's shared vocation and distinctive personalities influenced the paths their children took as they grew. For Ruth, an awkward, anxious, deeply sensitive child, growing up in China among uncompromisingly sacrificial parents prepared her for a life lived with sincere commitment to the right and compassion for the flawed. These impulses pulled her in different directions — sometimes literally. All her life, Ruth tried to make living sense of those tensions.

—◇—

Absalom Sydenstricker (the author Pearl S. Buck's father) founded Tsingkiangpu station in what is now Huaiyin, China, in 1887 for the Presbyterian Church US, a southern, predominantly white denomination with its roots in the antebellum era. The name Tsingkiangpu means "Clear Water Depot," and, as the North Kiangsu Mission's main station, it stood about halfway between Nanking (now Nanjing) to the south and Haichow (or Lianyungang) to the north. Situated on the ancient Grand Canal that connected southern provinces to Beijing in the north, the flood- and famine-prone area was "desperately poor."

Dr. James Woods, one of three brothers from a dynastic Southern Presbyterian family, came to Tsingkiangpu in February 1894 with his young wife, Bessie, who had also volunteered for the mission field as a nurse and evangelistic worker. He succeeded his brother Edgar as Tsingkiangpu's hospital chief and served in that capacity for thirty-three years. Mission chronicler Frank Price credited James Woods with building the hospital — the region's first, whose name in Chinese meant "Benevolent Compassion Healing Hall" — from a small 80-bed facility into a thriving, comparatively modern institution with 200 beds and a clinic that served several thousand patients per month. The local Chinese population lived among violent bands of outlaws and endemic black fever, a disease spread by infected sand flies. The hospital also trained Chinese doctors and nurses. True to his Presbyterian convictions, Woods never lost sight of the hospital's Christian purpose. When Nelson and Virginia Bell arrived, they dedicated their labor to this same mission of Christian witness.

The Bells were not unique in their mission-focused matrimony. Many matches led immediately to service in a foreign field. A veritable tide of denominational activism among American women raised funds to send single women into domestic and foreign mission work. Among the Southern Presbyterians, who, unlike their northern sisters, had no women's mission society per se, the "Women of the Church" raised money to fund missions, among other projects.

As for married women ambitious for mission service, some simply followed a husband into the field of his calling. But historian Jane Hunter notes that most married female missionaries in China had committed to Christian service independently from their mates, solemnifying in marriage "a vocational and religious decision along with a romantic one." The Bells reflect this very pattern. Virginia Leftwich Bell found in Nelson her partner in work, faith, and love. Their second daughter's marriage would reflect the same fusion of motives.

The young physician from Waynesboro welcomed technological advances that helped him do his work and do it better. Items that others (including Dr. Woods) might have considered luxuries, Nelson insisted on. For instance, Nelson had screens installed on the hospital windows while Dr. Woods was on furlough; the elder physician had rejected them because of the expense. But Nelson thought the screens would ensure airflow in the hot climate, while also ensuring hygienic conditions — in part, by excluding the infectious sand flies. Early in his time at Tsingkiangpu, Nelson purchased a Harley-Davidson motorcycle to facilitate his travels to the outlying stations; Virginia and the girls could ride along in the sidecar if necessary. In 1924, he sold it and bought a "Baby Austin" automobile (the Austin 7, produced in Britain as an economy car). Dr. Bell felt that he needed to make the best use of every minute. While rickshaws — two-wheeled carts pulled by local Chinese men — transported the bulk of material and people to and from the hospital compound, the sometimes impatient Nelson determined to make his rounds at will and speedily. Whatever tools helped him to accomplish his consecrated work, he embraced. This lesson, too, Ruth Bell would carry with her into adulthood.

In spite of its distance from major population areas, the mission at Tsingkiangpu sometimes fell under threat of violence resulting from internal Chinese conflicts. In May 1927, for instance, the Bells — Nelson, a very pregnant Virginia, Rosa, and Ruth — evacuated as fighting between Chinese Nationalists and their Communist adversaries drew close. The US State Department had recommended months earlier that Tsingkiangpu missionaries leave, but in his stubborn way, Nelson had resisted until the absolute last moment. He felt supremely confident that they could soon safely return. Before fleeing, Nelson had most of their belongings and furniture carried to the second floor of their house, then had workers plaster over the opening at the top of the stairs. He was obstinate, committed, and inventive.

The family made it to Waynesboro and Nelson's mother's home just in time for Virginia to give birth to her namesake, who would be called "MaiMai," meaning "little sister" in Chinese. By the fall of 1928, the Bells, now with this third daughter, were back in China, getting the house back in order. The first floor had been ransacked, but the sealed-up second floor had protected most of their furniture. Virginia redecorated with fresh paint and wallpaper ordered and shipped from Montgomery Ward. Her letters to "Mother Bell" described these efforts but also expressed an almost self-abnegating gratitude to her mother-in-law for welcoming them and letting the new baby be born in her home. Discerning the story from one side of this epistolary conversation is difficult, but one wonders if something extraordinary — besides the ordinary miracle of a baby being born — had happened at the senior Bells' home. Had it been unusually awkward or inconvenient for some reason to bear the child there, in those days when it was customary for women to labor and give birth at home? Had MaiMai arrived early? Was the birth complicated? Did Virginia experience difficulties during delivery? In any event, both Virginia and Nelson expressed newly deepened love for Mother Bell around the subject of MaiMai's birth.

—◇—

As much as the success of the Tsingkiangpu hospital depended on Nelson's skills as a surgeon, he depended mightily on Virginia not just as his companion but also as his professional partner. Virginia was her talented, headstrong husband's best ally and confidante. She set an example as a wife, mother, and professional that Ruth would emulate in her own way.

At the time of their marriage, Nelson was just shy of twenty-two years old — two to three years younger than the era's average first-time US husband — and Virginia was twenty-four — about three years older than the average first-time US wife. Their atypical age difference could suggest that Virginia saw in Nelson not only an advantageous marriage opportunity to someone she had known all her life, but also an opening to meaningful work for which she had prepared. Nelson, too, would have seen in Virginia a capable, deeply Christian woman equipped professionally and spiritually for medical work in the foreign field. The typical (and unpaid) work of a missionary wife was confined to child rearing and homemaking, although missionary theorists saw such activity as essential, both for preserving missionary children from the perceived dangers of the surrounding culture and for displaying the orderly piety of Christian domesticity. But because of her nurse's training, Virginia Bell also had responsibility for the hospital's drop-in clinic for women, managing the staff and seeing patients, while also managing the Bell family's domestic routine.

In 1922, before their first furlough, Virginia and Nelson had constructed a two-story Western-style brick house in the mission compound for their growing family. Virginia, Rosa, and Ruth, along with household workers, lived there, even during a period when Nelson ran the mission hospital 100 miles away from Tsingkiangpu, in the port of Haichow. Life inside the compound walls was relatively safe, but occasional dangers flared up and Virginia had to take charge in Nelson's absence. In the months after Ruth's first birthday, for instance, Virginia rushed to hide herself and the two little girls while a local mob raged through the compound. Virginia managed the household, the dangers, and the work of the clinic, soldiering on whether Nelson was close by or not. She was resourceful, steadfast, and clear in her beliefs.

Although her nurse's training set Virginia somewhat apart from other missionary wives, she nevertheless occupied an ambiguous position with respect to their denomination's mission agency, the Presbyterian Church in the United States (PCUS) Executive Committee of Foreign Missions. That entity governed the Bells' presence and work at Tsingkiangpu, but it was Nelson who communicated with them about matters such as salary, the chil-

dren's stipends, and furlough schedules. As Jane Hunter explains, women like
Virginia fell under the governance of the denominational board as filtered
through their husbands. For her part, Virginia's days focused on nursing
work at the hospital's clinic. Nelson highly valued and respected her work.
She functioned as a kind of physician's assistant to him and to Dr. Woods
both, learning from them but also advising them on courses of treatment.
Her skill, however, created more demand in the clinic. Nelson observed that
women came "more and more" to the clinic, to the extent that numbers of
female patients eventually equaled numbers of male patients. Nelson worried
perennially that Virginia was overworked, especially during a late-1930 black
fever epidemic. "She is busy from morning to night," he wrote worriedly
to his mother. Nelson was increasingly solicitous of her health as the years
passed. She suffered from severe migraines all her life; he eventually sought
advice about them from doctors at the renowned Mayo Clinic.

At home in Tsingkiangpu, the Bells' domestic existence was surprisingly homey, similar in some ways to how they might have lived back in
Waynesboro. The American missionary personnel constituted a community that functioned like a group of neighbors in a small town. They reared
their children together, shared tasks and household goods, supported one
another through sorrows, and celebrated each other's joys. Indeed, these
other families were extensions of Ruth's own family. She remembered years
later being deprived of her natural grandparents while in China, but thinking of the older missionaries as relatives. Ruth and the other Bell children
called veteran missionaries Jimmie and Sophie Graham (no relation to Bill's
family) their uncle and aunt; they adopted another missionary couple as
"Grandma and Grandpa Reynolds"; and they stayed overnight with James
and Bessie Woods when Nelson and Virginia traveled together. The families in Tsingkiangpu visited back and forth for a day's play or a sleepover
with Jim and Aurie Montgomery, who were stationed in Hwaian with four
children close in age to Rosa, Ruth, and MaiMai. Little Rosa wrote to her
grandfather Bell, "We go to Hwaian nearly every Sat. afternoon [to see the
Montgomery children] and we are going this afternoon too." Virginia and
Nelson hosted and attended birthday parties for young and old as well as
holiday celebrations marking Halloween, Valentine's Day, and the Chinese

commemoration of the beginning of the Republic, called "10/10." Games and costumes — especially if hosts threw a "tacky party" — featured in many of these revelries.

Just as Ruth later would enjoy pranks and jokes, Nelson loved playing tricks on others, and holidays gave him the perfect opportunity for hijinks. Sometimes Virginia was in on the fun. For example, with Rosa and Ruth away at school in the fall of 1936, Nelson wrote to them about Halloween at the mission. Their mother, he wrote, "fixed sheets and Ken [Geiser, fellow mission physician], your mother and I went over to the Woods' [home]" where all the children were having a party. They "moaned under the windows and then went in." Sometimes, the normally courtly Nelson was not above playing tricks on his beloved spouse. Once, feeling a bit under the weather, Nelson allowed Virginia to take his temperature. He wrote to the girls gleefully that while she looked away, he "stuck [the thermometer] on the hot water bottle and ran it up to 107," then replaced it in his mouth. Virginia clearly expressed her lack of amusement, Nelson wrote: "She said if I had not already been bald she would have made me so."

—◇—

In the ordinary days between birthday and holiday parties, life on the mission compound for the Bell family stayed busy. Nelson wrote a circular letter to the mission's US supporters in which he described his "regular morning routine" for weekdays. His daily life rippled out from a center of prayer. Ruth later remembered that there never came a morning that her father did not begin his day with Bible reading and prayers on his knees, afterward gathering the family together for more prayer. Upon first seeing her every morning, he would ask her, "Ruth, have you read your Bible yet?" and she would many times head back to her room, she said, "to begin the day as I should." The family had breakfast together, then prayed, in Chinese, with the locals who worked in their home, including Wang Nai Nai, who cared for the children, and beloved general factotum Ma Er, whose long hair hid scars from his ears being cut off, the "customary punishment" of Chinese army deserters. Then Nelson conducted prayers every morning in the hospital chapel for staff, ambulatory patients, and their visitors.

Nelson and his colleagues treated waves of patients suffering from medical maladies endemic to the area; deadly black fever (leishmaniasis, called kala-azar) struck those bitten by parasite-carrying sand flies. Nelson improved the hospital's approach to treating black fever in part by helping to identify the sand fly's role in transmission. He and the staff cured many locals, thereby building trust among the population. According to Bell biographer John Pollock, Love and Mercy Hospital, on its way to becoming the largest Presbyterian hospital in China and the largest mission hospital in the world, became the global leader in treating black fever during Nelson and Virginia's tenure.

Nelson worked entire days in the operating room; he regularly performed surgery on gunshot victims wounded in the area's unremitting violence among gangs of "bandits" involved in paramilitary warlords' battles for political and military control of China. These regional militias had arisen in the wake of the emperor's 1911 abdication and the 1912 establishment of a weak and severely fragmented Chinese Republic. Moreover, the Tsingkiangpu compound lay in a territory adjacent to several competing warlord groups. The Bells' arrival and tenure in Tsingkiangpu coincided with a decades-long period marked by the serial dominance of several major "cliques" — armies led by modern warlords who aimed to expand their territory as well as the number of men under their command. Victorious armies absorbed conquered troops along with whatever weaponry they possessed. These soldiers' evanescent loyalties, low pay, and spotty rations accounted for their involvement in ad hoc raids, kidnappings, and theft. One day, Nelson stitched up one of these men, only to see, hours later, the thief's bandaged head on display over the town gate — a warning to the man's posse from a rival gang. As tensions between China and Japan escalated during the 1930s, Nelson also operated on fighters wounded in military skirmishes, in 1938 attending to more than six hundred casualties after the Battle of Taierchuang (Tzierzhuang).

---♦---

Somewhat paradoxically given his particular concern for Virginia's health, Nelson shared with his mother his low opinion of another wife at the mission who grumbled about "only" being a mother: "children and home," he wrote, should "come first with all mothers." In another letter, he wrote to Mother Bell that "a *man's wife* is responsible to him and not to the [denomination's] Executive Committee" (emphasis added). In addition to reflecting the way that the PCUS viewed married missionary couples, the phrase Nelson used — "a man's wife" — showed his location squarely in the mainstream of assumptions about gender roles in marriage, at least in the abstract. (Ruth would inherit this bifurcated perspective; she, too, could be much more strident in the abstract than when confronted by the concrete.) Nelson made this declaration about the responsibility of a "man's wife" with the general run of wives in mind — not thinking about Virginia and her professional credentials and experience. Nelson did see himself as Virginia's protector, her shield against exhaustion when the Executive Committee asked too much of her. But he also relied on her to carry a significant workload in the clinic and at home. Nelson viewed Virginia as both an indispensable partner in work and a woman in need of his protection. He knew (and loved) her best, he knew her capacities, and in keeping with his suspicions of anyone directing their efforts from a distance, he claimed to know what she needed.

Nelson's contradictory feelings about Virginia and her work help illustrate the complicated position of married women in the mission field. Women without particular preparation for the mission field who married missionaries might aspire to contribute to the Christian work by conducting Bible studies or teaching (Western) domestic practices to local women. But those hopes took a backseat to the realities of managing meals, child care and schooling, and domestic upkeep in an unfamiliar setting. Some missionary wives, however, had been trained formally for medical or evangelistic work. The Assembly Training School of the PCUS had opened its doors in 1914 precisely to train Southern Presbyterian women for foreign work; indeed, Virginia had received training there.

Nelson's solicitousness of Virginia's health, therefore, could be fickle. In addition to her medical work and management of hospital and home accounts, Virginia supervised the domestic routines, including the children's education. Nelson worried a lot that her exhaustion would affect the girls' schooling. Virginia served as each child's primary schoolteacher through the fifth grade, beginning with Rosa in the mid-1920s and continuing through Clayton, who was about nine years old when the Bells left China for good in the spring of 1941. This task seemed to tax her patience and her skill more than her other duties. Keeping her children on grade level with their Stateside peers required materials and preparation time that were hard for Virginia to come by.

In the evenings, after a long day of surgeries, schoolwork, laundry, and food preparation, the Bell parents and children would spend "an hour of quiet" together, playing a game or listening to Virginia read what she and Nelson considered upbuilding stories. Sometimes while listening, Virginia, Ruth, and Rosa would knit, embroider, make rugs, crochet, or sew, leaving Nelson the job of reading aloud, often from classics such as Scott's *Ivanhoe* but occasionally something "frivolous" such as a story titled "Come Out of the Kitchen." Virginia selected reading material for her children with care. Nelson told his mother they "read the best books" because Virginia planned "their reading ahead and as a result they dont know what trashy reading is but have a fine store of classical literature already read." He continued, "Right now she is reading 'Hypatia' aloud," probably a reference to the 1853 novel by English author Charles Kingsley, a tale of Christian apologetics based on the life of the early fifth-century philosopher. They read *The Adventures of Tom Sawyer* aloud during Christmas holidays 1931–1932. Probably around the same time, Rosa and Ruth read *David Copperfield*, "a lengthy tale" that "the girls seem to enjoy" nevertheless. They had recommended *Pilgrim's Progress* and *Ben Hur* to one of their friends. Ruth wrote to her grandmother about reading "the 'ANNE' books," the series by L. M. Montgomery that includes *Anne of Green Gables*, *Anne of the Island*, and *Anne's House of Dreams*, among other titles. Virginia had Mother Bell send any *National Geographic* magazines she could spare for the girls to use in school; the older girls would "'sight see' after studying each country" in geography class.

Virginia also directed the work of Wang Nai Nai, the Chinese nurse, or "amah," who cared for the Bell children while she worked at the clinic. Virginia spoke of her as a "homely old soul" who loved everyone. As an adult, Ruth had almost a photographic memory of what she called Wang Nai Nai's "pleasant peasant" face. She remembered her as "a large, reliable, kind, and understanding Rock of Gibraltar," although once the children actually weighed her — she must have been indulgent of children's curiosity! — and discovered that Wang Nai Nai weighed less than one hundred pounds.

Only years later did Virginia tell Ruth and the other children how the Chinese woman had come to work for them. Wang Nai Nai and her husband "procured" prostitutes for clients, purchasing unwanted infant girls for brothels in Shanghai. By chance, Wang Nai Nai heard "Aunt" Sophie Graham preach there, perhaps as the missionary woman passed through the port city on furlough. Graham and her missionary husband, "Uncle" Jimmie, served in Tsingkiangpu for the length of their work in China, he as an evangelist who itinerated through the area around the station and she as a missionary devoted "untiringly" to evangelizing Chinese women. Fellow missionary and chronicler Frank Price credited Sophie Graham "with unusual facility" in speaking Chinese, able to persuade "even the most hostile" — such as, for instance, the denizens of a Shanghai brothel. Referring to an early leader depicted in Acts, Price called her "a daughter of Priscilla" able to teach "the way of God more perfectly."

Wang Nai Nai was moved to repent and give up her procuring work. Probably through arrangements made by Sophie Graham, she came to work at the mission for the Bells. That such kidnapping and child sex-trafficking were endemic in the area made this transformation and Wang Nai Nai's work for the Bells all the more extraordinary. Virginia and Nelson trusted her with their daughters, even knowing her past. Their confidence in the power of her faith confession rested their minds. Their trust in God calmed any worries they might have had about their children's safety. Ruth remembered that one evening the Bells discovered Wang Nai Nai trying to pick through the words in her Bible by firelight in the unelectrified house. They bought her an oil lamp to encourage her study, and according to Ruth, she taught herself to read the Bible. One might see in this early example of her parents encouraging a "baby Christian," as Ruth later called new converts, a pattern that the adult Ruth would work mightily to follow.

What did young Ruth think of other Chinese people she encountered? In the abstract, based on a letter she wrote at age nine to her Bell grandparents, she saw them in desperate need of Christian rescue: "The Chinese have not changed very many of their old habits," Ruth wrote breathlessly: "women still smoke they still gamble & play cards drink and do all other things which we do not do." The content as well as the somewhat resigned and imperious, prim tone from a nine-year-old signaled that the girl Ruth had imbibed the loving exasperation that her parents expressed (and that her grandparents expected). The Chinese peasants around her, she believed, needed her family's help. Her report also indicated that the Tsingkiangpu mission, characteristically for Southern Presbyterians if not for all white Protestant missionaries in those days, expected Christian converts to be transformed not only in religious commitments but also in ethics and behavior, along white American middle-class Protestant lines.

That young Ruth focused particularly on women's behavior indicated that she spent much of her time around Wang Nai Nai and the other women working in the Bell household. Given Protestant American gender norms, which held women to standards of moral and sexual purity that men did not have to meet, women gambling or smoking would have been of great consequence. Female propriety betokened Christian sincerity. The entire notion of women's involvement in missions — a nineteenth-century ideology that continued to govern the twentieth-century movement — specified that only women could "reach" other women, spiritually and physically. "Women's Work for Women" explained that Western missionary women could gain access to the harems, zenanas, and other private domestic enclaves to which women in the "Orient" were consigned. Once exposed to the spiritually and physically liberating message of Christ shared by their Western sisters, the thinking went, converted women would transform their own societies, household by household.

Ruth seemed to embrace, in emulation of her parents and grandparents and other adults on the mission compound, the notion of women's natural spiritual gifts and their importance in establishing and maintaining an upright Christian home as an outpost of a transformed Christian society. To see Chinese women playing at cards, smoking, and drinking, just like

Chinese men, would have signaled to her a crisis in Chinese culture, one that Christian conversion would correct. Nevertheless, given what she saw as the heathenish failings of the Chinese, Ruth was able to write to her grandparents a couple of years later, "How I long to see you although I love Chine *Very Very* much."

———◇———

Nelson was loath ever to rest from his work at Tsingkiangpu. Yet he made sure that the family took the missionary's customary furloughs over the years of their service, in part so that Virginia could have a rest from her ever-expanding clinic work. Many missionaries and foreign workers in the Bells' region left their posts for a period during the summer to enjoy the cooler climes of Kuling (romanized from Guling), a mountainous preserve about four hundred miles southwest of Tsingkiangpu. In 1924, Nelson and Virginia purchased a mountain home there, in anticipation of enjoying summers away from the exhausting heat of the hospital compound. It took some convincing for Nelson to make this purchase, and he never seemed content with it afterward. In fact, the Bells only traveled there in 1924 and 1925. Nelson groused about the distance and the difficulty of traveling there; they made at least part of their first journey in sedan chairs carried by what he called "coolies." Ruth had been terrified during this trip. Along with these complications, Nelson disdained the frivolity of a vacation destination where missionaries simply chummed around with one another. A vacation home in a colony where there was nothing to do but relax and indulge in gossip during endless idle hours was not the Bells' style. Virginia and Nelson both enjoyed good fun, and indeed sponsored a good deal of it on the mission grounds. But being in Kuling without useful work did not agree with them. The Bells sold their cottage there after only a few years of ownership, probably in 1931.

One could just as well stay in Tsingkiangpu and make creative use of materials at hand to create "a nice, comfortable home." Despite the difficulty and expense of obtaining things like schoolbooks, the resourceful Bells (supported, doubtless, by Nelson's generous and responsive mother) did create a somewhat idyllic setting for their children to grow up in. They had a piano on which Rosa and Ruth took lessons, and Ruth wrote to her Bell grandparents that she and Rosa had the "nicest doll's house you ever saw." In the summer of 1929, Nelson supervised Chinese workers who built a swimming pool for the missionaries' use. He claimed to have built it for about the same money that a trip to Kuling would have cost. It provided great relief from Tsingkiangpu's blistering summers to all the Christian workers. It held "5,000 gallons of water," Nelson detailed, and was about three and a half feet deep. He declared that the fresh, "very cold" water, pumped in by hand straight from the well — "it takes four men six hours to pump it full" — "makes one feel like a new person." This addition to the mission landscape might have seemed like a luxury to some — like window screens or a roadster car — but the refreshment it provided the workers and the diversion it gave to their children became almost essential to the work they did. Nelson's insistence on availing himself of such conveniences impacted his second daughter profoundly. As we shall see, as the wife of a man who habitually worked himself to exhaustion, Ruth Graham insisted on similar conditions — a roomy, secluded home; household staff; a swimming pool (eventually heated); frequent trips to warm-weather climes — as essential fuel to his Christian labor.

Nelson wrote his mother that the children had "a good time" in the swimming pool. Moreover, swimming "makes a real recreation for them and they get confidence and skill in the water." Ruth learned to swim that first summer; in a single week, Nelson reported, she learned to "swim completely around the pool twice without letting her feet down." In a letter she wrote to her grandparents, Ruth herself reported, "The swimming pool has been a great pleasure to us all summer, In it I learned to dive float swim and turn the summersult under water." She continued excitedly, "I also learned how to do the deadmans float and all other things that a duck can do."

This pair of letters deserves extra attention because Nelson's makes one of the few mentions of Ruth in this period (more on her absence from his letters below). Little Ruth had accomplished something that he could appreciate and describe easily to his parents. As an athlete himself, he may have especially enjoyed watching this daughter master such an important and daunting athletic skill. For her part, Ruth wrote to her grandparents carefully in pencil, asking them: "Please excuese my bad writing." She was also careful to avoid writing over the decorative illustrations on the paper of Chinese women in fashionable 1920s dress. (In a letter on the same stationery, Virginia's writing covered over the design.) Ruth's schoolwork — including her handwriting — was a subject of concern for her parents and her various teachers. Ruth had internalized that concern and saw her penmanship as problematic. She did not want to mar the stationery design with her "bad writing." Aside from that, she also loved drawing and other creative pursuits, and wanted the stylish Chinese woman to remain visible. In giving space to the design on the paper, young Ruth simultaneously withdrew from center stage and indicated art as a central passion.

Nelson brought another seeming luxury to the Bell household the summer after the installation of the pool, in August 1930, during the worst of the summer season's heat. He took delivery of a General Electric refrigerator purchased while the family vacationed in Shanghai. Virginia had wanted new chairs; over her objections, Nelson vetoed that idea and opted instead for the fridge, whose usefulness trumped any concern about expense. When it arrived, he "immediately assembled" it. To his mother, Nelson described "connect[ing] it up" and then the happy result: "we already have cold water and should have ice by night. . . . It is needless to say," he continued, "that we are thrilled with it and the anticipation of cold things to eat and drink. The butter has been like soup for instance." He reported Virginia's delight, in spite of herself: "she can hardly realize we have it. . . . She certainly feels humble having such a wonderful convenience here." Virginia and Nelson almost immediately took advantage of this "wonderful convenience" by making milkshakes for Rosa and Ruth. He created another gustatory delight when he rigged a discarded mortar gun to puff corn, rice, and wheat, in order to "supply the Mission with dry cereals." Nelson saw no reason for his family and colleagues to go without enjoyment simply because they were dedicated to Christian service. They had been called to serve as missionaries, not as ascetics. Again, Ruth would carry this sensibility into her life as an evangelist's wife.

Other missionaries on the compound followed Nelson's lead with respect to creature comforts and recreation. They built a tennis court, setting lines in the dirt, stringing a net across, and playing vigorous matches. Ruth later remembered the puzzled Chinese observers watching the refined Americans hit the ball back and forth. Why were the revered doctors working so hard? they wondered. During the Bells' 1935–1936 furlough, Nelson wrote, remaining missionaries even "fixed up a nine hole golf course" in the shared yards of their homes. Nelson enjoyed it upon his return: "it affords a lot of fun. . . . We need the exercise and change."

Nelson positively doted on MaiMai in his letters home. Perhaps he felt as if his parents had a special bond with his new little one because she was born at their house. No letters appear in Nelson's papers from the period of Rosa's or Ruth's infancy, so it is not possible to say that Nelson simply loved babies. Nelson's almost comically repetitive mentions of MaiMai in letters home take on a distinctive importance, however, because at the same time that he gushed about every detail of her development, activity, and appearance, and included regular updates about Rosa, this otherwise doting father remained all but silent about Ruth in those letters between 1928 and 1932. If Nelson did write about Ruth, he squeezed mention of her into the middle of fulsome descriptions of Rosa, who was a standout in all pursuits, especially academic, and MaiMai, the adorable baby. "Rosa has done so nicely in her music. She likes it and has been so faithful in practicing." But "Ruth did not like it at all at first but she has been right faithful in her practicing too and *the experience has been good for her*" (emphasis added). While Nelson did not specify the "good" derived from the "experience," other letters indicate that he saw her as lacking discipline and focus.

In one early summer 1929 report to his "precious mother," Nelson noted that he "stayed at home" and "did not go to the jail," where he often tended to the prisoners' health needs: "Virginia and Rosa went to church and I stayed with the baby." He goes on to describe what a "lovely day" it was. Not a word about Ruth. In another letter that opens with his account of performing minor surgery on his wife, Nelson wrote, "The children are growing so rapidly"; he then detailed how many inches Rosa had grown over the past three months. Moreover, he continued, about MaiMai, "the baby's arms and wrists are like little posts." Surveying the family landscape for his mother, Nelson puzzlingly left little Ruth unmentioned.

A similar silence appeared in a 1930 letter in which Nelson gave full details about a lingering fever zapping Rosa, MaiMai "the baby" enjoying the swimming pool, and more details about the cost of its construction. Nelson sandwiched in one brief sentence about Ruth recovering from a recent illness. In a 1931 letter, describing Rosa's thirteenth birthday party, Nelson detailed his own costume, as well as what Rosa, the teacher Lucy Fletcher, nurse Cassie Lee Oliver, Virginia, and Bessie Woods wore for theirs. But he was again completely silent on Ruth, neither including her in the fun-loving costumed ranks nor explaining her absence.

Even Ruth's joining the church, on Sunday, April 6, 1930, did not initially make Nelson's catalogue of the family's news. Although the PCUS's *Book of Church Order* leaves unspecified the age of "discretion" — that is, the age at which young persons can give "satisfaction" to the session and the congregation "with respect to their knowledge and piety" through examination and public profession of faith — Ruth would have been almost ten, although years later she recalled that she had been eleven. Nelson did not mention the event in letters written on April 9 or 11, nor did he note any preparations in letters before the Sunday in question. Only a week afterward did he ask his mother, "Did I write you that Ruth joined the church last Sunday. She went with me before the Session and stood a good examination. I had to interpret most of the questions for her as she does not understand a lot of the theological terms in Chinese."

Aside from providing evidence of Nelson's puzzling forgetfulness of Ruth, his description of translating for Ruth confirms that the missionizers insisted on "indigenizing" Christianity under Chinese leadership as quickly as seemed feasible. In the mid-1870s, the Southern Presbyterian Church had discouraged its missionaries from being voting members in the churches they helped plant, in order that the Chinese themselves would take the lead in building a "native church." By the 1920s at Tsingkiangpu and elsewhere, interactions between Chinese and American Christians had evolved — or "devolved," to use the missionaries' term for the hoped-for shift in control from the Americans to the Chinese — such that locals pastored the churches they all attended together and constituted majorities in regional church governance. The process of ceding authority to local leadership helped these churches to survive in the absence of the missionaries, who were forced to evacuate periodically by occasional violent flare-ups between Nationalists and Communists. Indeed, by 1925 the victorious Nationalists required Chinese leadership in these mission churches. The church that Ruth Bell joined in 1930 had come to be a Chinese church through both devolution and the Chinese government's insistence.

Just a couple of years before Ruth's admission into the church, "Uncle" Jimmie Graham reflected on the "striking" growth of Tsingkiangpu's Chinese Christian community. This expansion necessitated Chinese involvement and, it was hoped, made the church more enticing to potential converts. Uncle Jimmie had seen the population of Chinese Christians grow from "one station at Tsingkiangpu with not a half dozen church members" to stations across the Kiangsu Province boasting churches with "over seven thousand [members], together with many more thousands of enrolled inquirers."

—◇—

Rosa excelled in her schoolwork, her spiritual life, her attitude, her helpfulness. At the end of the school year in spring 1931, Nelson reported that "Rosa especially has done well" with her schoolwork, highlighting a 97 on her "especially good" literature examination. Anything less than what they considered excellent — and most anything would have been less than that — seemed hard for Nelson and Virginia to credit. In describing — not exactly praising — Ruth as "quite an artist" who "can draw such pretty etching scenes," Nelson wrote to his father, "It has never been a telent I have especially desired for a child of mine. Rosa is quite studious and reads a great deal." Nelson valued the intellectual over the artistic.

Nelson also may have found Ruth's behavior so challenging as to be unmanageable. He may have even feared that others disliked or avoided her. Describing a trip to Shanghai in early 1930 — curiously, during the same period when Ruth joined the church — Nelson reported to his mother that only Ruth came along with him and Virginia, while Rosa stayed with the Montgomerys at Hwaian and MaiMai stayed with the Woodses. "Ruth," he wrote, "is sensative and we feared she might have her feelings hurt down in Hwaian [with Rosa] and get all worked up so we brought her along. She is a great 'mother's baby' anyway, hates to leave us for a minute." Mother Bell must have expressed concern for Ruth because Nelson explained, somewhat contradictorily, in a later letter, "No, Ruth is not one bit nervous about conditions out here, neither of the children are, but she is sensitive and we did not like to leave her in Hwaian with the possibility of her not being thoroly happy all the time." (One wonders what the specific difference is between being "nervous" and being "sensitive.") When, a few years afterward, Ruth experienced acute homesickness during her first months at school in Pyeng Yang, Virginia remembered to Mother Bell that Ruth "was always anxious to come home after a few days in Hwaian, & she would often refuse to go." Being at home — in all of the senses of that phrase — held great importance to Ruth from early on.

Ruth was absent from other family letters as well. In a long, detailed letter from Rosa to her maternal grandparents — one of her only letters to them preserved among Nelson's papers — Rosa explained that she was "left to keep house" while "Mother, Daddy, and Mai Mai went to Shanghai." The older sister neither mentioned Ruth nor explained why she may not have gone to Shanghai with the rest of the family.

In a letter from late 1931, Virginia offered some insights into Ruth's temperament: she "is still somewhat scatter-brained, but *learning*." Virginia explained to her mother-in-law that she was helping teacher Lucy Fletcher by taking charge of Ruth and another child in several subjects, since "Lucy is so 'High Strung' that Ruth was a 'nervous wreck' over the thought of school." Ruth had trouble concentrating on her work, and Miss Fletcher was not as easygoing in redirecting her attention as Virginia was. Ruth later remembered that Miss Fletcher would give students a reward of five dollars — "a *lot* of money for a missionary's kid!" she recalled — for memorizing the Sermon on the Mount (Matthew 5–7). Ruth received the princely sum of $4.50 — she made one mistake — but years later, she declared that she "wouldn't take one thousand times that amount in place of having memorized it."

In February 1930, Nelson described Ruth to his father: "Ruth looks well ... is nice and fat." This brief description is squeezed between an assessment of Rosa's health on the eve of her twelfth birthday — "she is developed like a fifteen year olf child, weighs 107, is 5 ft. 3 and looks much older" — and another adoring, fulsome word picture of MaiMai's adorable mischief — "we all naturally make a lot over her." Nearing the time for Rosa's departure to school in Korea, Nelson reflects about "how the children have grown. Rosa is not only fully grown but she is so mature. Ruth [twelve years old at the time] is just about as large, weighs about 120 but she is still a perfect kid in her ways."

These descriptions of Ruth as sensitive and deeply pious help explain why, in 1931, a visitor to the mission compound from Tibet made such an impression on her. The Tibetan man, curiously named Jesus, was not a Christian, nor had he ever heard the gospel. This paradox might have spoken to Ruth and inspired her to consider Tibet as a potential field for service. She began to plan for a future as an "old-maid missionary" whose solitary work would be to evangelize nomads on the arid Tibetan Plateau. As Billy Graham biographer William Martin has written, Ruth zeroed in on this vocation "because it seemed like the hardest challenge she could possibly undertake." This kind of sacrificial ambition reflected her parents' influence.

As the years passed and Ruth grew, Nelson did develop some pride in his second daughter's creative gifts. In summer 1932, he sent his mother a sketch Ruth had drawn of Rosa, "a good likeness but not as good as some of Ruth's other work." Only much later, in the fall of 1936, when Ruth was in high school in Korea, did Nelson's sense of who Ruth was shift dramatically. Responding to his mother's observation that Rosa resembled him, Nelson demurred: "I don't think Rosa is particularly like me — she is so much more like her mother. I think Ruth much more like me in so many ways." While he did not enumerate the similarities he saw, the pronouncement foretold the bond that would strengthen as Ruth entered adulthood.

At the end of 1932, he wrote to his mother describing a "splendid" play that the children presented the week before. The focus of the action was the "cinversion of a Jewish family in New York." As usual, Nelson lavished praise on MaiMai, but then uncharacteristically turned to commend Ruth, who "carried the heaviest part and did it so well. She is such a scamp, so full of fun and life." Ruth had also designed the program's cover, which Nelson enclosed with his letter (unfortunately not archived with his papers). Nevertheless, he also fretted, "I fear she will be too popular at school." At least in Nelson's eyes, the twelve-year-old Ruth seemed to be coming into her own. Her energy, wit, and charm, a lot to handle in a seven- or eight-year-old, came into better balance as she matured. He could more fully enjoy and identify with her.

—◇—

Ruth's collection of animals at Tsingkiangpu constituted a focus for her attention during the late 1920s and early 1930s. She doted on them, bathing, training, cuddling them, and enjoying the attention they sometimes returned to her. The menagerie varied from year to year. She later wrote that she prayed to receive all kinds of animals — "a lizard . . . a puppy," even a bat. (When a missionary laughed at that last request, Ruth averred never to reveal that prayer again.) At the age of eight years old, Ruth had a pet rabbit that died. She solemnly buried him. But her continuing concern for him led her to dig him up every day afterward; she wanted to check that everything was okay. "The last time I saw him," she wrote in *Legacy of a Pack Rat*, "he was green." Ruth ornamented her animal cemetery with a trinket she found while playing outside; only later did the mission's groundskeeper realize that it was a hand grenade. Nelson disposed of it.

A nine-year-old Ruth described in a chatty letter to her Bell grandparents that they had "lots of pets," including two ducks, one each for her and Rosa. The ducks had been a gift from the kind people in the hospital kitchen, perhaps diverted from the dinner table. According to Nelson, Rosa and Ruth also had a "pet Magpie" named "Maggie" who was allowed to wander around the house but also flew around the yard, "much to the excitement of other magpies." A pair of "canarys," as Ruth labeled them, also featured in the Bell menagerie. Just as the family was deciding to skip the summer junket to Kuling, Ruth rescued a filthy kitten — bathing it in Lysol — and received two goats. As Nelson observed mordantly to his mother, "We prayed the children might have made up to them their missing [a summer in] Kuling but did not expect to see the prayer answered in the shape of two goats and a cat." The menagerie surely made more work and worry for Ruth's parents. But the creatures delighted her and Rosa and gave Ruth someone to shower with love and secrets.

In the spring of 1930, the Bell family made a weekend visit to neighboring Hwaian, where their friends and fellow workers Jim and Aurie Montgomery were stationed with their four children, close in age to the Bells' three girls. Knowing Ruth's love of animals, Jim and Aurie gave her a black dog. She carried the dog back to Tsingkiangpu, Rosa reported, "in her lap with her coat over it." Nelson elaborated separately to his mother that the dog "is only a mongrel but as far as [Ruth] is concerned it is the most beautiful dog in the world."

They christened the dog "Tar Baby." The name suggests the Bells' connections to southern literature and culture. "The Wonderful Tar Baby" appeared in Joel Chandler Harris's collection *Uncle Remus and the Legends of the Old Plantation* in 1886. Before he became a newspaper columnist in Atlanta, the white Harris spent the Civil War years as a teenager on a Georgia plantation, working on the owner's printing press and soaking up stories told by the enslaved black men and women who worked and lived there. Uncle Remus and the animal characters in Harris's stories spoke in a southern black dialect that delighted his white audiences and brought Harris national acclaim. As one of the so-called Plantation School writers, Harris depicted his southern region as governed quietly by whites' genteel paternalism that created an easygoing and harmonious atmosphere for all. Such an understanding, which glossed over plantation violence and underwrote racial repression that continued into the twentieth century, comported with how Nelson Bell viewed his home region.

Ruth wrote to her grandparents using the dog's nickname: "T.B. is getting less fierce and fatter," foreshadowing the litter of eight puppies that arrived in November 1930. When the puppies arrived, Virginia wrote drily to Mother Bell that "Mai mai & Ruth are spell-bound, with delight." She added, "I am spell-bound but *not* with delight." By February 1931, they still had three of the puppies: Mrs. Moore, Snow Ball, and the devilish Prinz, whom MaiMai described as "grab[bing] hold of the clothes of some bound foot woman & drag[ging] her off the walk."

In spite of Ruth's devotion, T.B. did not get along with other humans or animals. The dog's downfall came when she nipped at the son of the woman who cooked for the Bell family. Nelson, worried that the dog would cause further strife between his family and the local Chinese people, responded by putting T.B. down with chloroform. He wrote to his mother that he "did not tell Ruth until it was all over, and she was awfully sweet about it." He went on, "[She] said she was glad I had done it." Of course, Ruth buried her black dog in the yard so that she could attend to the grave and adorn it with flowers. Nelson observed of his animal-loving little girl, "She is such a tender-hearted little thing."

As a grown-up remembering this episode, Ruth recalled her beloved dog's demise in different terms than her father had described it. She had not been "glad," but instead called the dog's death "her first real heartbreak." She reflected on the intensity of her younger self's reliance on animal companions: "I doubt if there is any suffering more intense than a child's. T.B. was my first great love, and to me she was the most beautiful dog in the whole world. I used to tell her my troubles and she would listen intently, her brown eyes full of sympathetic interest, and she never betrayed a confidence." Whatever little Ruth's "troubles" — maybe related to the reason Nelson did not mention her in letters home — T.B. provided open ears and a dog's loving acceptance, at least to her. The grown-up Ruth remembered hearing adults complain about the dog's behavior: "It only made me love her the more. My love for her and hers for me was a very important thing at that time of my life." A little girl — misunderstood, misjudged, somehow wounded by the world already at the age of eight or nine — had lost her best friend to her father's well-meaning but drastic action.

As deeply as she felt T.B.'s loss, little Ruth could be indifferent about other animal hijinks. Cassie Lee Oliver, a nurse in the hospital, brought Ruth a baby turtle she had found while walking. Ruth wrote her grandparents excitedly about setting "it up on the swimming pool top in a doll Baby's tub & when we went to Church he got out of the tub & in to the swimming pool." Compared to the depth of her connection to T.B., she made but a

passing connection to the turtle, leaving it unclear whether the turtle escaped, died, or was rescued from the pool to live another day. This same
letter also included an even more extreme example of Ruth's matter-of-fact
attitude toward nature's indifferent workings. She described how she and
Rosa were playing with the Talbot boys — other mission children — who had
a "Kodack" camera. Rosa took a picture of the boys standing alongside Ruth
"with their [pet] dove" on her hand. Picture completed, William Talbot
threw the dove into the air, at which moment, Ruth narrated, "Mr. Hawk
swooped down from the tree where he was hiding & carried poor Mrs. dove
off for a feast with his wife." (Traditional domestic roles obtained in Ruth's
animal kingdom.) Ruth reported the children's "surprise." Then, without
missing a beat, she concluded, "but any how we got a picture of the dove
before it died."

Echoes of this dispassionate reaction occurred in another remarkable
episode when Ruth tried to rescue another helpless creature — an abandoned
infant rather than a helpless animal. She wrote about it in a letter to Rosa
in mid-October 1932, when she was twelve years old, Rosa was in Korea
at school, and Virginia was about seven months pregnant with the Bells'
fifth child. (Nelson copied a portion of Ruth's letter into one of his regular
missives home, adding, "It is so graphic in its description that I thought
you would like to read it.") Walking to school, Ruth saw a little baby boy
abandoned in a roadside ditch. The Bells later learned that the baby had
been "thrown out" by the parents because it experienced severe seizures.
Beckoned by a nearby woman who said that the infant boy was still living,
Ruth described "scrambl[ing] down to where it lay and [seeing] it breathe,
then give a tiny cry." She continued: "I ran for Dr. Woods (mother and
daddy were in Hwaian) and then came back, and Miss F." — their teacher,
Lucy Fletcher — "went to hurry things up a little, while I stood and fanned
off the huge green flies that had settled on it by the fifties." The baby's "eyes
were open and filled with pus so that all you could see was yellow. A few rags
lying by were all it had and its tiny naked body was blue from the cold." In
short order, Ruth and the other children who had gathered were hustled
off to school. "But," Ruth continued, "when we came from school we went
over to the hospital to see it, and honestly! you could hardly recognize it it

was so very clean, only pitifully white and thin." The adolescent girl, still so enamored of her animals, was similarly enthralled with this forsaken baby. Nevertheless, her concern mixed with detachment. She referred to the baby boy throughout this description as "it," even in her prayers to God "to let it live."

For all of her concern for the baby's earthly well-being, though, Ruth wrote to Rosa that she also "pled with [God] to take it home out of this vale of sin and tears (where the only mother it had did not care for it more than to throw it away before it died!), and He did. Friday night," she continued to Rosa, "it fell asleep." Young Ruth's initial calls for help, her concern, her prayers all displayed a connection and a sense of responsibility, yet by consistently calling the infant "it," she maintained that awareness at arm's length. She believed that the baby's earthly life mattered less than his eternal one. In practical terms, she knew that her family could not adopt it into their home without inviting scores of other unwanted children to be dropped at the door of the hospital or, alternately, incurring the wrath of locals who might suspect them of kidnapping. If Nelson's disposing of T.B. was her first real heartbreak, Ruth's attempted rescue of this little baby showed her at relative peace with life's brutality.

From a very young age, Ruth witnessed all manner of suffering that her Stateside peers would likely not have been exposed to. She later remembered how the whole mission compound prayed for the safe return of the hospital business manager's two kidnapped children; bandits returned the children unharmed. Rosa and Ruth knew personally about deaths by suicide, disease, criminal violence, and war. Years afterward, Ruth told of several tragic deaths among the missionaries: John Randolph Currie, a toddler who died after falling into a tub of scalding laundry water; his sister Lucy Calvin Currie, who died from eating contaminated beans; "Uncle" Jack Vinson, kidnapped and beheaded in 1931 by bandits. Nelson observed of his daughters, "They are hardened to things which few children at home know of outside of story books."

For instance, alongside news of MaiMai's growing vocabulary and her own stamp collection, Rosa matter-of-factly reported to Grandfather Bell: "Daddy took us out walking, and we saw part of a skull lying on the ground, a coffin with no dirt on the top, and a coffin with a hole in one corner of it." In another case, the family traveled to Shanghai "for a few weeks vacation just before Mission Meeting." Nelson described the "military guards (ten armed soldiers)" then newly aboard each boat. "We really had little fear of being held up altho there was a possibility of it so we all planned to lie flat on the floor the minute any shooting began." He continued, "Ruth was rather hoping we would be held up for the experience" — quite a change from her fright during the 1924 voyage to Kuling. Mother Bell must have expressed concern about another of the girls' experiences, their "shock" when they heard a "man call [out] who was murdered by his servant." Nelson protested: "I dont think it impressed them unduly as they only rarely referred to it afterwards and then as only a matter of course. They hear of so many things they are more inured to them than children at home would be."

As a grown woman, Ruth would remember that from childhood she had "loved storms" and always had the sense that near her parents in their "solidly built house . . . nothing really bad could happen." Gray brick, built according to Western standards and in a Western style, the two-story house represented to Ruth an outpost of southern hospitality and security on the Chinese landscape. One occasion illustrated this feeling vividly. During a string of hot August nights (maybe in 1932), Nelson, Rosa, and Ruth slept "on the top of the sleeping porch," where it was "much cooler" than inside the house. Nearby, volleys of gunfire lasted for "about twenty minutes." Nelson described it as "a regular battle." Tsingkiangpu's summer heat was oppressive, so much so that sleeping in the open during a shooting skirmish seemed reasonable, especially from the solid house's porch roof. Nelson slumbered peacefully until "Virginia called up from down stairs to know what was going on." At least in writing about the night to his mother, Nelson commented with typical sang-froid, "I *hoped* no bullets would land on us and our hopes were fulfilled. . . . God's promises of keeping in perfect peace are *true*." Here and elsewhere, Nelson displayed a somewhat magical view of God's protecting power over him and his family.

Ruth later recalled that this dangerous and high-pressure environment of missionizing in China during these times pushed some people to their limits. One of the missionary wives (stationed not at Tsingkiangpu but in

35

Taichow) died by suicide when Ruth was a little girl; "overworked and under unbearable pressure," the adult Ruth remembered, "this dear Christian broke." Nelson wrote home about Fannie Taylor's death at Tsingkiangpu, which came during the preparations for a 1933 presbytery meeting that found a dozen attendees staying at the Bells' home. Nelson had planned to attend the funeral, "but," he wrote, "I found Virginia was feeling the whole shock and sorrow so much more than she had shown." He decided, therefore, to remain at home to support her and help with the guests. In a section of his letter marked "**STOP** – DO NOT READ ALOUD – " Nelson explained that Mrs. Taylor "was very much disappointed at the news that they could not take their furlough" the following year as expected. The Taylors had also received "a letter from the Executive Committee" in Nashville, "urging the wives of the missionaries to do more work." Nelson felt outrage on behalf of this woman – "there was not a finer missionary on the field" – and protective of his own hardworking wife. The family's grief over Mrs. Taylor's death likely softened Ruth to the struggles that came with a life of Christian service and made her solicitous, in later years, of Christian workers – including Billy Graham.

Ruth learned from the example of her parents not to be afraid in the midst of such tumult. They taught and showed her that God was not unmindful of these human troubles, that somehow these adversities were to be offered up for God's sovereign wisdom to work out. Such an attitude might look to outsiders like resignation. But in Nelson's and Virginia's lives, acceptance of suffering brought renewed purpose for work rather than nihilistic surrender – and it was the work of a lifetime. For Ruth, too, the interpretation of suffering became lifelong work. She used the tools of her faith (including her knowledge of the Bible and a cherished Southern Presbyterian belief that God's sovereignty guided everything), her powers of careful observation, and her poetry to move toward a place where storms of troubles left her awed but unafraid.

—◇—

What were the Bells' ambitions for their daughters? Nelson wrote to his mother that he and Virginia both had a certain satisfaction about their children: "God knows we have no ambition or desire for them, other than that they should serve Him, how, and where He wishes." In one of the circular letters to mission supporters, he communicated a part of his and Virginia's perspective, which seems relevant for understanding Ruth's life: "a complete surrender to Him is the secret of the happy and useful Christian life, regardless of where we may be, and we do pray for that complete surrender of our wills." As Presbyterians who revered the tradition of a "learned clergy" and valued the life of the mind for laypeople, the Bells focused serious attention on educating their children. If in his letters Nelson obsessed delightedly over the adorable MaiMai, he also worried to death the subject of the girls' schooling. Both Bell parents expended unceasing effort toward obtaining sound instruction for them.

Several challenges confronted them on this front. They had the highest expectations for Rosa and Ruth, then MaiMai and later Clayton, from kindergarten through college. In early 1929, the quest began to find someone other than Virginia to teach the older two girls as they began moving past elementary-stage education. Nelson wrote to his niece Virginia Norris, his sister Norma Norris and her husband, and his mother, inviting the niece to come serve as Tsingkiangpu's station teacher for a three-year term. Uncle Nelson made a persuasive case that might have appealed to a young woman looking to make a meaningful contribution in the world: she would be helping them address "one of the most serious problems missionary families have to face," especially "in interior stations" like theirs. The tone Nelson struck in his several appeals was desperate, almost as if his wife's teaching was a deeply unsatisfactory compromise that was damaging Rosa and Ruth forever. By March, Virginia Norris had declined the offer, rather to Nelson's surprise, since letters had already passed back and forth about specific details of the job. After receiving this news, Nelson's tone changed. Perhaps he felt wounded by the failure of his extended family to take up the challenge of work in China. He also had to repair the negative impression created in Mother Bell's mind by his dire descriptions of Virginia's teaching. Rosa and Ruth were not, he assured his mother, "running wild without any school."

Another challenge for the Bells was that Ruth did not like school, while Rosa reveled in every part of it. Ruth did not fit into the mold of model student that Nelson and Virginia cherished. He wrote of her not "succeeding." Even if not spoken to Ruth herself, that label of unsuccessful student shaped father-daughter interactions with respect to homework and study. In those days before extra support or accommodations for students with learning differences, Nelson simply thought that Ruth needed to work harder.

One episode illustrates Nelson and Virginia's attitude both toward finding experienced teachers and prodding their second daughter to work her hardest. After their niece turned down the station teacher job, Virginia Bell continued to teach the girls, except for a brief period in October 1929 when a "Mrs. Bradley" took over "for the time being." Agnes Junkin Bradley and her husband, Dr. John Bradley, were stationed in Sutsien, about fifty miles from Tsingkiangpu. He fell ill and came to the hospital for treatment. Trained in "kindergarten work," Mrs. Bradley filled in for Virginia during this period. However, Nelson thought the girls were not "learning as much as when Virginia teaches them." Mrs. Bradley was "keeping Ruth back" with a less advanced child. In fact, after a few weeks, Virginia resumed her position as the girls' teacher. (Dr. Bradley died at Tsingkiangpu in November.)

Mrs. Bradley's approach evidenced that Ruth objectively lagged behind other children her age. But Nelson and Virginia were not having it. Ruth was not to be held back. She was to buckle down and meet the challenge of what they considered appropriate grade-level work. Virginia soon after reported reassuringly — and perhaps a little defensively — to Mother Bell that "Ruth is picking up very much, has learned how to go about studying and takes pride in it."

At least one other attempt to recruit a teacher for the Tsingkiangpu missionary children failed before the spring of 1930, when a recommendation arrived that Lucy A. Fletcher, a teacher working in Nashville, Tennessee, be brought to the station. She had a college education, Bible school training, and several years of experience, but she also was "deeply consecrated." The Bells valued that last quality as much as they sought skill in teaching. They planned for Lucy to live with them when she arrived. Nelson eagerly, even desperately, anticipated her arrival. When, in response to rising tensions in the area between the Chinese Nationalists and the antimissionary Chinese Communist forces, the Stateside mission authorities delayed Fletcher's departure for Tsingkiangpu, Nelson grew positively antic. In a letter to a friend, Nelson vented his fury toward what he saw as uninformed bureaucrats overreacting to exaggerated news reports of fighting. He sent a telegram to mission managers that sounded more like a call for emergency assistance than for a schoolteacher — "CONDITIONS JUSTIFY FLETCHERS IMMEDIATE SAILING URGENTLY NEEDED!" — and followed up with telegrams to other China missionaries, encouraging them in turn to lobby for Lucy Fletcher and other missionaries to be allowed to depart the United States. Nelson and his family were making out okay amidst the unrest, he thought, and he therefore saw no reason why others could not join them.

In addition to revealing his impatience for a trained teacher to arrive, Nelson's position here reflected a characteristic self-righteous rigidity. Nelson was determined that others either see things his way or, failing that, at least submit to his plan of action. Although he would not have used the term, he understood his work and his family's place on the front lines of gospel service as heroic. The Stateside bureaucracy was wrong to interfere with their sacrificial work. The pencil pushers needed rather to set aside their excessive concern for safety and instead trust in God's protection of those whom God had called to the field. They must forge ahead in faith, without fear.

Finally, on the last day of October 1930, the long-awaited Lucy Fletcher arrived in Shanghai. Ruth and nurse Cassie Lee Oliver had traveled there from Tsingkiangpu to replace Ruth's lost glasses. They met Lucy and escorted her back to the mission compound. By Monday morning, November 10, class was in session. Rosa could "hardly wait" to begin, Virginia wrote to her mother-in-law. She made no mention of Ruth's feelings on the matter, suggesting that regardless of the teacher, in Ruth's view school was nothing to get excited about. As eager as Nelson had been for Fletcher's arrival, his reviews of her work were tepid. He admired her knowledge and capabilities but saw her as "not especially fitted temperamentally" for teaching. Perhaps she was less than patient with certain dawdling students.

Lucy Fletcher continued at Tsingkiangpu until the spring of 1933, when her term of service ended. In late August 1932, Rosa had followed the customary route of missionary children and left China to attend boarding school — in her case, at the Presbyterian-run Pyeng Yang Foreign School in what is now North Korea. At the time, Japan controlled the Korean peninsula, its repressive rule creating, ironically, relative safety for the school's students. The Bells hoped that Ruth would follow her sister there by the time Lucy Fletcher finished her service at Tsingkiangpu. That meant that Nelson and Virginia expected — unbelievably, given Ruth's laggard academic performance — that Ruth would advance through two grades in a year. Her previous academic record gave little reason to hope for such rapid progress. But the Bell parents perhaps saw Lucy as their best hope and saw the value of safety and companionship if Rosa and Ruth could travel back and forth together. Nelson reported to his mother in November 1932, "Ruth is doing so well at school this year, making excellent marks and showing evidence of real study and work." Reflecting a year later about Ruth's academic journey, he wrote, "Ruth was slow in starting but the last two years she did well in her books." By that time, MaiMai had herself evidenced a less-than-stellar commitment to her studies. Rosa was a hard academic act for her younger sisters to follow, but Nelson was, by late 1933, beginning to accept and even lovingly appreciate the fact that Ruth and MaiMai were typical students and Rosa was the unusual one.

Nelson and Ruth accompanied Rosa the first time she made the almost 2,400-mile trip to school in Pyeng Yang, a city that boasted Korea's most diverse, concentrated missionary population. The huge Presbyterian missionary installation there featured schools for boys and girls, a gymnasium and athletic fields, a hospital, a seminary, a college, dormitories, houses for instructors, and a machine shop for vocational training. Stopping in Shanghai on their way to Korea, the father-daughter trio attended what the former professional baseball prospect declared a "jam-up good" baseball game between a Japanese college team and a team of US Marines. They must have found themselves in a group of teachers from both the Shanghai American School and the Pyeng Yang school, for Nelson wrote a self-satisfied letter home containing his comparative assessment of the two schools, based on what his assumptions about the teachers' appearance led him to conclude about their moral probity. Although the missionary-sponsored Shanghai American School constituted one of the leading institutions in Asia for children of expatriates employed in business, diplomacy, and missions, Nelson found its teachers too worldly for his tastes: they "had bobbed hair and were painted" — that is, they wore makeup. (By contrast, as David Hollinger has noted, some children of US business executives experienced schools like Shanghai American as "stiff and hypocritical.") Nelson also indicted the school for disregarding Sabbath observance. He wrote his mother in late 1932 of poker being played on Sunday during a Shanghai school trip, citing it as evidence of "a great deal of bad behavior in the school."

On the other hand, "Rosa's [future] teachers" at Pyeng Yang "had long hair and no sign of paint" — these women, in Nelson's opinion, properly valued plainness and sincerity. Nelson went on: "their general attitude was that one would want for one's children to have as teachers." The teachers at Pyeng Yang had been educated at places Nelson approved, such as Moody Bible Institute and the Bible Institute of Los Angeles. Although Northern Presbyterians attended the school in Pyeng Yang, and indeed the city itself was in the Northern Presbyterian mission zone, Nelson was relieved to discover that those particular northerners "back Westminster Seminary," which was founded by antimodernist J. Gresham Machen in Pennsylvania in 1929 after his break with Princeton Seminary. For that reason, Nelson concluded that they were "good sound people." He was excited and reassured by the vibrant Christian community in the city of Pyeng Yang, which boasted a score of Presbyterian churches, some seating thousands. "I never saw anything like it," he enthused.

In spite of her father's enthusiasm, Ruth only reluctantly followed her sister to Pyeng Yang Foreign School, entering in early September of 1933. Ruth, her parents, teacher Lucy Fletcher, and several other students heading off to the Korean high school constituted the traveling party. They stopped over at the "very British" missionary home in Shanghai, overseen by the also "very British" (and very old, Ruth remembered) Miss Edith Spurling, who had a particular fondness for the Southern Presbyterians — perhaps because they possessed a formality that she appreciated. Ruth, however, dreading the imminent separation from her parents, could not enjoy the relative comforts of the missionary home. She later recounted her last night in Shanghai, "lay[ing] in the stifling heat . . . praying earnestly [to] die before morning." Death was to her preferable to being separated from home, especially for anything as distasteful as schoolwork. Mournfully, Ruth recalled, "Dawn broke over the great, gray city, and obviously, God had not seen fit to answer my prayer." She was still alive, still in the middle of a weeklong voyage from Tsingkiangpu to Pyeng Yang Foreign School. She would join Rosa there, after all. Characteristically "eager to try her wings," Rosa had adjusted and flourished. But when faced with the distance that would separate them, Ruth hated to leave behind Daddy, Mother, MaiMai, and her infant brother, Clayton — not to mention her Chinese friends and the tight-knit missionary community.

Arriving in Pyeng Yang, Ruth felt a "sense of finality" as she rode through the city's streets toward her new school. The "spartan" gray building where the school's female students lived held no charm for her. Almost immediately, Ruth fell desperately homesick. During the days, with classes and homework to distract her, she muddled through. But "the nights," she later remembered, "did me in." She sobbed, head buried in her pillow, trying not to wake Rosa and their roommate Helen Meyers, but aching from the separation she felt deeply. "Night after night, week after week," she later confessed, "I cried myself to sleep, silently — miserably."

Distressed to the point of illness, Ruth soon landed in the school infirmary. Virginia had written to Nelson's mother, "Our hearts just ache for poor little Ruth, a letter from Rosa of Sept. 25 said Ruth hadn't failed a single night to cry herself to sleep, and she looked so badly & was so thin that [Rosa] was taking her that afternoon to see a doctor." While convalescing, Ruth turned for solace to her Bible. She read through the entire book of Psalms, ensconced in the infirmary bed, surrounded by pillows. She read Psalm 27, her eyes coming to rest on verse 10: "When my father and mother forsake me, then the Lord will take me up." As an adult looking back, Ruth dismissed the idea that her parents had "deliberately forsaken" her. She came to recognize that her mother and Lucy Fletcher had taught her everything they could. "There was," she realized, "no alternative now but to send us off to the best school they could locate" — significantly, not the closest, which was in Shanghai. To the Bells, "best" meant not only academically rigorous, but forthrightly Christian in moral rigor. For decades afterward, the comfort and strength that the Psalms brought Ruth during that period stayed with her — as did that very Bible, well-worn and eventually placed on a shelf above her desk in Montreat, North Carolina.

Ruth prayed assiduously to God and implored her parents: she wanted to leave school and return to Tsingkiangpu. But the Bells did not relent. They did feel for their tenderhearted girl. Nelson wrote in a confidential letter to "My dear Miss Axworthy" — the appropriately stern name for the girls' dean — "Mrs. Bell and I have been distressed and disturbed by three long letters we have received from Ruth during the past week, all so home sick and urging us to permit her to come home." Virginia recognized Ruth's old anxiety and clinginess, but, she said, "I never dreamed she would suffer so long" from this homesickness. For her part, Ruth persisted; she kept praying to be allowed home. Nelson wrote to his mother: "<u>We</u> too had been praying & we could find no reason for her to go home and *many* for her to stay at Pyeng Yang."

Her parents concluded that Ruth was engaged in too much "introspection" and was not finding ways to enjoy other students' company. Nelson's letter to Miss Axworthy went on at length: "Ruth is a precious child, so loving and sympathetic, and kind. She is also sensitive and emotional and we feel she has been staying in her room writing too much; not only has she written these long letters to us, but she has also written long letters to other members of the station. They are really exceptional in their descriptive character, but they take time she should be spending either in study, or in play."

This description stands out all the more given Nelson's persistent silence about Ruth just a few years earlier. It shows that as the years passed, Nelson grew in his ability to appreciate Ruth's "exceptional" gift for capturing life in words. He recognized Ruth as a "sweet, sensitive child," Rosa as "so dependable and self reliant." Both were "two *precious* girls" to their parents.

This passage also reveals an important aspect of Ruth's character that would stay with her for life: in times of loneliness, frustration, or sadness, Ruth wrote. Later, she would tell readers that writing was the alternative to developing an ulcer. Her oldest child would confirm that Ruth gave her children only "sunshine," putting her feelings of stress and loneliness into her private writings. All her life long, Ruth poured her anxious desolation onto the page in letters, musings, and poems.

Nelson and Virginia wanted Miss Axworthy to counter Ruth's tendency to isolate herself. Coax Ruth out of her room, Nelson recommended; get her "out-of-doors," and perhaps rearrange Rosa and Ruth's living situation. A little unfairly for Rosa, the Bells worried that her rooming with Helen Myers "caused Rosa to neglect Ruth without realizing it." They left this aspect of the situation to Miss Axworthy's "sense [of] the situation." The concerned parents expressed great respect for Axworthy and her school. That was high praise, coming from Nelson.

His letter to the girls' dean included another significant clue about Ruth's temperament: "We feel that Ruth has a slight tendency to revel in the sad side of things, letting her religion (which is exceedingly real and precious to her) take a slightly morbid turn." Triggered by her desperate homesickness, a "crisis of faith" struck Ruth during that first semester in Pyeng Yang. Neither God nor her parents had responded to her pleas. Later Ruth recognized that she had arrived at a developmental inflection point. She had followed her parents' guidance in matters of faith up to then. Away at school, it was up to her to discern the path her faith would take. And she realized that, while intellectually she knew what her parents had taught her about Jesus dying to redeem human sin, "somehow," she said, "I did not feel included." All those years of sensing herself as the odd daughter out were festering. Did she belong in the Bell family? Did she belong in the Christian family? Her homesickness catalyzed an existential isolation. As much as she implored God for forgiveness and a sense of God's presence, she "felt nothing." She recalled, "I wasn't even sure He was listening."

So, as she had before and would again, she turned to Rosa, her "ever-practical sister," for counsel. What to do?

"I don't know what to tell you to do," Rosa said, "unless you take some [Bible] verse and put your own name in. See if that helps."

Ruth took her sister's suggestion to heart. Isaiah chapter 53, a passage Ruth treasured, seemed a good pick: "He was wounded for [Ruth's] transgressions, He was bruised for [Ruth's] iniquities: the chastisement of [Ruth's] peace was upon Him; and with His stripes [Ruth] is healed."

Rosa's advice worked. Ruth reported, "I knew then that I was included."

Writing years later, Ruth recognized this bleak episode in Pyeng Yang as her "training period," her "boot camp," "preparation for [her] future." Again and again, she would turn to that Bible and to companionship with God in her isolation and doubts as a mother and a faithful Christian. She would continue to use Rosa's method and recommend it to others. She recognized that without living through and eventually thriving in Pyeng Yang, she would have had an infinitely harder time enduring the challenges of her life as long-distance wife and mostly solo parent.

By the spring of 1934, Ruth had settled into life at Pyeng Yang more comfortably. Her powers of description continued to enliven her letters home: Virginia described Ruth as a "scream," able to capture so perfectly her observations about others at school. Ruth would later write that she could not recall a time when she "wasn't scribbling something. Bits and pieces." Her letters home might include long newsy stories depicting recent goings-on. But for her own purposes, she tended to jottings. Ruth was never one to write lengthy diary entries. Every new year, she later remembered, "I began . . . optimistically on the first of January," determined to keep up a daily habit of recording the day's memorable events, but then her determination "flickered out shortly after." In her poems, though, Ruth captured feelings and events that she wanted to remember. Her process, she wrote later, was "like snapping pictures."

Chapter 2

College and a Calling

—◇—

1937–1943

Nelson and Virginia planned another furlough to begin in mid-1935. Their main goal was to prepare for Rosa to enter college in the fall of the next year. The Bells wavered about where they should live. The family could settle in Wheaton, Illinois, where Rosa could perhaps start at the college and Ruth could attend Wheaton Academy. Or, Virginia suggested, they might go to Montreat, North Carolina, outside of Asheville, where many furloughing or retired Presbyterian workers made their homes. Both Virginia and Nelson wanted to avoid returning home to Waynesboro but needed also to avoid offending their families. Nelson refused his mother's offer for them to live with her, giving a strange reason, considering the future close relationship and proximity to his Graham grandchildren: "I don't believe older people should be forced to live in the same house with lively youngsters." MaiMai was about seven, and Clayton was a toddler at "the most lively age." Other housing was available in the town, but it was not up to Virginia or Nelson's standards. At the root of Nelson's worries lay his desire to protect Virginia's health. If they settled close to home and family, it would be hard to ensure that she got sufficient rest and privacy.

In the end, the academic quality and Christian tone of available schooling greatly influenced the Bells' decision. "We do want [Rosa and Ruth] with us" during the furlough, Nelson wrote, "and yet we do not care about sending them to the local [Waynesboro] High School" because "it is a small town and our girls will have practically nothing in common with the girls there." Virginia dismissed that public school as "not Christian"; therefore "the influences are not good." Montreat seemed a good alternative.

And so, by the spring of 1935, the Bells worked out their plan: they would live in Montreat for the year, but instead of attending the college there, Rosa would proceed to Wheaton and begin taking classes. Ruth would remain at home with her parents, attending the high school program at Montreat College. (Her parents were gratified to discover that Ruth was one grade level ahead of her classmates, owing to the rigorous curriculum at Pyeng Yang.) At the end of that furlough year, in August 1936, Nelson and Virginia bade farewell to Rosa, who would begin her premedical studies at Wheaton. The parents, along with Ruth, MaiMai, and Clayton, made their way back to China, stopping in Yokohama, Japan, so that Ruth could sail for Pyeng Yang and her last year of high school year there.

In contrast to the homesickness Ruth experienced during her first semester at Pyeng Yang, she flourished in her last. She returned from the furlough year to settle into a private room, "for which she [was] very thankful." Ruth had grown in self-confidence about her academics and her ability to contribute to the school community. She was happy and popular, taking algebra and participating in Christian Endeavor. A short prayer-poem, titled "Gift," written in 1935, reflected Ruth's spirit of surrender and her desire to live as a joyful Christian:

> Lord Jesus, take this life of mine,
>   worthless as it may be,
> cleanse it, and fill it, and make it shine,
>   that it may be bright for Thee.

Ruth suffered in the fall from a boil under her arm, and much to Nelson's chagrin, received unsatisfactory treatment from the female doctor at the school. He wrote about the experience to Rosa at Wheaton and cautioned her to avoid making similar mistakes when she became a doctor.

Ruth's letters back to Tsingkiangpu that fall of 1936 evidenced enthusiasm about her studies and about the school's strong "spiritual tone." She still did not excel in her schoolwork, at least not to Nelson's high standards, although her performance in Bible courses — she was enrolled in four different ones — proved an exception. At least on this score, Nelson felt pleased and reassured.

Ruth also observed and reported on local Korean Christian communities and their internal disputes. One major source of tension arose from the Japanese government's requirement that traditional Shinto shrines be maintained; imperial Japan annexed Korea in 1910 and undertook wide-ranging efforts to "Japanize" the country's economy, language, culture, and religious practices. By enforcing the Japanese tradition of Shinto observance, the empire aimed to temper Korean resisters' embrace of Christianity. When some Christian laypeople nevertheless complied with the imperial order, the local Christian leadership responded with disciplinary action. Young Ruth reported this controversy in her letters home, signaling her attention to matters beyond her schoolwork and social life. She figured that the news would be of interest to her parents, and she was right. Nelson found the disciplining of the laypeople "distressing," since he recognized that Korean Christians lived between the rock of faithfulness and the hard place of Japanese domination, but Nelson also "rejoic[ed] in the courage of those [among the Korean Christian leadership] who are taking this strong stand for the right." Nelson's Christian rigor brooked little compromise with geopolitics.

Another exchange of letters, however, showed what looks very much like Christian compromise with another kind of local custom. For Halloween 1936, Ruth and a friend dressed as blackface minstrels for the school costume party. Word reached Nelson through the grapevine not only of her costume, but also of the difficulty Ruth had removing the blackening cork soot she had smeared on her face: she "had rubbed part of the skin off getting rid of the black." He jocularly included in his next letter to Ruth a "word from an old minstrel hand" — presumably Nelson himself — to "always put on grease of some kind before putting on burnt cork or other black, otherwise it is almost impossible to get clean." The "old minstrel hand," the product of a southern culture that saw minstrelsy as entertainment rather than hateful provocation, knew how to "black up" and calmly schooled his teenage daughter in the practice. His matter-of-fact advice helps set Nelson and the Bells — including Ruth — in a context of white privilege and white supremacy that was still the norm in the 1930s. They shared the practice of this masquerade, revealing conventional attitudes about race and whiteness while working among a nonwhite, largely non-Christian population.

The fall 1936 semester was not only about Bible classes and Halloween parties. Ruth also mourned the apparent suicide of a fellow student, the son of Northern Presbyterian missionaries who jumped into the path of an oncoming train. She wrote in several letters to Virginia and Nelson about the boy's death and the funeral, highlighting words that the boy's father spoke to the Pyeng Yang students advising them to, as Nelson reported, "give their hearts entirely to God." This tragedy perhaps was one spur to Ruth's prayers for a Christian revival at the school, prayers that Nelson noted in early 1937. The school did indeed experience "a real revival" that spring, an awakening that Ruth apparently played an active role in guiding and encouraging. Although her specific contribution remains unknown, Nelson and Virginia received reports "from others" that Ruth had that year exerted a "wonderful influence . . . in the spiritual life of the school."

Still, after Ruth's graduation from high school, Virginia and Nelson worried about her readiness for college, with its intensified academic and social demands, not to mention its greater distance from Tsingkiangpu. (It was a given that she would follow Rosa to Wheaton in part as a buffer against Ruth's tendency to homesickness.) They considered keeping her with them at the mission for what we might today call a gap year. Both Nelson and Virginia felt like Ruth might need the time to mature further. Nelson even wrote to his "precious nineteen-year-old daughter" — Rosa, at Wheaton — to ask her advice: Did she think that "a year of seasoning at home" would better prepare Ruth for college-level work and campus life? (No response from Rosa appears in Nelson's papers.) Ruth's parents worried still about her moodiness, the possibility of homesickness, and her academic abilities. She had been close enough to them in Korea in case of some crisis, but if she were in the United States, she would be beyond their reach if she fell into a sulk or became seriously ill. With trepidation but trusting God to guide, Nelson finally wrote to Ruth in early 1937, "We cannot tell what the future holds but as the Lord seems to have opened the way for you to go there [Wheaton] next year we will just take things as they come." He had already planned out a course schedule for her that omitted all math classes. Algebra gave her fits. Nelson wondered in letters to her if she could possibly maintain a B average (there was scholarship or perhaps missionary stipend money at stake, not to mention family pride). His confidence in Ruth's academic abilities still flagged, although he tried to bolster his conviction by putting ultimate confidence in the Lord.

Her parents registered Ruth as a first-year student at Wheaton and made travel arrangements for her to enter in the fall of 1937. Their decision rested on both educational and financial concerns. Ruth might have a harder time adjusting to the college workload if she took a break from school. Moreover, her missionary stipend would end, as it did for all missionary children, at the age of twenty-one. If she could complete college study before her twenty-first birthday in June 1941, the Bells would not incur extra expense trying to cover that amount themselves. (She did not.) Nelson, ever thrifty, made peace with any concerns about Ruth's academic or emotional readiness for college, and made ready to send his second daughter off to the States.

Wheaton College, founded by Wesleyan Methodist abolitionists as Illinois Institute in 1852, aimed to offer students college-level study and encourage their embrace of social reform. The college's first building — now incorporated into Blanchard Hall — opened its doors in December 1853, although construction on its upper rooms had not yet been finished. The institute welcomed antislavery activist Jonathan Blanchard as president at the beginning of the academic year in fall 1859, and was renamed Wheaton College in January 1860. Andover Seminary had expelled Blanchard because of his antislavery work; he graduated from Lane Seminary, then led by none other than Lyman Beecher, who would face down his own abolitionist student rebels, Theodore Weld among them. Wheaton College was from the start open to both women and men, black and white.

In the 1930s, when Nelson and Virginia would have been deciding where to send their daughters for college, Wheaton was "the fastest-growing col-

lege in America," according to one history. Its 1931 accreditation by the
Association of American Universities, which recognized its solid academics
and professionally trained faculty and administration, bolstered its growth.
Periodic religious revivals stirred the campus community. In 1936, the college experienced a revival after a January visit of prolific author and evangelist J. Edwin Orr, detailed in his book *This Is the Victory* (1936). Nelson
sent seven of Orr's books — accounts of his evangelistic tours — to Mother
Bell the following year, possibly including *This Is the Victory*. (He may have
later recommended Orr's work to his son-in-law, who in 1951 wrote an introduction to Orr's book *Full Surrender*.) In that decade, too, Wheaton was
adding new buildings — including a new women's dormitory, built in sections beginning in 1936.

Wheaton appealed to Nelson and Virginia for a variety of reasons. Its
evangelical bona fides were impeccable, and the college continued to insist
on training every student in the Bible. The college also insisted on personal
conduct and engagement in evangelistic work befitting its standard for young
Christian women and men. But Wheaton also encouraged the regular fun of
college life. It had a long tradition of literary societies, beginning in 1855 with
the founding of what became the Beltionian Association, a coed debating
society. Beginning in 1893, Wheaton fielded a football team, and many of the
attendant festivities followed — parades, pep rallies, and a marching band.

Their parents might have preferred originally that Rosa and Ruth attend a college closer to Mother Bell in Waynesboro. Indeed, Mary Baldwin
College, in Staunton, Virginia, just fifteen miles from Waynesboro, showed
up first as Virginia's suggestion in 1931 — quite a while before Rosa would
actually depart for college — "in order," she wrote to her mother-in-law,
"that [Rosa and Ruth] shall be near you." Virginia worried about sending
her "girls" away: "little do they know the *force* of evil at home" in the United
States. If Mary Baldwin did not suit them, Mother Bell offered to move
from Waynesboro to be near wherever Rosa, and eventually Ruth, ended
up. Virginia was deeply touched by this offer, writing, "There isn't anyone
else I want to trust them to."

Nelson expressed his and Virginia's strong preference for "a southern
school" with theological commitments and social expectations that he and

Virginia recognized: a belief in the Bible's inspired origins and the "spirituality of the church" — a Southern Presbyterian idea rooted in the antebellum era that opposed church involvement in social reform, particularly around civil rights. The Bells also expected white and black students to be segregated from each other. Nelson may not have known that Wheaton had welcomed black students from its founding. Or perhaps he knew, and he and Virginia ended up caring less about that than about what they judged to be the school's correct theological and moral stances.

Or still further, perhaps Wheaton in the late 1930s and early 1940s had embraced the broader culture's segregationist habits. The college's *Bulletin* for 1936–1937 listed the International Students' Association among the various campus organizations for students; it "promote[d] a better understanding among races and nationalities," according to the brief description. This wording suggests Wheaton's openness to racial "understanding" existed within the international frame consonant with its mission imperative. The *Bulletin* also described the college's "outlook" as "conservative in its political and economic views." Photographs in the *Tower* yearbooks of Rosa's and Ruth's Wheaton years show an overwhelmingly white student body, faculty, and administration; throughout her college years, Ruth appeared in group pictures showing almost uniformly white students, except one 1943 *Tower* photo of a large coed club that included one Asian female student. Even Ruth's 1940 *Tower* picture with the Student Council, a supposedly representative body, showed no students of color. In his 1950 history of Wheaton, Wyeth Willard included forty-three pictures, only one of which showed nonwhite subjects — African American children attending a "Colored Sunday School" being taught by a young white female student. The photo's caption notes with self-congratulatory pride, "The [college's] founding fathers would rejoice" — one implication being that little black children particularly needed the intervention of white Christian womanhood. While determining race and ethnicity from photographs is an inexact way of determining student demographics, it seems safe to assume the surpassing dominance of white students in this era. Wheaton, although not located in the South, reflected the kind of white space that the Bells were accustomed to and approved of.

Moreover, as Nelson wrote in late 1932, Wheaton defended the gospel "unswervingly, even aggressively." The choice of a college was not a casual decision (if anything were a casual decision for the Bells), but one with eternal consequences: "I am convinced that in these days an institution" — a college, or a mission hospital, or a religious denomination — "cannot simply *stand* for the right, or try to take a neutral position. Satan," Nelson warned, "is actively fighting thru men and women unfaithful to God and His Word and we must fight back, in His power."

Sending Rosa then Ruth to Wheaton constituted yet another leap of faith for these parents, given the college's distance from Mother Bell and from the familiar customs, including racial codes, of the South. Yet Nelson and Virginia valued excellence. They demanded it of themselves, their coworkers, and their children. Wheaton's up-and-coming reputation as a Christian institution with rigorous academic standards would have impressed them. By 1933, Nelson had zeroed in on Wheaton as a uniquely attractive institution: "These days," he wrote to Mother Bell, "when there are so many compromises and when so few schools will come out and say what they stand for in a positive way" — perhaps here taking a jab at the militant fundamentalists of Bob Jones College — "I like the way Wheaton makes its unequivocal stand for God, the Bible, the Savior, and clean, honest moral living." Indeed, Wheaton's 1936–1937 *Bulletin* declared, "The general curriculum of the College is correlated with the fundamental principles found in" the Bible. Moreover, the Bells found Wheaton's stated purpose, to educate future Christian workers, to be in line with their daughters' vocational interests. The *Bulletin* announced, "The curriculum as a whole, with special emphasis in Christian education, prepares students to be pastors' assistants, directors of religious education, home and foreign missionaries, leaders of church schools, and for various other types of Christian work." The Bells wanted a college course that would prepare their daughters for serving God.

—◇—

Nelson intended to accompany Ruth to Shanghai in mid-August 1937, when she would board a ship bound for Seattle and then travel east to Wheaton in time for the start of fall semester. For her part, Ruth felt that her plans required nothing more than "a utilitarian knowledge of Tibetan and the Bible." She later recalled, "By 1937, I had my future securely planned. I would never marry. I would spend the rest of my life as a missionary in Tibet." She "certainly didn't have to sail halfway around the world for that" — although Nelson and Virginia had clearly been preparing to send her to Wheaton College to follow Rosa. Virginia wrote that "everything is in order, and Ruth has a lot of pretty new clothes, nothing elaborate, mostly prints." Her material preparations, at least, were complete, and she was prepared for departure. The Japanese, however, had other ideas. Japanese soldiers had engaged Chinese forces near Beijing. Japanese air forces had bombed Shanghai and deployed soldiers on the ground there. The conflict reached as far south as Tsingkiangpu, which experienced its first air raid warning just as Ruth was supposed to be departing the mission. Concerns for their safety kept the Bells hemmed in at home. Rather than fret or fear for their lives, however, Virginia wrote to Mother Bell, "when war broke out the very day [Ruth's] baggage was to leave, we just kicked up our heels in joy & decided to have a good time."

Then, in early September, the US ambassador in Nanking strongly recommended that all Americans evacuate Tsingkiangpu. The Bells followed the directive. Ruth later recalled singing "God Be with You till We Meet Again" with the household workers at Tsingkiangpu before she and her family left the mission compound. Because the Japanese had laid mines in the Ch'ang Jiang (Yangtze) River and bombarded the railroad from Nanking to Shanghai, the Bells headed to Haichow instead. "Each succeeding day" of delay, Ruth later professed, "was like a reprieve — a stay of execution." After Haichow, they made their way to Tsingtao (Qingdao), where they spent "happy days" together in a house on the beach. Virginia described Ruth's surprisingly carefree attitude: "Ruth has enjoyed all the excitement of Air Raids, vicissitudes of travel etc. etc. She isn't the least bit nervous." Indeed, Ruth would have preferred staying there and apparently hoped to get stuck in China, air raids notwithstanding. Then she would not have to leave for the United States, she would not have to go to college at Wheaton, and she could bide her time until she could enter the mission field herself. She could remain with her parents in her familiar surroundings. Virginia, too, enjoyed the unexpected delays in Ruth's departure, writing with emphatic feeling from Tsingtao to Mother Bell, "My, but it is *hard* to see her leave, she is timid and would far rather stay home."

By late October 1937, it was safe enough for the Bells to relay Ruth from Tsingtao to Shanghai. Nelson found space for Ruth and her acquaintance Betty McLaughlin on a naval vessel being used to transport servicemen's families back to the United States. While Betty looked eagerly forward to seeing her Stateside fiancé again, Ruth remembered "looking back" toward family and home in Tsingkiangpu. She claimed to be "more mature" than when she had gone off to Korea for school, but she still hated to leave her familiar life behind. In a gloomy prayer-poem she wrote before her departure, Ruth tried to consecrate her desperation: "Spare not the pain / though the way I take / be lonely and dark . . . for the flesh must die."

Decades later, Nelson's biographer John Pollock somewhat melodramatically wrote that Ruth sailed for Wheaton "and her destiny." At the time, however, no one, least of all Ruth herself, knew what lay ahead. She looked only with dread to the future. She still felt that "her destiny" was the mission field and Christian work among Tibetan nomads. Perhaps she also worried that her desperate homesickness would resurface.

More immediate troubles arose during the journey. Betty and Ruth shared a cabin in steerage with four missionary women; the room, "just in front of the propellers," vibrated constantly with mechanical rumbling. A good night's sleep, never Ruth's strong suit, likely was elusive during the journey. More seriously, two passengers died by suicide during the voyage. News reports in the United States only relayed the bulletin of "the loss of two passengers at sea" — no names or other details. "Needless to say," Ruth recalled, "our families breathed a sigh of relief when they learned we had safely arrived in the States." One imagines many prayers being said between the time of learning of the deaths and finally hearing from Ruth.

Another artifact from that journey presents a different side of Ruth's outlook: a list she created detailing the kind of man she would choose "*If*" she married — "odd," she later noted, "for a 'confirmed spinster.'" Certain desirable physical features appear on the wish list — height, broad shoulders, kissable lips — woven into features of Christian commitment or at least good character. His height should be such that "when he is on his knees . . . he reaches all the way to Heaven." The strong shoulders should "bear the burden of a family," strong arms should be fit to "carry a little child." The lips should not only be "tender" but also be "strong enough to smile, firm enough to say no." Perhaps aware of the distraction such a man might present to her missionary aspirations, Ruth placed one particular requirement at the center of her inventory: "His love must be so deep that it takes its stand in Christ and so wide that it takes in the whole world." She wanted someone who could share the dimensions of her Christian devotion.

Upon reaching Wheaton, Ruth immediately sensed the place's "warm Christian atmosphere": "[I] felt as if I had come home as soon as I arrived on campus." She may have felt a little self-conscious, though, later recalling her "hand-me-downs and size 7 saddle shoes." A week into her college experience, she wrote a prayer-poem asking God for "contentment . . . what'er my lot, / keeping my eyes on You in trust, / knowing Your love is true, Your way is just." She then asked for "discontentment, Lord, with what I am." She concluded her prayer:

> Contented, Lord, yet discontented make me,
>   both together working, blending
>   all in Your own glory ending.

The new college student strove to balance trusting faith and a lack of complacency.

Nelson hoped that Wheaton would give her some credit for the Bible courses she had excelled in at Pyeng Yang. He continued to worry to his mother about Ruth as "rather a plodder" academically, "not a bright student." Ruth described herself as "an indifferent scholar." However, "the horror of failing" kept her working away, year after year. Determined to stay on top of her classwork, Ruth made a schedule that began with devotions at 3:00 a.m. and did not stop until 10:30 p.m. bedtime. During these punishingly early mornings, so as not to disturb her roommates, she studied in the bathroom, with her lap as a desk. Unsurprisingly, she struggled with staying awake. One early morning, as she read Genesis, she fell asleep. Waking up some time later, she read the first verse that her eyes fell upon: "Cain went out from the presence of the Lord, and dwelt in the Land of Nod." Ruth had to laugh at herself.

She later professed having "learned more from people than . . . from books" at Wheaton, with the exception of her major and minor subjects, Bible and art, respectively. She apparently spent hours in classroom discussions zoned out and read pages of textbook assignments that did not sink in. But her "classmates, roommates, friends, teachers," and people she met in the town of Wheaton were her "primary influences," especially those who showed her kindness. At Wheaton, Ruth still had her "sensitive nature" and was therefore "vulnerable to hurts," even unintended ones. She gravitated toward those who treated her with tenderness. She also tried to derive lessons from those who acted insensitively. "Each time something unpleasant happened to me," she later reflected, "there was the subconscious decision never, if possible, to hurt someone else that way." Outside of the classrooms and library stacks of Wheaton, Ruth gleaned this "valuable bit of training" that, in retrospect, served her well.

Ruth remembered in later years some of the people who influenced her the most during her college years. Professor Henry Thiessen, the head of Wheaton's Bible department, delivered lectures that left much to be desired in excitement. His sincere depth of faith, however, sometimes brought tears to his eyes as he taught, signaling to Ruth "that true scholarship and deep love for God frequently go hand in hand." Ruth's favorite chapel speaker was Dr. V. Raymond Edman — then a professor in the history department, but later Wheaton's president. His messages, Ruth recalled, were "always brief (a nice quality) but right on target."

Edith Torrey, daughter of evangelist and scholar R. A. Torrey, whose brother served as a missionary in China, taught in the Bible department, adding "luster in her own right," according to Wyeth Willard in his history of the college. Torrey had herself graduated from Wheaton College in 1919 and taught at Wheaton Academy after that until moving to the college in 1924 as a Bible instructor; among her courses were "The Life of Christ" and "Records and Letters of the Apostolic Age." She taught "with a thoroughness," Ruth remembered vividly, "that frightened you." That stern pedagogical style, however, belied "a heart of gold." "I owe her," Ruth recalled, "a debt of gratitude not only for the sound Bible instruction which I received in her classes but also for the surprising fact that she prayed Bill and me together." This bit of information came to light only after Ruth and Bill "were safely and surely engaged." Torrey had not pulled any matchmaking hijinks. She had, instead, simply placed the young pair together before God. Her niece years afterward found evidence of these prayers in her aunt's Bible on a handwritten list of intercessions. (Torrey also apparently prayed for Billy Graham's grammar to improve for his *Hour of Decision* radio sermons.)

The presence of women among Wheaton's faculty was not unusual during these years. Wheaton's Bible department faculty included one other woman during Ruth's time there. Alice Knowles Spaulding, a longtime Bible instructor, taught the Bible survey and classes on Hebrews and Romans. Katherine Shapleigh, whose husband and sons had died of smallpox during their second mission stint in China, briefly taught Bible as well as serving as the women's dean in the late 1930s. During the Bell sisters' college years, about one-third of the faculty listed were female. They were, however, almost all single ("Miss Torrey"), although "Mrs. Shapleigh" stood out as an exception. And the women were labeled as "instructors" rather than as "professors," who were exclusively male.

In the 1939 yearbook (which covered the academic year 1937–1938), the photo of Ruth included among other first-year Wheaton students showed her softly smiling, wearing black, looking spirited and Audrey Hepburn–chic. That this photo is the only one of her included, according to the yearbook's index, suggests that she joined no clubs during her first year of college. Multiple suitors may have kept her too busy for other activities, but she had also briefly been "campused" — restricted to academic activities only — for part of her first semester. Returning from a date, Ruth unknowingly violated curfew. Finding her dormitory building locked, she climbed in through a window. When Ruth was caught, she tried to explain herself. But Dean Wallace Emerson imposed the campusing penalty and "rebuked [her] so harshly" that, she later reported, she felt "completely demolished," and fled to Rosa, who was sick and in bed. (At Wheaton, Rosa struggled with various lung ailments — including tuberculosis — and periodically even had to take a semester off to rest and recover.) Ruth sobbed to her sister in shame.

Of course, any student caught breaking the curfew rule would have been severely reproved. Ruth took the admonishments personally, and probably existentially. Once the dean was able to communicate with Nelson and Virginia, however, the situation was sorted out and Ruth received a reprieve. The relevant communication does not appear among Nelson's letters, but maybe her parents explained to the dean about Ruth's "sensitive" nature and pleaded for lenience. The Bells had complete confidence in Ruth's upbringing and her moral rectitude, rooted as it was in her strong personal faith. She had not meant to break any rules. She might not have even paid attention to the rules since she had lived, survived, and thrived on the Chinese frontier. Next to the bandits, air raids, and encounters with death she knew from Tsingkiangpu, Ruth probably thought that Wheaton was a quiet paradise that ran of its own accord without rules or precautions like curfews.

Aside from such extraordinary episodes, Virginia and Nelson occasionally received reports about how the girls were doing from friend Ken Geiser, an eye surgeon from Tsingkiangpu on furlough in Wheaton. Rosa and Ruth themselves also kept up a regular correspondence with their parents. They were "good about writing about all their doings and problems," Nelson reported to his mother. These letters meant the world to him. He lamented to his mother, "Certainly the one hard thing missionaries have to do [is] have their children so far away during these important years" of growth and maturation.

Nelson and Virginia felt that they knew "all that [was] going on" with their daughters, the good and the bad. The honesty and open communication that flowed between the parents and their daughters had its roots in the family's shared life in Tsingkiangpu — the unique intimacy forged by many mission families when work, home, and faith overlapped so thoroughly. One aspect of what was "going on" during Ruth's first year of college was a love affair, or at least a serious crush. Nelson shared the details with Mother Bell: "a senior, eight years older than Ruth" — a puzzling and perhaps concerning age difference — "has fallen desperately in love with her." Describing the young man as "one of the outstanding Christian leaders in the school," Nelson may have been referring to Harold Lindsell. Although Ruth's date on the night of her curfew violation was neither identified nor sanctioned, it might have been Lindsell, who, as a twenty-four-year-old senior in love, could have dismissed such regulations as beneath him when compared to his ardor. Nelson reassured his mother that both Rosa and Ruth had written Virginia and him about it in a "most sensible and satisfactory way."

Lindsell had conspired to meet Ruth after seeing her across the college cafeteria. Knowing that his friend Rosa was sick in the infirmary, he contrived a sickbed visit as a way to meet her lovely younger sister. The subterfuge worked, and Ruth and Harold became an item. Both girls shared news of this relationship with their parents, who gave cautious advice about taking it slow even while expressing confidence in Ruth's good judgment and Rosa's sisterly wisdom. Prayer and calm counsel — shared in letters traveling back and forth across the Pacific Ocean — proved a central tool in managing such issues across thousands of miles. Neither Virginia nor Nelson was in any obvious hurry to marry off the girls, to Harold or anybody else: "we hope things will not get too serious now and have written Ruth fully in regard to it," Nelson reported to Mother Bell. Although the Bells lacked confidence in Ruth's academic ability and emotional fortitude, they seemed to hold firm to a sense that Ruth and Rosa had deep resources of faith and character to help them navigate the social side of collegiate life. Nelson assured his mother about Ruth's relationship: "Both [girls] have left it to the Lord and we have prayed and also sent some good advice." Nelson was able to express gratitude that Rosa and Ruth were together and supporting one another, and that they were at Wheaton rather than at an institution with less demanding moral and theological standards.

Nevertheless, just as Ruth's homesickness had stirred up spiritual unrest in her first year at Pyeng Yang, so did the new, if more comfortable, surroundings at Wheaton stir new doubts. Harold coached Ruth through this crisis, which arose from a conversation with one of her high school friends. This friend had encouraged Ruth to lighten up a little by not taking her Christian commitments so seriously — indeed, she counseled Ruth, just set those commitments aside. Ruth responded by saying that atheism was an empirical impossibility for her, because the world around her testified to a knowing creator. The book of nature spoke clearly to her of a generative power — an affirmation that Ruth explored in poems her whole life long.

But Ruth was beginning to question the power of redemption, the subject of the other book she was at Wheaton to study so closely — the Bible. "I could not be sure," she recalled, "the Bible was God's message to man, and if I could not be sure of that," she continued, "I could not be sure that Jesus was who He claimed to be." The very foundation of Ruth's life, from her morning devotions to her life's goal of mission work, came in for reexamination. No wonder that she "began to argue . . . with anyone," she later wrote, "who was willing to argue." The tension in her mind must have been tremendous — and expressed unpleasantly: "It got to where friends would avoid me, knowing confrontation was inevitable." These arguments were all the more frustrating to everyone because, Ruth remembered, "I wasn't arguing to win, I was arguing desperately to lose. I wanted them to come up with valid reasons that I was wrong and they were right." Ruth's expectations of her interlocutors were probably set too high, given that her familiarity with the Scriptures was already so extensive. Harold must have realized as much. Ruth needed to talk with someone more experienced, he thought, someone more knowledgeable about the Bible. So he suggested they go talk with one of their professors, someone never named in her recollections but whom Ruth recalled as "a deeply spiritual" presence on the campus.

She initially resisted Harold's plea. "He will talk with me," she objected, "and pray with me, and it could even get a little emotional." Such a scene was not what Ruth was after. "All I want," she declared to Harold, "are cold, hard facts." She preferred a visit with Professor Gordon Haddon Clark, a Calvinist thinker who taught in Wheaton's philosophy department. Ruth admired "his logic, his unemotional brilliance." He would give her the "cold, hard facts" she wanted.

In the end, Ruth and Harold apparently called on neither scholar. Harold made his best argument and then proposed "the final step": "There is still the leap of faith," he told Ruth. She expressed gratitude and acceptance: "It was exactly what I needed: the clear, terse arguments, the merciless logic" that Harold was able to marshal about the status and trustworthiness of the Bible as God's word to human beings, "and finally, the 'leap of faith.'" At last, Ruth accepted the proposition that intellectual inquiry could only bring a person so far in the Christian journey. The leap beyond ostensive knowing, beyond logical understanding, required wordless trust. Ruth would call on that trust innumerable times in the decades to come.

This spiritual hurdle overcome, Ruth dove with new fervor into life at Wheaton. Using Wheaton's yearbook, the *Tower*, as a guide, one can partially reconstruct her involvement in certain organizations that show her abiding focus on evangelism and especially her plan for entering the foreign mission field. Ruth was pictured among members of the Foreign Missions Fellowship (FMF), part of a national student missions organization that "promot[ed] close association of students looking forward to missionary service on the foreign field." This group heard talks from guest speakers, prayed together in small groups ("definite intercessory prayer"), raised money for missionaries abroad, and conducted their own mission work off-campus. Ruth seems to have belonged to the FMF for at least three years at Wheaton.

Ruth also participated in the International Club, which gathered students from around the world, often with missionary connections. She joined the Rural Bible Crusade, which had been organized in the town of Wheaton in 1937 with the project of helping children to memorize Bible verses. She became a member of the Philalethians ("Phils" for short), one of Wheaton's "literary societies," and served as their Prayer Meeting chair during her sophomore year. Rosa was also a member. Wheaton did not allow traditional Greek life because of the secrecy and oath taking involved in such organizations, but the literary societies for women and men allowed for social events organized around poetry readings, debates, and literary discussions. Ruth rose in rank and served as the Phils' "sergeant" during her senior year. In that role, she took responsibility for tracking members' meeting attendance and keeping an eye open for disciplinary infractions.

The Dixie Club, founded during the 1938–1939 school year, provided another outlet for Ruth's energies during her second year on campus. This group of almost one hundred students came together "as a direct result of a little breakfast table discussion in Williston Hall among some of the students from the 'Deep South,'" the *Tower* reported. The club "was organized to maintain Southern customs and ideals, to promote social unity among the members, and to uphold the high Christian standards of Wheaton College." Although the yearbook's blurb continued by describing its main activities — a skating party and a breakfast featuring grits, "'patty' sausage," and "the kind of coffee that grandma used to make" — one imagines that the "Southern customs and ideals" promoted might have included the exclusion of Black people from the group. Indeed, no Black students appear in the yearbook photo. Ruth's involvement was apparently short-lived; her senior activities summary in the *Tower* index made no mention of it.

Like any college student, Ruth experienced her share of "live and learn" moments. Some, like the curfew debacle or the relationship with Lindsell, were of more consequence. Others were hiccups that imparted practical information about how things worked. During required morning chapel in her first snowy winter semester, for instance, Ruth ended up on the first row, "right under the speaker's nose." As the service continued, Ruth looked down at her feet to see disaster engulfing her brown and white saddle shoes — her "pride and joy," she later recalled, handmade for her in Tsingtao during her travel delay. Ruth habitually polished the beloved shoes every night, but that morning, after walking to chapel through fresh snowfall, she confronted an undeniable reality: "The snow," Ruth recalled, "had melted and with it the white shoe polish. There I sat, my feet planted firmly in a slowly expanding white puddle." A practiced nonchalance was her tactical reaction: "I kept my eyes intently on the speaker, hoping everyone else was doing the same."

Three poems Ruth wrote in 1939 and 1940 reflected her struggles with some deeper, unnamed setback. Ruth composed "Exodus 14:14" (untitled in *Collected Poems* but given this title in *Clouds Are the Dust of His Feet*) at Wheaton on January 8, 1939, but specified no more about what prompted it. Some adversity had come her way, causing her to doubt. Was it personal? Or, given the martial language of the verse from Exodus and the poem's other images — "The battle is the Lord's," "we must / watch for His victory" — was Ruth concerned about Japan's continuing aggression in China, which had reached a new peak of intensity in the fall of 1938? Was she eyeing the growing power of Adolf Hitler in Germany? In any event, the poem showed Ruth chastising herself. "Look up, O you of little faith; / let doubting cease." Whatever the conflict, personal or global, "The battle is the Lord's." Let God fight, "fearful one, / be still, and trust."

The other 1939 poem, "Only You," suggested a more personal distress. (This poem, unlike "Exodus 14:14," appeared only in *Clouds Are the Dust of His Feet*, discussed more fully in chapter 8 below.) Ruth there described her soul as "Dusty," her attitude one of bewilderment. The poem voiced an anguishing list of "Idols . . . dreams . . . pains . . . suspense . . . memories . . . thoughts" that vexed her "aching" heart, "all crumpled by care." After enumerating these causes of her suffering, she pleaded with "Father God," "everything, everything / take it away." She begged God to "take them each one away — / mind not my tears" and replace her grief with "Yourself alone — / nothing beside — / so will I be with You, / content, / satisfied!" As a young woman, Ruth met with challenges typical for the era's coeds — perhaps of any era. She strove to balance the demands of Wheaton's academic rigor and a lively social life. (Billy Graham later remembered that Rosa had a list of fifty-two different men that Ruth had dated during her college years.) But typical of Ruth, she carried that burden to "Jesus alone," confident that he would restore her contentment.

The third poem, which Ruth wrote in the spring of 1940 at Wheaton and titled "Psalm 61:2," again lamented her "helpless . . . overwhelmed" heart: "long it has struggled on, and now at length / is crushed again." Her sorrow sounds deeply personal, something that touched her "oh, so small" heart profoundly. One of those suitors, perhaps? She had been "eager with expectation" about something. But her hope failed to materialize. "Wearily," Ruth nevertheless turned to God, "that great Rock," for comfort. "With Your Strength absorbing every shock, / calm shall I lie." In these poems, as she would so many times in decades to come, Ruth wrote her way to surrendered refuge in what she believed was God's sure, strong plan for her.

Ruth's junior-class picture, from the academic year starting in the fall of 1940, showed her again wearing black. She wore pearls and smiled coyly. Did she smile about anyone in particular? Billy Frank Graham, from Charlotte, North Carolina, had come to Wheaton that fall by way of a nonaccredited Florida Bible college. His mother, Morrow Graham, had prayed for him to choose Wheaton or Moody back when he was first preparing for college; he was there at last. The stories of how Ruth met him — or how he, like Harold Lindsell, engineered a meeting with her — proliferated over the years.

In a 2012 interview, Ruth's housemate and friend Helen Stam remembered one version of events that led to the couple's introduction. During the 1940–1941 school year, Ruth and Helen boarded in the Scott House with another student named Ruth. One evening, Helen answered the door to find a tall, handsome fellow with a southern accent calling to pick up his date, Ruth. Which Ruth? Helen asked Billy Frank. They discovered that "somebody got him a date with the wrong Ruth." Helen reassured him confidentially, "Oh, I can fix that up. I'll get you one with the right Ruth."

Ruth Graham later frequently recalled her own "first impression" of this person who would become her husband. He was just "a blur," a new student who hurried down past her as she climbed the steps in East Blanchard Hall. Blurry, but noticed. "He's surely in a hurry," she thought without stopping. One Sunday morning soon after, before students left in their "gospel teams" for street evangelizing work, Ruth heard an unfamiliar voice utter the group's parting prayer. Ruth again thought to herself, "There is a man who knows to Whom he is speaking." She gave credit to fellow student Johnny Streater for finally introducing her to Bill, who soon asked her out. Ruth seemed not to have known about Helen Stam's promised intervention.

Johnny Streater had already described Ruth's beauty to Billy Frank. The latter had long been nursing a wounded heart, broken a couple of years earlier when the Florida woman he planned to marry, Emily Cavanaugh, changed her mind and married another Bible college student. Billy had sworn off women altogether, at least until he could definitively identify the one for him. When Streater introduced the pair, Billy later remembered, "I fell in love right that minute," immediately writing to his mother in Charlotte to tell her so. "Mother," the smitten son wrote, "the reason I like Ruth so much is that she looks and reminds me of you." His mother wrote later that she took that explanation as a "compliment": "then when I finally did get to meet Ruth, I was really touched — Ruth is far above me!" she enthused.

For their first date in December 1940, Ruth and Bill attended a Sunday afternoon campus concert of Handel's *Messiah*. Bill later reported that Ruth pulled her hand away from his when he tried to grasp it as they returned to her house afterward. Back in her room, Ruth knelt for a prayer to her guiding God that revealed layers of seriousness about love, service, vocation, and marriage. Her prayer also sounded more clearly than ever an idea that was coming into sharper focus: "If you let me share his life," she prayed, "I'll consider it the greatest privilege in the world." Something about him had loosened her hold on aspirations of independent missionary work. He had her thinking about embracing partnership and marriage. The prayer seemed to spell the beginning of the end of Ruth's solitary missionary dreams.

She knew that she and Bill together would commit to serving God. The idea of following in her parents' footsteps, of marrying her partner in Christian service, would have appealed to her. It was what she knew. She had seen such a partnership flourish. Nelson and Virginia enjoyed a kind of consecrated love affair. Ruth wanted that, too, and prayed for God to allow it. Years later, Ruth puzzled over her girlish decisiveness about this handsome and godly fellow: "Now one does not get to know a person by sitting and listening to a group singing, however inspiring the music. Yet that night [after the concert] I knew he was the one. Someone has said, 'Feminine instinct is a great time-saver: it enables a woman to jump at conclusions without bothering with the facts.' So I laid it before the Lord and left it there." (Incidentally, Ruth here misquoted author and editor E. B. White, who had skewered prejudice rather than "feminine instinct" as the great time-saver.)

Ruth did not just "leave it there," however. She had clearly studied Bill, describing him at the time as "a real inspiration, . . . a man of one purpose & that one purpose controls his whole heart & life." He had become, she later recalled, "the most popular subject in my journals, my poetry, and my letters." Ruth wrote to her parents in January 1941 about this man she might marry, highlighting traits that would appeal to them. Bill, she wrote, lived with total Christian commitment, "dead in earnest" without being a grind — someone not unlike Nelson Bell himself. He was, she observed, "richly endowed with the fruit of the Spirit," which gave him a significant combination of traits: "humble, thoughtful, unpretentious, courteous." In her eyes, Bill possessed the appealing leadership virtue of not thinking too much of himself. He seemed to anticipate others' wishes and needs. Ruth was in love with Bill, and also probably in love with the notion that this much-admired man-about-campus, who outstripped all others with his easy enthusiasm for Jesus, had zeroed in on *her*.

The relationship — or, in her view, the fact that it "went nowhere" even for all her fixation on it — had devastating effects on Ruth's studies. She ruefully remembered beginning the year "1941 by flunking Greek and ancient history." At the beginning of February, Bill finally asked her to accompany him to church and hear him preach. It was a date — Ruth recalled "the firmness of his hand beneath [her] arm as he guided [her] through the crowd at the church" — but it was also an occasion for him to signal further what he was really about. She expressed "surprise" at the combination of "authority" and "humility" that his preaching displayed. "The star," she wrote in *Footprints of a Pilgrim*, "seen and admired from afar, became a human, personal thing — within reach." For his part, Bill confessed to her as they returned to her house that day that he was "more than interested" in Ruth and had been "since the day Johnny Streater introduced" them months before. He wanted her to pray about their relationship — little did he know — because, he told her, "I know you have been called to the mission field, and I'm not definite."

Indeed, Ruth's desire for the mission field had not completely faded. Since 1931, when the Tibetan visitor named Jesus had so impressed her, Ruth had labored to discern a path to that field, from her participation in the revival at school in Pyeng Yang to her engagement with FMF and Bible Crusade groups at Wheaton. She began working to convince Bill that he, too, was being called as a missionary to Tibet. In her mind, partnership with Bill necessitated that he follow her into foreign mission work. Why would God have brought them together so powerfully if the intention was not for Bill to accompany her? Yet the young preacher was "not definite" about this call. "It was obvious," she later remembered, "that I was doing the calling, not God." For Ruth to abandon that long-held vocation for the pleasures of love must have seemed to her an almost impossible shift. She must have persisted for quite a while in her efforts to convince Bill of his foreign calling.

The theological and social conservatism of the Southern Presbyterian Church meant that, even compared to other southern Protestants, Presbyterians were slow to organize women's mission efforts beyond local horizons. Not until 1912 did the PCUS form a woman's auxiliary to its foreign and home missions boards — almost fifty years after the first women's missionary societies began funding "woman's work for woman." By the time Ruth Bell needed to decide between marrying and moving to Tibet, the whole face of Protestant missions had been transformed by a contest between strict evangelizers and social service missionaries, and denominations had moved to incorporate the vigorous (and solvent) women's missionary societies. Perhaps Ruth sensed on some level that her determination to evangelize would be better spent in a different kind of mission field — as the mooring for a wandering preacher.

Ruth reflected later that her ambition "could have been a pipe dream." Indeed, the region would close to foreign missions in just a matter of years. But, she figured, it also could have been a stirring from God, "checking out" her willingness for sacrificial service of any kind — including a life of supporting an evangelist-husband. At Wheaton, she felt herself willing. The many missionaries who had spoken in Wheaton's daily chapel services reinforced Ruth's longing for distant fields of work generally, and Tibet in particular. One draw of that work for her was its solitariness. The challenge and purity of such isolation held deep appeal for Ruth. If her parents had helped create a community and an institution that transformed their region of work, Ruth would go them one better and work in isolated obscurity as an "old-maid missionary," which she labeled "the highest call there is." Her idols, the missionary authors Amy Carmichael and Mildred Cable, had lived out such callings. A single woman eschewing marriage, children, and worldly pleasures offered the satisfactions of unheralded, undistracted, unquestionable devotion. How could a romantic relationship compete with such ineffable rewards? Would it be possible for Ruth to transfer her own ambitions for arduous Christian service to someone else's project?

All of these heady concerns happened alongside the petty, fickle, feelings-on-the-surface complications that typify young passion. Even as she prayed about sharing a consecrated life with Bill, Ruth complained privately at the time that he had not yet "mentioned caring for" her. A faculty wife cautioned Ruth — who had a campus reputation for naïveté — that this

Billy Graham had worked his way through a number of relationships already, leaving a trail of broken hearts in his wake. The woman had a list to prove it! (Even after Emily Cavanaugh, Bill's renunciation of romance might have been less thoroughgoing than he had intended.) For his part, Bill did profess to be "more than interested" in Ruth. Yet her missionary calling daunted and even annoyed him. At the time, Bill told Ruth, "I have asked the Lord, if you are the one, to win you for me. If not, to keep you from falling in love with me." Ruth responded to this callous bluster by going on a "flurry of dates" with other Wheaton students. In doing so, she was in effect answering his egotism with a little Bell self-righteousness of her own: Why not pray, Bill, for God to relieve *you* from loving *me*? Yet if Ruth's reignited social life had been part of a plan to move Bill past his resistance to her Christian vocation, the plan went awry. "Either you date just me," Bill fumed, "or you can date everybody but me!"

He believed that God made women for marriage and motherhood. As his early biographer John Pollock put it, Bill felt that Ruth did not have the "stamina" to be a "pioneer" missionary. Ruth saw herself as one of the "exceptions" to the traditional gender roles he hewed to, and her love for Bill made her "afraid," she wrote in *Footprints*, that "I was losing myself." Bill could not accept her insistence that mission work might be her calling. "You should search the Scriptures," he told her, breaking off their relationship, "and pray until you find out just what is God's place for woman in this life. And when you find out" — and agree with me, he implied — "and are willing to accept God's place, you can let me know." Then and only then, he declared, could their relationship continue.

The early relationship was characterized generally by the interaction of two stubborn personalities. Bill would insist on micromanaging every minute of Ruth's time when they were together at Wheaton, a habit that frustrated Ruth no end. She had, after all, managed quite well as a headstrong child on the Chinese frontier, a teenager making her way back and forth between Pyeng Yang and Tsingkiangpu, and a young woman coming halfway around the world to college in the United States. Her parents had the utmost confidence in her judgment. Why could Bill not credit her in the same way?

This point brought the most serious rupture in their deepening relationship, as Ruth's friend and biographer Patricia Cornwell later recounted. In April 1941, the couple fought bitterly, Bill's controlling nature clashing against Ruth's determination to live out her vocation. Ruth wrote confidentially that Bill made it clear: "until I understand more clearly what the Lord would have me do, and until I am in the center of His [i.e., God's] will, Billy won't see any more of me." Bill left her with an ultimatum, forcing a choice between her own feelings and fidelity to Bill and God's will, which in his mind were fused. The demand plunged Ruth into despair until she could talk with Bill again. Several days passed. When they met again, five days after Bill drew his line, Ruth could not help but confess her love for him. He was — strikingly, she thought at the time — surprised and delighted.

By June of 1941, Bill had proposed to Ruth and then left Wheaton for a revival meeting in Florida. At her insistence, Bill sent a telegram to the Bells asking for their blessing. They had returned for good from China in May and were staying temporarily in Waynesboro. In a letter dated July 6, 1941, Ruth wrote Bill to accept his proposal. In the pages of her diary, Ruth tried to be realistic — and verged on dour — about the life she was signing on for. Being with "Bill in this type of [evangelistic] work won't be easy," she reflected. "There will be little financial backing, lots of obstacles and criticism, and no earthly glory whatsoever." These dire (and ultimately inaccurate) predictions could not sway her, however. Indeed, Ruth perhaps emphasized the difficulties in order to rationalize her all-but-surrendered aspiration to suffer sacrificially in the desolate Tibetan field. At the bottom of everything, she confessed, "Somehow I need Bill. I don't know what I'd do if, for some reason, he should suddenly go out of my life." So complete was her need for him that she was willing, at least at this watershed moment in their relationship, to "slip into the background. . . . In short, be a lost life. Lost in Bill's." Self-extinguishing love is not an unfamiliar concept in a tradition focused on a God who died for the sake of others. Neither is it foreign to anyone who has ever been young and in love. If Bill found in this godly young woman part of God's plan for him, then she found in Bill an alternate path to the sacrificial Christian life she had prepared for all her life.

She did make that sacrifice for a man she loved. Ruth penned a poem titled "Dreams Come True" in 1941, probably in the spring before leaving Wheaton for the summer. "It was so very good of God / to let my dreams come true," she mused. The poem depicted Bill as her ideal in every way, crafted by God even down to "little, detailed parts" of his physical appearance. God had "let" Bill be "tall and slender . . . with waving hair more blond than brown / and eyes of steely blue." Not all of those specific attributes had appeared on the list that teenaged Ruth had made years before, while sailing for Wheaton. Back then, she had wished for a man with height and kissable lips and strong arms, yes, but also with a strong Christian love "so deep [and] wide that it takes in the whole world." Ruth had come to understand Bill's presence in her life, after all, as a blessing from God, down to his lanky frame, his golden curls, his brilliant eyes, and his evangelistic calling.

In late summer 1941, Bill drove to Montreat, where the Bells had settled, with an engagement ring he had purchased with love-offering proceeds collected at Sharon Presbyterian Church in Charlotte. Ruth, like her father a lover of jokes and tricks, conspired with a friend to dress up like a gap-toothed, barefooted mountain girl and surprise him on the road. A nervous and preoccupied Bill drove right past her, focused on his mission to the exclusion of all distractions. Unlike Ruth, Bill would never be one to joke in the midst of serious matters. As he drove along Montreat's main road, Assembly Drive, something familiar struck Bill about the "snaggle-toothed mountain girl" he passed. He stopped the car and, laughing, collected his beloved faux hillbilly. That evening, he gave her the ring and they shared their first kiss. When nine-year-old Clayton Bell met his big sister's fiancée and got a look at the ring, he asked, "Is it a diamond or a grindstone?" Billy himself later described the diamond in *Just as I Am* as "so big, . . . you could almost see it with a magnifying glass!"

Even after she accepted the ring, though, Ruth's love for Bill continued to battle with her lifelong missionary calling. She almost immediately regretted having committed to him. What was worse, her health had become a concern. Nelson worried that she was experiencing a flare-up of malaria.

He and Virginia arranged for her and Rosa, sick with tuberculosis, to recuperate at the Southwestern Presbyterian Sanatorium, a small facility in Albuquerque, New Mexico, founded in 1908 by the Reverend Hugh Cooper specifically for patients with the stubborn and highly contagious disease. At that great remove, Ruth pondered again the wisdom of surrendering her long-treasured missionary dreams to marry Bill. At the same time, she hoped to deserve his love for her. A prayer-poem she wrote in November 1941 expressed this very longing. Ruth asked God for strength, clarity of mind — "clear as the dew, and just as kind" — and the ability to help and encourage Bill during difficulty. She prayed to be cheerful, courageous, "quick to yield, and glad to share." She also petitioned God to make Bill aware of her love for him. She so admired what she saw as Bill's self-assurance: "His head's held high as he faces life." Repeating the poem's opening line at the end, Ruth closed by perhaps asking for her own share of this confidence: "God, make me worthy to be his wife."

Ruth rested, reflected, and recovered in Albuquerque all through the fall of 1941, leaving Rosa behind as she returned to Wheaton for school in January 1942. Upon arriving, she again shared her hesitations with Bill. She later recalled that an exasperated Bill asked her, "Do you believe that God brought us together?"

That was the root of the problem. If Ruth had not felt guided by God into this relationship, she would have more easily been able to drop it and recommit herself to her mission vocation. Yet she did feel God leading her to be with Bill. She answered him: Yes, "unquestionably."

He volleyed back: "In that case, God will lead me and you will do the following." Bill's quick reply took advantage of her answer and tried to quash any doubts.

Ruth Bell did "follow" Bill. That decision, however, would require sacrifices not unlike those of an isolated mission worker: unwanted separations, arduous travel, nonstop labor that she embraced dutifully.

Curiously, Bill did not record the above exchange in his 1997 autobiography. He instead presented his own cheeky version of events. Reluctant to forsake her missionary aspirations, Ruth had changed her mind about marrying him, he wrote, but she nevertheless refused to give him back the little

72

ring. She wanted to keep it, but he insisted on its return. "She was emotional about the ring," he claimed, "and would not give it back to me. And that," Bill drily concluded, "was the end of her doubt." His account sounded the tone of a long-married man reminiscing teasingly about his devoted wife's ulterior motive for marrying him. Her plans for missionary service, in his cheeky account, were no match for her "emotions" about the ring.

One of her poems, dated 1942 and titled "Common Things," revealed more about Ruth's work to set aside the self-sacrificing but somewhat grand missionary dream for the life of a preacher's wife. "Lord," she again poem-prayed, "let mine be / a common place / while I am here." Jesus himself lived just such a common life, setting an example that Ruth declared herself ready to embrace.

> Give me the things to do
> that others shun,
> I am not gifted or so poised,
> Lord, as some.

Her love for Bill had shifted her perspective on her purpose:

> I am best fitted
> for the common things,
> and I am happy so.

In these lines, Ruth contented herself with the knowledge that occupying a "common place" would give her a greater connection with Jesus, "Who learned / to do the lowly things / that others spurned." To live and dress simply, to care for children, to heal and care for rejected people, to serve — this work, which Jesus himself did, Ruth could devote herself to while being Bill's wife. She drove the point home at the end of the poem: Jesus had even "upon the city dump . . . die[d] for me / in view of all who passed." Not that Ruth intended to die a similar humiliating death — she had by 1942 tempered her girlhood prayers for martyrdom. But she continued to take very seriously Jesus's example of unadorned obedience. Once again, as in poems she wrote before even meeting Billy Frank Graham, Ruth used her poems as prayers where she could invoke God's perspective and reframe her experience. She would surrender her missionary ambitions, yes. But in doing so, she would embrace this man and the godly plan she believed he embodied.

—◇—

In later years Billy Graham said he might have gone with Ruth into the mission field if that was the only way they could have been together. But that seems to have never been a real possibility at the time. For her part, Ruth later declared that she "wouldn't have had the nerve to marry" Bill if she had known how his extraordinary career would unfold. The unique partnership they did create mirrored bits of their parents' unions. As Frank Graham had depended on his wife, Morrow, Bill would rely on Ruth, if not to run a family farm, then at least to run the family. And while Ruth did not become the Virginia to Bill's Nelson, working side by side as a visible, public partner in his work, she served indispensably as the compass that kept him oriented. She had surrendered her missionary goals for the sake of his evangelizing work, and she rarely let him forget it.

The stage was set for the young couple to begin a life together; a few more semesters at Wheaton, and they would wed. She dreamed about the wedding in a poem published only in *Clouds*, anticipating her dress and veil, flowers, music, all the trappings of a traditional midcentury ceremony — including, she mused, Bill's "firm, sweet kiss." Ruth's only photo included in the *Tower* yearbook for 1942 (issued in 1943) showed her without her customary black garb and pearls, broadly smiling, very much like the Ruth Graham of her mature years. Ruth appeared relaxed and healthy, not exactly looking "lost" in Bill's life. She seemed ready for her next chapter.

Chapter 3

Marrying the Ministry

—◇—

1943–1954

While Ruth and Bill negotiated the terms of their relationship in spring 1941, the Bells faced the end of their sojourn in China. The Japanese threat to Chinese sovereignty intensified, and Virginia's health was deteriorating under the stress of continuing headaches and persistent malaria. When Japanese troops occupied Tsingkiangpu, Nelson decided that his family would decamp to the United States. Unsure if they would ever return, in May the four Bells — Nelson, Virginia, MaiMai, and Clayton — began their journey back to the States. They made their way first to Wheaton, where Ruth met them at the train station on the morning of July 3.

The Bell family needed somewhere permanent to land. They could have stayed in Wheaton and remained close to Rosa, Ruth, and their future son-in-law. But Montreat presented them with a more familiar option. They had lived there before, having purchased the old Abernethy house during their furlough in 1936–1937. (Montreat continues to be a place where houses are known less by addresses than by previous or even original owners.) The community consisted largely of active and retired Southern Presbyterian clergy, missionaries, and leading laypeople. Moreover, as a southern town, Montreat reflected the segregated social arrangements that the Bells were comfortable with.

—◇—

On March 2, 1897, the Mountain Retreat Association received a charter from the North Carolina legislature to create an interdenominational Christian retreat modeled on Ocean Grove, New Jersey. A few months later the group, comprising predominantly northern pastors and businessmen, purchased a 4,500-acre valley east of Asheville. In July 1897, the first religious gathering was held there. The Southern Presbyterian Church (PCUS) bought the property in May 1906, an effort spearheaded by Charlotte's First Presbyterian Church. The denomination planned to host religious conferences and continuing education opportunities in "Montreat" for white Southern Presbyterian pastors and laypeople.

Until 1911, this mountain venture stood on shaky financial ground. Then, Presbyterian minister R. C. Anderson engineered a new debt-resolution plan, took charge as president of the association in late 1911, and put his full effort into establishing a sound financial and programmatic foundation, gathering ideas from visits to Bible conference grounds at Winona Lake, Indiana (made famous by evangelist Billy Sunday), and Northfield, Massachusetts (where D. L. Moody played host). In 1916, the regional synods established a normal school for women that would make use of Montreat's facilities during the school year. Its two-year College Department became Montreat College in 1934. The denomination took full ownership of Montreat in 1922 and began holding its annual General Assembly there in 1923. Anderson's historical account of Montreat, published in 1949, credited the conference grounds as the setting in which "every forward movement of the Church" began. C. Grier Davis, a later president of both conference grounds and college, observed a tension that still filters across the community like ripples on Montreat's Lake Susan: the conference center was "firmly in the hands of the 'liberals'" while the college typically "depended on 'conservatives' for support."

In his day, Nelson Bell represented a foundational rampart of Montreat conservatism. Grier Davis remembered that before he was hired in 1959, Nelson, a member of the search committee, called him early one morning. He told Davis, "Virginia and I have been praying about Montreat. We

were led to say to you that we think you should be called to be President."
Recounting this conversation in his own history of Montreat, Davis said
that he would have turned down the job if he had not known of Nelson and
Virginia's support, so influential were they in town. Davis wrote fondly of
Nelson. He acknowledged that their friendship made him suspect to other
"liberals" in the PCUS. They viewed Davis's friendship with the archcon-
servative Bells "as a betrayal of the Liberal Cause."

Nelson's influence began to take root soon after the Bells' arrival in
1941. He bought a lot right on the town's main street, Assembly Drive. The
property included a summer house and a chimney that had been part of the
town's first building. Nelson winterized the house, and Virginia set to work
creating a garden around the leftover chimney. Retired from the mission
field but hardly ready to retire — he was not yet even fifty years old — Nelson
bought a surgery practice in nearby Swannanoa. With hospital privileges
in Asheville, he began seeing patients and quickly achieved a success that
allowed the family to enjoy a new level of material comfort. Still fascinated
as ever with machinery, speed, and adventure, Nelson also took flying lessons — without Virginia knowing. Young Clayton eventually made his father
confess this secret. His passion for evangelism and defending Presbyterianism against liberal encroachment also was undiminished. He planned that
first summer in Montreat to launch a publication focused on Presbyterian
doctrine, history, scholarship, and testimonies of Christian faith. In March
1942, with five colleagues he formed the board of the Southern Presbyterian
Journal Company. They published the first issue of the *Southern Presbyterian
Journal* in May 1944 to represent what Grier Davis later characterized as the
PCUS's "Conservative point of view." It aimed to counter the *Presbyterian
Outlook*, the "voice of the Liberals," published by the denomination.

—◇—

With her parents setting down roots in North Carolina and her health much
improved after a season in the New Mexico sanatorium, Ruth returned to
Wheaton in January 1942. She penned a poem in late October 1942, perhaps
about pre–wedding night jitters:

You held my hand
and I,
feeling a strange,
sweet thrill,
spoke to my heart
a sharp rebuke,
told it —
Be still.

You held me close
and I
gasped, "Oh, no!"
until
my heart within rose
and told me —
Be still.

Ruth was excited but also nervous about her physical attraction and emotional connection to Bill. The formerly clingy child had committed herself to solitary mission service. Now she was again almost desperately connected to someone. He had shaken everything up, but she did not want him to stop.

Ruth wrote other poems in which she meditated on their relationship and on the man she had promised to follow. One undated verse spoke "To Bill" of her desire to express the unique character of her feelings for him:

There are so many thoughts on love
all carefully penned out . . . [ellipses in original]
But it was not I wrote them, dear,
nor you they wrote about.
I wish my heart — all over-full
might add one little line.
Something expressed for only you
something that was all mine.
It would not be original,

nor one with subtle powers,
nor would it live through endless years
But dear — it would be ours.

As her wedding date in summer 1943 drew closer, college friends feted her. One celebration was hosted for Ruth by the women at Wheaton's "Tab," the student-run United Gospel Tabernacle where Bill had served as pastor since 1941. The attendees presented Ruth with bits of marriage advice. Some of Ruth Graham's famed gems came from these women. "Where two people agree on everything," Ruth later advised, "one of them is unnecessary." It was one of her favorite axioms, affirming her in expressing her opinions: "How often that saying came to mind and how necessary I felt!"

Such bits of marital wisdom germinated in Ruth's mind and were fertilized by her experience of life with Bill — someone, she observed, who had not been reared in a household where women necessarily spoke their minds. After all, Ruth observed, she came "from a long line of strong-minded people — strong-minded and outspoken." In her childhood home, Virginia and her daughters held their own in face of Nelson Bell's occasional bullheadedness. By contrast, Ruth noted, Bill's father, Frank, and his sons were not "accustomed to strong-minded and outspoken women. So," she concluded somewhat ominously, "there were Times."

One of these "Times" boiled up when, early on, Bill said to his young bride, "I have never taken your advice before and I don't intend to begin now."

Ruth had a gift for the verbal ace — the unanswerable response that burst from her carbonated wit. Now was a Time for one of them: "I'd be ashamed to admit," Ruth answered ("rather disrespectfully," she later regretted), "that I had married a woman whose advice I couldn't take."

The point went to Ruth, and the argument ended.

Building on her mother's example and her own experience of figuring out how to live with Bill, Ruth eventually worked out a kind of formula describing a "Christian wife's responsibility": maintaining equilibrium "between knowing when to submit and when to outwit." Being married, she later advised, required "adapting to our husbands," but that adaptation "never implies the annihilation of . . . creativity, rather the blossoming of it." Navigating the real constraints of partnership, especially in an ethos that expected "conventional" gender behavior from nurturing women and stoic men, called for imagination rather than robotic obedience.

—◇—

Ruth married Bill in Montreat in Gaither Chapel (renamed Graham Chapel in 2015) on the campus of Montreat College. "'With this ring . . .' / your strong, familiar voice / fell like a benediction / on my heart, that dusk," Ruth wrote. The scene seemed to her a gathering of time-honored words and music and lifelong friends. The only new part of the ceremony, Ruth observed, was her wedding band, with

> its plain gold surface
> warm and bright
> and strange to me
> that candlelight . . .
> unworn — unmarred
> Could it be that wedding rings
> like other things,
> are lovelier when scarred?

Ruth looked forward to the years and experiences to come in a life shared with Bill.

The wedding reception took place in the Assembly Inn's Galax Dining Room, across Montreat's Lake Susan. The newlyweds spent their wedding night in Asheville, then headed for a honeymoon week in Blowing Rock, a small mountain resort town about seventy-five miles northwest of Montreat. After a brief visit to Charlotte, the pair set off on the long drive back to the Wheaton area. A stop overnight in Indianapolis featured a memorably dirty room in a hotel with an improbably snobbish restaurant — the manager required Bill to put on a jacket and Ruth to remove her pigtails. In *Just as I Am*, Bill remembered, "We were as disgusted as could be at the management, and as happy as could be with each other!"

After they returned to the Chicago suburb, their youthful idyll soon ran into complications. Ruth became feverish with a bug. (Bill Martin suggested that Ruth may have contracted a mild form of polio from Bill's sister Jean, who was diagnosed with the illness soon after the wedding.) But Billy had a preaching engagement in Ohio, filling in for their beloved Wheaton president Edman. Rather than cancel or try to care for a sick wife on the road, and perhaps loath to prevail on church members to look in on her, Bill checked Ruth in to a hospital, where she stayed briefly. She was back in their newly rented apartment by the time Bill returned from his trip.

This early episode offered one forecast of what "Billy leading and Ruth following" would look like in the decades to come. Ruth was sick enough to need medical attention, but not so ill that Bill felt constrained to remain at her bedside to care for or even console her. Bill had decidedly not followed Ruth to Tibet. He had extolled the rightness of her following him as he pursued his calling. And after tying the knot, he left her almost immediately in the care of others — incidentally, the Seventh-day Adventists who ran the hospital. Following him would often look like staying put — in a hospital bed or at home in a mountain cove. Sometimes following, especially when it meant staying put, could be a lonely slog.

Ruth found herself back in Illinois because Bill had accepted a call to the pulpit of Western Springs Baptist Church, about twenty miles southeast of Wheaton. He had done so without Ruth's knowledge or input. Bill simply wrote her a letter informing her of his decision. She was taken aback, not only because he had not talked with her about whether to take the offer — which, she later wrote, "doesn't mean I didn't express my opinion" — but also because she did not see him serving in congregational ministry. He was, in Ruth's view, called and fitted for a particular kind of evangelistic work, not to committee meetings, building campaigns, or the fine points of administering a parish. Delivering a convicting message of God's love for human beings was what he was meant to do, in Ruth's eyes. Some critics have highlighted the difficulty Billy Graham sometimes had in turning down an opportunity, even a questionable one. His acceptance of the Western Springs call was an early example of that impulse.

The newlyweds took up what sociologists later characterized as a "two-person career." Vocations such as medicine, corporate leadership, and the ministry "require the active participation of the wife in the husband's work," to the near exclusion of her involvement in an independent career. In historical perspective, the "prototype" of this phenomenon is "the Protestant ministry." "The ministry," Mary G. Taylor and Shirley Foster Hartley argued in 1975, "stands alone in the nature and extent of the demands made on the wife" as an "extreme case of the two-person career."

Ruth's introduction to her part of Billy's "two-person career" happened at Western Springs. In the first decades of Billy's work, Ruth represented a fairly traditional, not to say old-fashioned, embodiment of the clergy-wife ideal: she served as a supportive helper, handling tasks that fed into his preaching and management; she presided over congregational events that called for a hostess; she budgeted his salary frugally; she kept herself attractive but not too attractive; and, as children came along, she kept them clean, quiet, and well behaved. As his evangelistic career expanded, she continued to comply with the demands of Bill's work, "adjusting" to them but also setting limits to her availability to public scrutiny and expectations. She had surrendered her own missionary vocation for his evangelistic one, and had few regrets about having done so. But she resisted — for herself, and later for their children — being put on display.

Ruth, however, did not enjoy being the wife of a congregational pastor, especially under the circumstances that put her in Western Springs. She had had no voice in Bill's accepting this call. He had chosen their apartment in nearby Hinsdale, describing it in a letter as "just . . . lovely." When Ruth inspected the place, however, she found what their eldest daughter Gigi later described as "a small, dingy apartment — on the railroad tracks." Ruth's solution was to create at least the illusion of coziness by tacking a piece of red cellophane on the wall in place of a fireplace. She would sit beside the ersatz hearth to read. The cellophane, while creative, offered no warmth against the Chicago-style winters.

The church building itself, the congregation's starter sanctuary in a roughly finished basement, was "sort of junky," she thought. But Ruth set to work anyway, searching for sermon illustrations in *Reader's Digest* and similar popular, middle-brow publications. They worked together on his sermons and taught an afternoon children's Bible class on Wednesdays. At the beginning of 1944, they also took over the Sunday night radio show of popular Chicago evangelist and Youth for Christ founder Torrey Johnson, broadcasting from the Western Springs church. Ruth and Bill together wrote out the scripts for the program, *Songs in the Night*, presented in front of a live audience. The broadcast featured a Bible message from Billy and music from rising regional star George Beverly Shea, whom Billy had recruited for the show. Ruth sat close by during the broadcasts, sliding notes to Bill about what to say next. Reflecting later on this period and Ruth's acceptance of a less-than-ideal situation, Bill reasoned that they both thought it would be for the short term only. They anticipated that Bill would soon join the US Army as a chaplain, and then, after the war ended, they would indeed head into the mission field. Ruth and Bill could put up with a taste of parish life until then.

As time wore on, the Baptist church folk at Western Springs became increasingly uncomfortable that the pastor's wife was not Baptist. Ruth determined not to leave her lifelong Presbyterian affiliation behind. She admitted that differences such as her and Bill's disparate denominational choices could be divisive, especially early in a marriage. Ruth's family on Nelson's side, she later explained in *It's My Turn*, "had been Presbyterian for generations." (For her part, Virginia had grown up Baptist but also had Presbyterian roots.) Bill, reared in the Associate Reformed Presbyterian Church, had become a Baptist in 1938 and would, in his own politic way, join W. A. Criswell's First Baptist Church in Dallas in 1959. As for Ruth, once she joined the Presbyterian Church in China, she moved her membership affiliation only once — in 1944, to Montreat Presbyterian Church (then a part of the PCUS, now affiliated with the Evangelical Presbyterian Church and since 2012 called Christ Community Church). All of her life, she would proclaim "loyalty" to her Presbyterian faith. Her daughter Bunny later said Ruth borrowed another famous evangelist's phrase and called herself a "PTL" — a "Presbyterian That Lasts."

That loyalty grew from lifelong connections and exposures and from theological rationales that reflected and helped interpret and shape Ruth's experience in the world. By following Presbyterian practice in having the infant Ruth baptized, the Bells had "claim[ed] God's covenant promises" for her. When she had joined the church in Tsingkiangpu in 1930, she took on responsibility for that claim, embracing it for herself by passing the session's examination. She would that day have given a public profession of faith, acknowledging her hopeless sinfulness and her complete dependence on Jesus Christ for salvation. Ruth would have then promised to depend on the Holy Spirit for guidance in living "as becometh the followers of Christ," supporting the "Church in its worship and work" and acceding to its "government and discipline." (These phrases appear in the *Book of Church Order* from around the time Ruth joined the church.) A child whose shortcomings were the subject matter of family letters, who lived in a country deemed "heathen" that was riven by deadly violence, among a missionary community devoted to sharing the gospel that she was taught would save them all — Ruth Bell's Presbyterian profession had given the components of her life an order and a purpose from her earliest years. The binary star of Presbyterian belief — human sinfulness and God's universal sovereignty over the visible and invisible world — made sense of her world. As we have seen in some of Ruth's youthful poems, she understood herself as sinful or at least lacking and imperfect, in need of God's rescue; moreover, she had faith that a provident God had a plan that even she had a part in. If she trusted in God and acted in obedience to his guidance, he would use her life for his purposes. As a much older woman with grown children and grandchildren, she would frequently advise others to "trust in the promises of God" — promises of purposeful guidance through life's difficulties and salvation from sin and death after earthly life's end. She felt confident in giving this counsel because she had tried to live it out herself over the decades.

Yet Ruth's deeply rooted Presbyterianism did not deter Bill or some of the members in the Western Springs congregation from trying to persuade Ruth toward a Baptist profession. She could not comply with their wishes to be immersed and make things officially Baptist: "the more the Baptists tried to make a Baptist out of me," she later recalled, "the more the old Bell stubbornness rose to the surface." She held her line, albeit privately and with restraint: "I prayed and I studied" and perhaps even researched the legitimacy of Baptist insistence on immersion. Bill publicly had to take "the heat for having a 'disobedient wife.'" Part of Ruth's insistence on Bill itinerating rather than settling into parish ministry may have grown from her desire to escape such accusatory scrutiny.

Along with this hassle, which simmered along even past their time at Western Springs, this first and only congregational pastorate brought what Ruth later remembered as the "first major disagreement" of their life together. The spat was neither theological nor denominational, but just plain marital. Some out-of-town "bachelor friends" of Bill's came through for a visit, and the men planned a day trip into Chicago. Ruth asked to be included. She did not want to horn in on their manly fun. She just wanted to accompany the group as far as the city, where she would spend the day by herself window-shopping — "all I could afford to do," she recalled years afterward.

"No," her husband replied coldly. "We guys just want to be alone. No women today." His rebuff sounded as if Ruth had asked for the "guys" to spend the day holding her purse while she tried on new clothes.

The men left, "taking the only car," while Ruth, in tears, watched them drive away.

She returned to the apartment not only alone but also desolate, "tears pouring furiously" from her eyes. Far from feeling privileged by her marriage — remember her first-date prayer after the Wheaton concert — Ruth knelt and prayed what she later labeled as "undoubtedly the dumbest prayer" she ever prayed: "Lord, if You'll forgive me for marrying him, I'll never do it again." An inarticulate fury, perhaps tempered by a comic sense for the absurd, skewed her feelings into nonsense. Was she tempted to divorce Bill over this insensitivity? Probably not. But in that moment, this frustrated prayer suggested that she felt compromised. These men had negated her freedom and good faith. And not just any men — *her* man, with whom she was to serve the Lord, for whom she had postponed if not renounced her lifelong ambition, had dismissed her. Did she feel then as she had as a "sensitive" child, unheard and misunderstood? She did not pray for calm or a sense of submission. She prayed for forgiveness for marrying a bullheaded patriarch. Her biting sense of humor intact, in some sense she prayed that Bill never get the better of her again.

Friends and admirers who followed the Grahams through more than sixty years of marriage know that this episode must have ended happily. Indeed, Ruth later recalled, Bill returned from his day with the "guys" realizing "how thoughtless he had been and," she confirmed, "apologized profusely." Ruth drew from this early incident wisdom for her own children's marriages. Newly married men, she counseled, "unable to see things the way new brides do . . . can be thoughtless." These disagreements, she knew, were par for the newlywed course. She later advised her children and their spouses using words from South Carolina journalist Robert Quillen: "A happy marriage is the union of two good forgivers."

The Grahams' success with *Songs in the Night* prompted far-flung listeners to invite this stirring evangelist to their churches. Western Springs Baptist Church, by now less identifiably renamed at Bill's suggestion the Village Church, did not relish the frequent absences of its sought-after minister. His many junkets came to a halt suddenly when he fell seriously ill with the mumps. The army had just commissioned him as a chaplain, and he was headed for training. But after Bill suffered six desperate weeks of illness, the army rejected its weakened and underweight recruit. What was worse, Bill's doctors prepared the Grahams for the eventuality that Bill had been left sterile (incorrectly feared in those days as a complication of mumps in adult men). Torrey Johnson swept into this professional and personal vacuum to offer Billy a job as full-time traveling field representative for Youth for Christ (YFC). This time, Bill discussed the opportunity with Ruth before committing to Torrey's project. She occasionally accompanied Bill on his travels, but only if revivals were within driving distance, for lack of travel funds in the YFC budget to fly both of them.

At the time, Ruth wrote in her journal about the doctors' sterility fears. "It helps to write," she confided, "since I can't unburden to anyone but the

Lord." Ruth wrote, "Bill took it the hardest — he felt that he had let me down. Bless him," she continued, "as if he could help it. If possible I loved him all the more." She tried to see the news in a positive light. "I pretended I didn't care. We'll have more freedom, more money, less responsibility." It was hard news, "but one can't brood." She landed not on an explanation but on what was for her a comforting realization: "And anyway, it's from God. Somehow," she concluded, "it's easier to drink the bitter when it's God's hand that holds the cup." Given Bill's calling, Ruth reasoned: "It may be that God knows Bill will be too busy in His work to be a real father and," moreover, "that I'd do a poor job alone." She was deeply disappointed but clung to her God's guiding to lead her to different expectations.

By the following spring, however, Ruth had a surprising new topic to journal about: "I'm going to have a baby." So much for worries about Bill's infertility. She informed him in a letter about the news: "he was so thrilled," she recounted in her diary, "(more than I have ever known him to be over anything ever)." Ruth confided to her diary that she and Bill "had buried" their hopes for children. But, crediting God for making the impossible happen, she rejoiced. "It doesn't make the tiniest peck of difference" if the baby were a boy or girl or, she mused, "if it's homely as an anteater." Ruth even professed a willingness to accept "if God should call it home right away" because "the sweetness of these months" being pregnant had been so rich. As the time approached for Ruth to deliver the baby, she wrote excitedly and with perfect precision, "Strange how a girl can look so absurd, feel so uncomfortable, and be so happy."

Facing the reality that Bill's new role with YFC would only intensify his travel schedule and looking ahead with dread at the solitary months of pregnancy to come, Ruth moved to Montreat, where she lived upstairs in the Bells' Assembly Drive home for the next couple of years. She prepared by knitting, sewing, and decorating a bassinet with the netting of her wedding veil. Frugal practicality and unsentimental style had indeed passed to a new generation. Bill tried to spend as much of summer 1945 in Montreat with Ruth as he could between revival engagements. September kept him working mostly in the South. She wrote, "Know when he is here my little world must seem very small to him; my interests are as broad as his, only

I view them from the sidelines while he is down in the thick of it." Following him meant that she often had to do so at a distance.

The baby, a girl, arrived near the end of September 1945. Bill was working in Alabama but sent Ruth a telegram that declared, "The baby has the sweetest mother in the world." Ruth named the little one Virginia Leftwich for her mother, but they would call her Gigi. As an adult, Gigi recalled Nelson and Virginia, whom she and her siblings called by Chinese names Lao I and Lao Niang, as such fixtures in her life from the start that she never realized "it was all that unusual." Nelson and Virginia became for Ruth the constant supporting presence that none of them could have imagined twenty years earlier.

Ruth was ready to undertake the domestic project of marriage, housekeeping, and motherhood. But in the fall of 1946 Bill insisted that she travel to meet him in Europe — without one-year-old Gigi — where he was attempting to evangelize in Great Britain and France. Ruth boarded a flight bound for Europe and her Bill. Unlike her mother and father, who had usually taken one or more of the Bell children with them on their travels together, Ruth left her little girl behind. She carried a picture of Gigi with her as a gift for her husband and naïvely presented it to the customs agent who asked what she needed to declare.

Billy Graham's success with Youth for Christ had caught the eye of another maven of Christian revival. Baptist and fundamentalist William Bell Riley (no relation to the Bells) had founded and presided over the complex of institutions known as the Northwestern Schools in Minneapolis for decades but was aging, frail, and looking for a successor. He thought he had found one in Billy Graham. Ever conscious of Bill's call to evangelism and not higher education leadership — or anything else, for that matter — Ruth disagreed. Billy tried to negotiate a compromise with Riley but ended up as the interim president when Riley passed away in December 1947. His temporary status continued through 1948, but then he was named as the institutions' full-time successor to Riley.

For the most part, Ruth remained in Montreat with her parents. With her husband traveling for YFC, and her father busy with his medical practice and the *Southern Presbyterian Journal*, Ruth and her mother doted on Gigi and kept up with domestic, church, and neighborhood projects. Ruth soon was also preparing for the arrival of another baby. Anne McCue joined the family in May of 1948. Like millions of other young couples in the United States, Ruth and Bill Graham participated in a demographic shift later called the baby boom.

Not long after Anne was born, Ruth purchased the old Parks home, which backed up to Assembly Drive and stood at the corner of Louisiana Road, just across from Nelson and Virginia's house. She paid $4,500 for the lot and stone house. The charming story-and-a-half cottage featured a large main sitting area with a real stone fireplace to read by. This feature hinted at what was to come a decade later, when Ruth would build a log home with a surfeit of stone fireplaces inside. This house, though, like most in Montreat, had been used originally during cool mountain summers only. It was uninsulated against snowy winters. So with the help of one Mr. Sawyer, "an old mountain contractor" and "dear personal friend" who had worked on Nelson and Virginia's house, Ruth remodeled the first floor.

She later remembered that after spending every penny they had on that part of the project, she "had nothing left over" to redo the upstairs or to buy furniture. So she and Virginia scoured the area for suitable hand-me-down materials, used furnishings, and what Ruth later called "junkyard discoveries." Ruth had inherited both parents' ability to transform roadside finds and secondhand items. "I apprenticed under Mother," Ruth explained. "We did the housework together and we shopped together. We cooked together and just had great fun. She taught me a whole lot."

During these years of "combing junk shops," Ruth revealed, "I lost my taste for new furniture. We didn't have antiques, it was just the fun of doing second-hand furniture over." Ruth could spot the potential in a cast-off table or fixture and coax it into new life with some polish or paint. One of many interesting finds Ruth admired was the curved display window of a defunct shoe store in nearby Asheville. She salvaged it and had it installed in the corner of the house's dining area. She also made lamps for the renovated house. Bill later teased that he could "always tell which lamp [Ruth] had made because when he turned it on, it went off." In a 1978 interview, Lois Ferm offered that Ruth just grew up learning to stretch materials at hand.

Ruth demurred: "Right, but it's just more fun to be creative." Indeed, Ruth contributed many practical and aesthetic elements to the home's interior design: a Dutch door opened into the first-floor nursery, useful for keeping an eye and ear out for sleeping infants or playing toddlers; a pass-through allowed easy communication between kitchen and dining area. Each stair tread on the flight leading to the home's upper level featured a hinged opening for storing clothes or toys. Ruth could spy the potential in a forgotten window or an ordinary flight of stairs.

At least early on, Ruth loved the home's location, across the side road from her parents. Ruth used Montreat's party telephone line as a makeshift baby monitor, leaving her own phone off the hook and listening in to napping children while she visited or helped out at Virginia and Nelson's. The property featured a stream that ran parallel to Louisiana Road, shaded by trees and dozens of large rhododendron bushes. While she valued the buffer that the mountain growth provided, Bill saw the trees and shrubs as many midcentury suburban men were encouraged to: wild growth in need of taming. With Ruth still in the hospital after Anne's birth, he ordered the yard men to cut down the rhododendron bushes so that passersby could better see their pretty little stone cottage. "Fortunately," Ruth later explained, "the workmen knew how much store I set by the trees on the place, particularly the protective wall of rhododendron." She loved the mountain's native shrubs not only for the beauty of their flowering shade, but also for the screen they provided from Montreat's main thoroughfare. Ruth remembered that when one of the landscape workers "blurted" that they "ought to wait till Mrs. Graham gets back," Bill sensed that he was not actually "leading" so much anymore, at least at home.

Bill experienced this creeping sense of being sidelined, according to Ruth, only one other time, again at an early point in their marriage. Was he not supposed to be the "head of the house"? he wanted to know.

Ruth — like her parents, practical and perhaps only tactically compliant to authority — asked Bill if he "would like [her] to come to him whenever the furnace needed fixing, the house needed repainting, the cesspool needed to be cleaned, or repairs needed to be made." Ruth declared herself "more than willing" to seek Bill's guidance and approval on every little maintenance project. But, she explained, "I hadn't the heart to bother him with these details" when his work was so all-consuming. Bill understood. It made sense to him for Ruth to take charge of home matters, even those typically identified as men's work. Always able to marshal Scripture as her guide, Ruth interpreted Proverbs 31 as a passage that "substantiate[d] this division of labor" between wives and husbands. "A woman assumes the household responsibilities to free her husband for his." If his job was to travel widely, evangelizing millions, hers was to make that work possible, by keeping everything at home running smoothly.

—◇—

The call eventually came to Montreat from Northwestern Schools to ask when they could expect Ruth and her daughters to join President Graham in the campus residence. "Never," Ruth replied. She had settled in so fully with her parents and daughters surrounding her that she saw no need to live in a house that even Bill, still traveling continually with YFC, did not consider home. Her curt declaration displayed her determined independence, but also a certain discomfort with asserting herself. Her demurral also showed Ruth's continuing insistence, at least implicitly, that Bill was an evangelist and not a college president. She had relinquished her own missionary ambition, but she could still throw her weight around. Bill's home and family would remain in Montreat.

This fact prompted some of Grier Davis's "liberal friends" in town to fear that Billy Graham harbored a secret plan to "get control of Montreat and establish the headquarters of his evangelistic enterprise there." Davis, however, understood that the Grahams wanted to be in Montreat not in order to take it over but rather to enjoy it for what it was: a "home, a refuge, a place for rest and renewal." Ruth's agenda had been to settle near her parents, rear her children away from Bill's growing fame, and provide him a quiet retreat. (Billy's organization did construct what became a small office complex on the Assembly Drive property adjacent to the stone cottage. The main headquarters, however, remained in Minneapolis until 2005.)

Ruth loved Bill. She had committed to "follow" him and had dedicated herself to serving God by supporting his evangelistic work. As she looked back years later, however, on her "old premarriage love poems," she had to laugh at herself a little. "I wrote them so earnestly," she recalled, "meaning every word." But the realities of marriage — even marriage to someone she so adored and felt called in partnership to — meant that the ideals of those poems were not simply unattainable for her but also "really unfair" to Bill. "It is a foolish woman," she later warned, "who expects her husband to be to her that which only Jesus Christ Himself can be," that is, completely forgiving, understanding, patient, gentle and loving, and able to anticipate and fulfill every need. "Such expectations," she advised, "put a man under an impossible strain." If a woman must be ever-needful, she must surrender some if not all capacities for accomplishment; if a man must be the ever-competent provider, he is not allowed to lean on anyone else. In Ruth's view, such an arrangement would not be sustainable.

Nevertheless, Ruth insisted that wives "adapt" themselves to their husbands. She understood Genesis 2:18 as describing God's creation of women as "helpmeets" for men. She read Adam and Eve's story as paradigmatic for relationships between all men and women. Wives, Ruth advised, should "study" their husbands and devise their own plans for how to enact that helping role. Taking the lead was simply not God's design for women. In later years, Ruth would claim, "Some of the most beautiful women I know, as far as character goes, have developed from adapting to difficult men." She did not outline the precise nature of those "difficult men," but Ruth had managed her own demanding, forgetful, sometimes self-absorbed partner.

As a college student in love, Ruth had committed to a life "lost in Bill's," but she grew to see women's adapting work as creative and energizing. Adapting, she observed, was no simple feat; it took "skill and imagination." Ruth kept Bill grounded, supplied him with the fruits of her constant reading and research, ran the household, cared for the children, and tended her own spirit.

The arrival of Gigi and then Anne added another dimension to Ruth's experience, one shared by many ambitious young women in love. She had to prioritize numerous worthy but potentially all-encompassing devotions. Just as marrying Bill had meant at least the delay of her vocation as a foreign mission worker, having children during the postwar resurgence of nineteenth-century gender norms implied the acceptance of stay-at-home motherhood. With other white women married to upwardly mobile men, Ruth was expected to keep her focus almost exclusively on her children. A woman's domestic (read private) concerns were to consume her energy as the country tried to reinstate prewar divisions of female and male labor, space, and roles. Historian Nancy Cott has observed that even with the transformation of many women's lives by the ratification of the Nineteenth Amendment in 1920, Americans in the late 1940s continued to look on white middle-class women more as wives, mothers, and homemakers than as citizens with public duties. White men were to occupy the public landscape and be the primary economic support of their wives and children. Even though broader educational and employment opportunities opened to women during the Second World War and following, popular opinion — and governmental measures such as census forms — held that a "normal" white woman would choose to marry and have children rather than seek paid employment outside the home. A white mother working for pay evidenced economic "trauma." After the war, any broader opportunities for women's education and employment occurred alongside a continuing insistence in magazines, movies, and religious communities that women "retain their femininity," that is, the appearance of frailty that supposedly awakened the male protective instinct. Even wartime icon Rosie the Riveter had a boyfriend.

—◇—

In the fall of 1949, Ruth again left Montreat to accompany Bill to a series of revival meetings in Los Angeles. Gigi stayed in Montreat with Nelson and Virginia, Lao I and Lao Niang. Ruth took Anne, just a toddler, to Los Alamos, New Mexico, to leave her with Rosa and her husband, Don Montgomery. Billy's services in LA would be a turning point for his career. Ruth saw for herself, perhaps for the first time since hearing and being convicted by his prayers at Wheaton, how good Bill was at delivering the plain gospel message. "This was without a doubt," Patricia Cornwell reported Ruth as realizing, "what God had called Bill to do." Ruth did have feedback for him, though. She emphasized to Bill that he needed to keep it simple, to not be so "much of a ham," according to Billy's later biographers. "Bill," his bride advised, "Jesus didn't act out the Gospel. He just preached it. I think that's all He has called you to do!"

These LA meetings, originally slated for three weeks but stretching to fill two months, kept the young mother and father away from their little daughters. Such separations Ruth later called "the price" they all paid for Bill's successful work. Week after week the Los Angeles crusade boomed on, as the organizing committee kept voting to extend their work. Rosa and Don eventually brought Anne to LA to rejoin Ruth. When they appeared at Ruth's hotel room door, and Ruth moved to embrace her, Anne buried her face in Rosa's neck and refused to let go. She did not recognize Ruth. That night, Ruth held Anne while the baby "sobbed for her aunt." A sad coda to this story occurred when Bill did not recognize Anne but instead mistook her for someone else's little girl, lost and wandering around the hotel.

The cost of stretching parent-child bonds to breaking, especially when young children were involved, stayed with Ruth. She reflected on the effects of those separations years later. God had warned her, she believed, that long distances and months apart would mark her life with Bill but that she should remember the "privilege" that came with the price. She felt, she said, "that God put me here to take care of the children when they were small." Nevertheless, in retrospect — and like many folks who marry or have children — Ruth declared, "It's a good thing I did not know exactly what lay ahead," for she "would never had had the nerve" to pray, as she had, for such a life.

When Ruth became pregnant with their third child in 1950 — whom they would name Ruth and nickname "Bunny" — again the growing family reflected a general trend in the United States. Historian Stephanie Coontz notes that "the birth rate for third children doubled" in the two decades after 1940. With Ruth's fourth pregnancy, resulting in the July 1952 birth of son Franklin, she participated in the tripling of the birth rate for fourth children in that era. These were fertile times for American parents. Nevertheless, public talk or even acknowledgment of pregnancy was taboo. As noted, Nancy Cott described mid-twentieth-century "femininity" as a measure of a woman's modesty. A "feminine" woman exhibited discreet rather than overt sexual appeal. A pregnant tummy belied the sexual innocence expected from even married white women. A history-making 1952 episode of *I Love Lucy* solidified the point: central character Lucy Ricardo revealed her pregnancy but in deference to network censors was euphemistically described as "expecting." (Intensifying their concern was the fact that the show's star, Lucille Ball, was, in real life, "expecting" a baby with her costar husband, Desi Arnaz.) The same program took care to show "Mr. and Mrs. Ricardo" sleeping separately, each chastely in their own twin bed.

A news story about Ruth from 1950, aimed at promoting a Minneapolis crusade, anticipated the treatment that Lucy Ricardo's pregnancy received. Photos accompanying the story showed Billy Graham's "lovely wife, Ruth," seated in the main living area of the stone cottage on Louisiana Road, with preschoolers Gigi and Anne strategically seated in front of her, hiding her pregnant tummy. The pregnancy went unmentioned in the story. In 1958, Bill and Ruth Graham's bedroom appeared in a picture announcing the arrival of their youngest child, Nelson Edman ("Ned"). In the image, Ruth cradled the newborn in her arms, while gazing adoringly at Bill (who returned her gaze). The other children fawned over Ned. These images of maternal asexuality capture a midcentury paradox about female sexuality: women were to strive for marriage and motherhood but were not to revel in or even allude to the sex that traditional culture (including that reinforced by religious culture) expected they "save" themselves for.

—◇—

The year 1950 brought many other changes. With Bunny's arrival by the end of that year, Ruth Graham had three little girls at home, all under the age of five, with Bill's work and travel schedules intensifying. Accompanying him was becoming more of a challenge for Ruth. Nevertheless, the couple traveled to Portland, Oregon, during a crusade (rebranded from "campaigns" that year) to sign documents incorporating the Billy Graham Evangelistic Association (BGEA). They launched a small-scale but national radio show, dubbed by Ruth the *Hour of Decision*. Although Ruth's dating of poems was irregular, her dated published poems seem to come mostly from before 1950 or after 1967. An exception was quoted in the tribute to Ruth that Julie Nixon Eisenhower published in 1977. It was a poem Ruth wrote for Bill after ten years of marriage:

I met you years ago
when
of all the men
I knew,
you,
I hero-worshipped
then.

Ruth had idealized Bill, but after the decade and more of their relationship,
she wrote,

I know you better now:
the faults,
the odd preferments,
the differences
that make you *you*.

This deepening knowledge made Ruth more, not less, enamored of Bill:

That other me —
so young,
so far away —
saw you
and hero-worshipped
but never *knew*,
while I,
grown wiser
with the closeness of these years,
hero-worship, too!

After ten years of married life, four children, and a closeup view of Bill's
quirks, Ruth not only loved but admired her husband.

Ruth produced other written work (discussed in later chapters), but her
poetry writing seems to have mostly paused during this period of her life.

Childbearing and child rearing dominated her landscape. Almost as soon as Bunny arrived, the Grahams were expecting yet a fourth baby. Of Franklin, Bill said, "I'd have loved another girl, but every man needs a son." Bill's career was taking off and his family was growing. The Grahams looked like millions of other white middle-class American families in the 1950s, down to the loneliness that Ruth sometimes felt. Motherhood's demands often proved isolating and exhausting.

According to Stephanie Coontz, in the 1950s, divorce ended from one-third to one-half of marriages in the United States. Twenty percent of married couples polled reported that they were in unhappy marriages. Another 20 percent said that they were only happy in their marriages part of the time ("medium happiness"). The signal book of second-wave feminism in the United States, *The Feminine Mystique*, came out in 1963 but detailed research that Betty Friedan conducted in the 1950s. Friedan catalogued the unnamed misery plaguing many educated, increasingly affluent white wives and mothers. Demographically, Ruth belonged in this cohort and felt some of these same frustrations. Yet she, with Bill, became a powerful American role model for happy marriage. In newspapers, magazines, and broadcasts about Billy Graham's crusades, Ruth and Bill seemed to enjoy an exemplary marriage that gave them both maximum happiness.

Many are the stories of Billy's fans coming through the stone Montreat gates to catch a glimpse of him, his home, his wife, or his children. Decades later, Ruth joked about their Assembly Drive home being "on the sight-seeing tour, especially from Ridgecrest," the Southern Baptist retreat over the mountain. "If the bus drove by and stopped" in front of the little stone house, "we knew it was from Ridgecrest." Presumably, Ruth implied, Southern Baptists wanted to see up close where one of their own lived. "If the cars just kept going, we thought they were probably from the Episcopal center," Kanuga, in nearby Hendersonville. "If they just slowed down," she continued, "we thought they were probably Presbyterians!" Her observation of varying denominational interest evidenced Ruth's barbed humor and a residue of disdain for the earlier Baptists' pressuring her to leave her restrained Presbyterian clan. The Southern Baptists came to Montreat in tour buses, "look[ing] in the . . . bedroom windows and wander[ing] all over" their yard.

Stylish Episcopal folk did not want to be caught gawking. The same went for Ruth's own staid and formal Presbyterians, who lived alongside the Grahams and stood theologically at a remove from Billy's crusading work anyway. Ruth said, "Bill said I was prejudiced against the Baptists. But that's the way they were. They were so friendly," she observed, "too friendly."

Ruth had felt pressured to switch denominational affiliations at Western Springs. Leaving that pastorate did not bring to an end the attention to her Presbyterianness. At one point the pressure Ruth felt to become a Baptist was so great that it brought her to tears — privately. "Why the emphasis on denominations?" she had prayed. "Isn't Jesus Himself the issue?"

Bill tried to broker a deal — not a compromise, for he certainly hoped that Ruth would simply become a Baptist and remove this particular barb from his colleagues' criticisms. Instead of trying once again to convince her himself, he invited someone that Ruth later described as "a leading Southern Baptist minister" to their Assembly Drive home for breakfast in order to persuade her. Surely that would work.

What this minister failed to understand was the strength of Ruth's extended Presbyterian roots as well as the depth of her practicality. The town of Montreat, geographically if not theologically coextensive with the Presbyterian conference center, has "only one church," Ruth pointed out — "a Southern Presbyterian church" to which she and her parents belonged. If one of the Graham children fell ill and she needed to stay home, Ruth depended on her parents to take the other young Grahams to church. But if she became a Baptist and took her children to the church in Black Mountain (admittedly only a couple of miles away), she would not be able to call on Nelson and Virginia to accompany the children if they needed to go without her. Lao I and Lao Niang could not be expected to attend a Baptist church. They would surely take the children to Montreat Presbyterian. Under those conditions, Ruth insisted, the little Grahams "would become confused." If, on one Sunday, they saw an infant baptized by sprinkling and, on the next, saw a young person or an adult immersed, they might begin to question if any claim made by either tradition could be trusted. To the casual observer, Southern Baptists and Southern Presbyterians might not seem too different from one another. But neither Ruth Bell and her parents nor Bill and his Baptist minister-friend claimed to be casual observers. This business was serious, especially because it involved the children. Ruth stood on her Presbyterian heritage and that "old Bell stubbornness," and finally her desire "for the children to grow up, not so much aware of denominational differences, but aware of the reality of the Lord Jesus Christ himself."

The breakfasting minister, too, had a bit of stubbornness himself, and resisted Ruth's reasoning. He had a perfect horror, apparently, of the children growing up as Presbyterians. Years later, Ruth identified her children's various locations across the American denominational spectrum. Through their ecumenism, Ruth had the last word, long after that Baptist leader had had his Montreat breakfast.

As for others who had pressed the issue of her denominational affiliation, Ruth recalled that those "Baptist friends eventually began to realize that" she belonged to Jesus, "if not to them." She grew philosophical about the painful experience of feeling pressured to "switch," seeing in her and Bill's divergent affiliations a witness to the relative unimportance of denominational identities, and the central importance of unity in Jesus. True to form, in her 1982 memoir *It's My Turn* Ruth eventually joked about Baptist intolerance, playing on a popular 1960s and 1970s cigarette advertising slogan (incidentally part of Barry Goldwater's 1964 presidential campaign — a campaign that Billy Graham came close to getting drawn into): When it came to becoming a Baptist, she wrote, "I'd rather fight than switch."

Chapter 4

Creating a Log Home in the Age of Levittown

—◇—

1950s

Although Ruth's declaration that she would "never" move to Minneapolis had settled the question of where she and the children would reside, Bill rendered the entire issue moot in late February 1952 by resigning from the presidency of the Northwestern Schools. He had traveled frequently during his tenure, first for YFC and then for the newly incorporated Billy Graham Evangelistic Association. Ruth had stayed on her husband to focus on his evangelistic work. There was where his gifts and calling lay, in her view. Billy Graham should not try to be all things to all people.

And there were opportunities aplenty because the early 1950s brought several enticing offers Billy Graham's way. Why not run for the US Senate to fill a seat from North Carolina that, because of deaths and unsuccessful election bids, changed hands among Democrats numerous times from 1946 until 1958? Or why not aim higher — for the office of president of the United States? (A decade later, in 1964, Ruth put a definitive lid on Bill's presidential ambitions by telling him, with pointed Bell understatement, that a divorced candidate would not succeed with voters.) A handsome, articulate man could also do worse than hosting a nationally televised morning show (the forerunner of NBC's *Today* show). But none of these options were what Ruth — or Nelson Bell, who had by then become one of Bill's closest advisers — wanted him to undertake. Ruth had surrendered her missionary ambition to "follow" an evangelist, not a politician, even one with the backing to run and perhaps win a race. Ruth functioned as the better angel of Bill's ambition. Her counsel, rooted in her clear vision for his aptitudes combined with stubbornness on behalf of what she had given up, kept Bill from entering work in politics or media where he might have been subject to the manipulation that his critics faulted him for.

Having held out against moving to Minneapolis, Ruth could have decided to live in Charlotte, where Bill had grown up and where his parents still resided. She could have chosen to live in Asheville, near enough to Montreat and her parents to see them frequently. But the modulated urban settings of the New South were not her cup of tea. Nor was the burgeoning 1950s phenomenon of suburban neighborhood developments, which historian Barbara Kelly later called "instant communities." Like the "Soul" in Emily Dickinson's poem, Ruth "select[ed] her own Society" — her parents, her children, a few Montreat friends, and the Blue Ridge Mountains — then at least tried to shut the door.

Indeed, after moving from her parents' home into the little stone cottage across Louisiana Road, Ruth kept her eyes open for the opportunity to move away from Montreat's "main drag," Assembly Drive. This main street remains the only route for vehicles to enter and exit the retreat town. As Bill's fame grew, those seeking a private audience or a photograph with him became bolder: Ruth remembered that her young family "had practically no privacy at all" in their little house on the corner of Louisiana Road and Assembly Drive.

When a parcel of mountainside property became available in the spring of 1950, Ruth laid out the asking price of twelve dollars per acre for a rugged, impossible-to-survey plot of between 150 and 200 acres. The land included at least one simple "pole shack" — a log cabin that had been set up hastily in days past for quick shelter until a more permanent structure could be built. Shacks like these were made with unhewn (that is, round) logs, with each log simply notched to sit like a saddle over the one beneath. Perhaps this little pole shack sparked an idea in Ruth about the character of the house she would erect in the mountain cove. One of these shacks is pictured in the 1951 book *America's Hour of Decision*; in the photo, Bill and Ruth — "the evange-list and his wife," the caption read — sat on the edge of the front porch look-ing wistfully into the distance. The caption also explained that this structure would be renovated into Bill's study. In the years before construction began, Ruth sometimes took the three girls to the pole cabin for rustic overnight stays, complete with hot dogs and cocoa prepared over a campfire.

Ruth later recalled that after the land transaction had closed, Bill asked her, "Ruth, what did you do it for?" He had been out of town when she made the deal, but he had also given her permission to make the decision before he left. She elaborated, "He was horrified because we didn't have the money. We had to borrow it. But," Ruth opined, "I figured it was a good investment." Bill's crusade work consumed increasing amounts of his time and energy. Bill's schedule significantly intensified in the early 1950s: he made a trip to bolster US troops fighting in Korea (1952), released Worldwide Pictures' first theatrical film (*Oil Town U.S.A.*) in 1953, led record-setting evangelistic campaigns in London's Harringay Arena (1954) and New York City's Mad-ison Square Garden (1955), accelerated expansion of the *Hour of Decision*, and launched *Christianity Today* magazine (1956).

The day-to-day running of the household fell to Ruth — including care and feeding of children, handling home repairs (even with caretaker John Rickman and housekeeper and "assistant mother" Beatrice Long on hand), building and maintaining neighborly relationships, and of course paying bills. So even though the purchase of the land was a large one, it was not completely unexpected that Ruth would have made such a step more or less independently of Bill. And besides: she really wanted to move off Assembly Drive.

Billy Graham also published his first best-selling book, *Peace with God*, in 1953. In a short portrait of Ruth included in her 1977 book *Special People*, Julie Nixon Eisenhower wrote that Ruth served as the "main researcher" for *Peace with God*, a book that has never been out of print. Perhaps that also explains why the book was dedicated to Nelson Bell. Billy biographer Grant Wacker has detailed more recently the process by which the book came into being, a process that involved Ruth not only as a researcher but also as a coauthor. The book's publisher had tasked Janet Baird, author of a practical guide to aging well, with organizing piles of Billy's sermons and radio messages into a short book summing up his presentation of gospel truths. But what Baird generated — which had come to her, she recounted, as if someone were "telling [her] the words to write" — did not meet Bill's expectations. The writer had no feel for Billy's message or tone. He took the project back and, with Ruth, put the book together. *Peace with God* was an extraordinary success, eventually selling between two and three million copies and appearing in more than fifty languages worldwide. (Ruth single-handedly revised the book for a new edition published in 1983.)

While Ruth's role in writing *Peace with God* was only lately acknowledged, Billy Graham's part in purchasing the mountain property and building the family's log home was early on much exaggerated. Stanley High and John Pollock both credited Billy with the land purchase; according to them, Billy's supporters had contributed to cover the house's construction costs. A 1954 *Parade* profile of Ruth reported that "they" — that is, Billy and Ruth Graham — "built the house in 1955," seeking privacy. (Curiously, Bill later presented the land's purchase and the home's construction as a move to "deny . . . ourselves," as he put it. His interpretation of the house's out-of-the-way location and American frontier aesthetic substantiated Ruth's observation that her husband found anything less than the Holiday Inn or Marriott to be roughing it.) The *Parade* story quoted Billy Graham to the effect that a wife must fit into her husband's life, so logically the story had to include him as an equal partner in the home's construction. Nevertheless, all of these accounts also revealed that Billy had been in India while Ruth scavenged building materials and home furnishings from the surrounding mountain communities. His input had been minimal at both the planning and the construction phases. Little Piney Cove was Ruth's project.

—◇—

Ruth's construction of the family's permanent home on the mountain may have been jump-started by her experience accompanying Bill to England in early spring of 1954. After a rocky start, the crusade team lit up Harringay Arena north of London in March, April, and May. Two episodes from her Harringay experience capture both Ruth's sense of being on display and her determination to resist the unwanted publicity. She longed to reclaim her privacy and her agency even as Billy Graham's notoriety intensified interest in and expectations about the evangelist's wife.

Upon their arrival in England at the end of February 1954, Bill curtly asked Ruth not to wear any makeup. He was aware that some Christians there suspected the godly bona fides of "painted" women — shades of Nelson Bell back in Shanghai passing judgment on the unsuitable teachers. Ruth objected. "Who wants to emulate frumps, no matter how Christian they are?" she might have said. But Ruth complied, at least initially. A few days after the crusade began, Ruth returned to wearing her simple Tangee lipstick — a moderated rebellion. Growing up, Ruth never had the budget or the taste for extravagance, but her mother had an eye for what looked good on her daughters and the sewing ability to create the children's wardrobes. Rosa and Ruth dressed simply without being dowdy. In contrast to later icons of evangelical culture such as Tammy Faye Bakker, Ruth's lifelong aesthetic favored understated classics. So her determination to wear at least a little lipstick demonstrated her resistance to being told what to do or how to look, even by Bill. She wanted to present an attractive exterior, to show that it brought no "credit to Christ to be drab," as she later put it.

Ruth agonized over another experience during this long Harringay sojourn, more painful than Bill's makeup prohibition. The young mother of four had agreed to travel to Britain with him, stay for several weeks, and then return home alone to Montreat. She felt like the children needed her with them. She longed to return: "I couldn't bear to look at their pictures on the dresser," Ruth later remembered, "and when bedtime came with little more than a quick, 'Dear God, please bless each one,' I would dive into bed and try to fall asleep." Bill had his team to support him, after all.

Having stayed in England for a month, she made her return trip arrangements. When Bill found out, he canceled them. He declared that he needed her to stay. He effectively pulled rank — his needs as a husband outranked the children's needs for their mother. Bill then reversed himself and allowed Ruth to make plans for an early April departure. A letter soon arrived from Virginia, who was caring for the little Grahams. In it, she wrote that Anne had prayed, "Dear God, please bless Mommy and help her not to be so homesick for us." Ruth also received another letter simply offering this advice: "You have the right to ask the Mighty One to do more for [your children] than He could if you were with them." Reassured and bolstered by these messages, Ruth canceled her own travel reservation. She felt obligated to remain for the crusade's duration, but she also embraced God's protection and comforting of her children.

In London, Bill also gave Ruth a taste of the limelight — an experience that she did not seek or enjoy. Without clearing it with her first, Billy announced that Ruth would speak from the podium one April evening. When he informed Ruth of his plan, extreme anxiety threatened to overwhelm her. Bill coached her, and, on the fateful night, Ruth stepped to the microphone. "I could kill you," she intoned. Perhaps surprised and clearly delighted by Ruth's frank rejection of the era's compliant wife script, the crowd roared with laughter.

Ruth rebelled at the invasiveness of curious strangers, rude criticisms from Bill's detractors, and intrusive questions from reporters. She tried to parry these assaults as best she could. Ruth wrote later of an encounter in the Harringay arena with a "rather attractive young woman" who "was staring off into space." Taking the seat next to her, Ruth tried to strike up a conversation. Finally, the woman dreamily answered her: "I was just wondering what it would be like to wake up and find yourself married to that man!"

Ruth deadpanned, "You asked the right person. . . . I've been doing it for the past eleven years." The woman ended the conversation and left "rather hurriedly," Ruth chuckled.

On another London afternoon during the crusade, Ruth found a small crowd gathered to listen as a well-known critic of Billy's held forth loudly. She inched forward through the throng, but clouds rolled in and rain started to fall.

As Ruth walked briskly back to the hotel, a man — a "wolf," Ruth's Montreat neighbor Betty Frist called him — caught up to her and invited her out for a cup of coffee. Ruth tried to walk away but he persisted. Then he noticed her American accent. "You aren't by any chance with the crusade, are you?" Ruth said she was. And she invited him to attend.

"Are you married?" the man persisted.

"Yes," she said.

"Not to one of the team members?" he asked, realizing that this beautiful woman was way out of his league.

Frist continued the story: "Ruth again said, 'Yes' and was thoroughly enjoying the look of incredulity gathering on his face. He began to stutter, 'Not to . . . not to — ?'"

Ruth finished it: "Yes . . . to Billy Graham," and the fellow bolted.

This unnamed "wolf" was not the only one in London in 1954 to arrive at a more positive estimation of the American Grahams. Ruth served as a counselor to inquirers at Harringay and invited people she casually encountered — including "wolves" — to come hear Bill preach. Busy as she was, though, she continued to pine for her children and her solitude. Her absence from aging parents also probably weighed on her mind: Nelson had suffered the first of several heart attacks in 1951, and "Mother Bell" — Ruth's ever-attentive paternal grandmother — had died in 1953. The wildly successful London meetings finally concluded at Wembley Stadium at the end of May 1954. Being an ocean away from her children and Montreat's relative serenity was hard on Ruth, but she could finally return home.

Returning finally to Montreat in the summer of 1954, Ruth reflected in her diary about the path her life had taken: At Wheaton, Ruth Bell had "surrendered for the obscurity of the mission field." She added, "I thought the height and depth of surrender was to lose myself in heathen obscurity for God." After the exhausting stay in London, however, trying to evade the scrutiny of reporters, critics, and fans, Ruth Graham realized solemnly that an even greater level of commitment was called for: "I find my surrender was neither high enough nor deep enough. All summer I have rebelled at this publicity." Yet, sure that God continued to lead her as Bill's wife, she recommitted herself: "I belong to God and He placed me here, and He will undertake for me and give me poise, grace, love, wisdom all I need to bring Him honour in the life He has appointed."

Ruth aimed to provide Bill a place to rest and recuperate from his exhausting work. But she also craved for herself the restorative protection of the mountaintop. Ruth was scrupulously aware — burdened by her awareness — of how closely her behavior was watched by Billy's admirers and, especially, by his critics. Her spending habits, her style of dress, her child-rearing methods all came in for examination. Patricia Cornwell later described "the resentment that boiled to the surface when tourists invaded their property and their privacy"; Ruth "knew that any unkindness . . . would not be forgiven" — neither hers nor Bill's. She had to protect her children and her husband, and in her view, the best way to do that was to move up the mountain, off the tourists' beaten path. She committed to do everything she could to shelter the family from the glare of fame.

Moving from Assembly Drive to the mountainside spot west of Little Piney Ridge, Ruth was just slightly ahead of other famous, if imaginary, sisters-in-homemaking. Lucille Ball, whose wildly popular television show *I Love Lucy* began its run in 1951 set in New York City, moved to a suburban setting in 1955. Other family-focused sitcoms such as *Father Knows Best* (1954), *Leave It to Beaver* (1957), and *The Donna Reed Show* (1958) left the city around the same time. Living in the town of Montreat, Ruth and Bill typified the upwardly mobile midcentury white American family, bidding farewell to high-density living in favor of solitude (or the illusion thereof).

Just as these personal experiences and cultural trends of the early 1950s help us understand Ruth's land purchase, so too did the house she built express Ruth's sensibilities and will. Biographer John Pollock emphasized the retreat's role in helping the evangelist relax and recharge. But we can say more and perhaps better understand Ruth's relationship to the house. Pollock briefly assessed the house's design as growing from Ruth's "romantic sense of history." True enough. As Ruth demonstrated with the house on the corner of Louisiana and Assembly, she did love old things and loved bringing them back into everyday use. Yet the house Ruth built in the mid-1950s and dubbed "Little Piney Cove" stood as the backdrop for Graham family life into the twenty-first century. As a major creative undertaking on her part, its design, construction, furnishings, and representation speak volumes.

Why did Ruth Graham want to build a log house — from reclaimed materials, no less — just as most other young white middle-class families were longing for modern convenience and uniformity? She once wrote, "All I want for my old age is a log cabin with a loft." Her choices of design and decoration all but rejected the taste trends of the mid-twentieth century.

Ruth's decision to build a home from logs was highly unusual in the 1950s. In the 1930s, the Civilian Conservation Corps had constructed log structures designed by federal Park and Forest Service personnel, and in the 1950s, according to one historian, "an increasing number" of log buildings were being dismantled for reconstruction elsewhere in decorative or historical displays rather than for residential use. Log homes would not gain their current popularity and marketability, especially as vacation homes, until the late 1960s. Ruth went her own way in choosing the style of her home.

She may have been inspired to build a log home simply by seeing such structures on the property and in her roving around the North Carolina hills with Montreat friend Betty Frist. These simple structures dotted the southeastern mountain landscape. White settlers built them in the eighteenth and nineteenth centuries from trees at hand, without plans, nails, or tools other than an axe. The home Ruth eventually constructed featured hewn (squared-off) logs and half-dovetail corner-timbering, which southern housing historian Henry Glassie identified as characteristic of the mountain cabins in Montreat's environs.

A more typical residential housing choice in the mid-1950s could be found in developments like Levittown, on Long Island, New York. The construction of Levittown marked the beginning of the "greatest boom in domestic building" in US history, according to Levittown scholar Barbara Kelly. In 1949, brothers Alfred and William Levitt began selling their panelized homes for $7,900 (furnishings cost an additional $1,200). Kelly described how government officials made it attractive for developers and constructors to create "instant communities" that could house returning military veterans on a massive scale. Like Ruth, white women staying at home with small children and rearing growing families sought affordable housing in good condition, which was in extremely short supply after World War II. According to another housing historian, in the early 1950s, *Life* magazine featured the prefabricated three-bedroom Levittown ranch home as the "wave of the future," providing modern convenience while evoking (or trying to create) a meaningful connection with the past.

Levittown-style developments boomed with models dubbed "Cape Cod" and "ranch." Architect and scholar Robert Stern has labeled such evocations "architecture with Memory." Nostalgic model names tried to create connections to a particular American past, according to Stern, peopled with brave, determined settlers. These evocations offered inhabitants certain cultural scripts to follow. Levittowners were to balance self-sufficiency and neighborliness. They were to hold their own even as they sustained community ties that substituted for traditional family connections of bygone days.

In most ways, the house that Ruth built spurned Levitt-style design. Where Levittown houses prioritized gathering space for the family's together time over space for cooking and laundry — women's work — Ruth's kitchen included one of the house's five fireplaces (more on them below) and was a cozy place to linger. When efficient and affordable construction dominated the calculations, the Levitts' designs devalued space for housewives' tasks. Levittown's house facades varied slightly within a limited set of options, and a limited number of interior options made mass off-site construction possible and dramatically reduced construction costs. Ruth's house was one of a kind, built from unique, salvaged materials. Levittown houses included back porches rather than front — for the sake of privacy in the instant community — and yards landscaped with fruit trees that paid homage, however attenuated, to the American agrarian ideal. Ruth's mountaintop home could afford to have its porch in the front, where they welcomed guests and enjoyed a view of the whole valley. Levittown residents frequently converted attic space to a workshop for dad or closed in the carport for another bedroom. Do-it-yourself projects such as these renovations gave Levittown homeowners, particularly men, bragging rights as well as additional space. They might not have to fight off wild animals, but they could wield a hammer. But Ruth Graham was not married to a Levittown man. The very existence of Little Piney Cove demonstrated who the do-it-yourselfer in the family was.

Given the scale of media attention focused on Levittown and other mid-century suburban developments, it would have been hard for Ruth to be unaware of this trend in American housing, even if it held no appeal for her. Although thirty-six-year-old Ruth fit the age and family demographic of a mid-1950s Levittown housewife, she did not fit other typical demographic traits of that group. Ruth, for instance, had a college education and a husband working in a profession rather than a trade. She had more in common with a group that the federal government convened in spring 1956 for the Women's Congress on Housing. The Housing and Home Finance Agency consulted congress attendees about the features they wanted in a home; like Ruth, these women were generally looking for "move-up" rather than first homes. They desired more space overall, but especially for their domestic work.

Ruth's Montreat aerie ensured her privacy, expressed her individuality, and allowed for her domestic focus. She wanted neither the sameness and close proximity of a Levittown, nor the sleek modern design that many women of her age and stage sought. She wanted space for her housework and study, and she wanted room for the children to run and play. She also wanted to build for the long haul. Ruth intended to plant her family for good on the side of that mountain, where bears and bobcats were still common sights.

Ruth loved that wildness. Levittown's ersatz Cape Cods and stripling fruit trees would have represented too much conformity. Her mountainside location and log design clearly rejected that. She was going to embrace consummate domesticity, yes, but in her own distinctive way. No cookie-cutter suburbia for her. She wanted the privacy that designers could only gesture at in high-density Levittown. She felt relatively unbound by the accommodations to convenience or cost that the Levittown developers made.

Nevertheless, Ruth's log house design constitutes another example of Stern's "architecture with Memory." Ruth's home became a place where she could try to reclaim a connection to the past — her past. She built a retreat, yes, but she also built a stronghold for her large family, close to her parents, and eventually, with some additions and expansion, ample enough for the next generation to enjoy.

—◇—

Ruth intended originally to design the house herself. But her contractor Zeb Sawyer, who had worked on the Assembly Drive house, brought in an architect from Jackson, Mississippi. The two men formed an alliance to talk Ruth out of certain notions. Ruth embraced the role of "counterarchitect," as she called it. Ruth did not simply deputize Sawyer and the architect to build her home. She also read about log cabins and scrutinized the ones she encountered in her wandering for desirable features to incorporate into Little Piney Cove. She had originally envisioned a two-story structure — like the house Nelson and Virginia had built in Tsingkiangpu. Sawyer and the architect convinced her that such a house "on the mountain looks like a skyscraper." They settled on a design that Betty Frist called a "layer and a half type," with an upper half-story for the children's quarters. A later story in *Parade* magazine called the house's upper floor "a regular dormitory of bedrooms and bathrooms." Anne later remembered how, because her bedroom was directly above her mother's, she could look out and see Ruth's light on, sometimes late into the night; she would sneak down to see her mother kneeling in prayer.

Ruth was sensitive about the size of the house. She did not want it to give off the air of grandeur or extravagance, and as she told Bill Martin years later, the architect told her not to count rooms but to focus on the function of each given space. They should build, he advised, for what the family needed and not worry about the total square footage. Patricia Cornwell observed that in the decades after the home's construction, rumors abounded about its massive size, its "hundred acres of arable land" — an impossibility given that the craggy property hung on the side of a mountain — and its "Olympic-sized swimming pool," also a virtual engineering impossibility on that site.

In contrast to the gleaming newness of much midcentury home-building materials, Ruth, frequently accompanied by Betty Frist, scoured the coves around the Swannanoa Valley looking for building materials. Ruth could find usable materials in sufficient supply because, according to Glassie, people continued to build simple log homes in the area "well into the twentieth century." In the late 1930s, more than 10 percent of homes in the region Glassie examined were log — a much higher share than in other regions of the country. One of Frist's daughters said many of their finds came from around Lake Lure, about twenty-five miles southeast of Montreat. Log cabins, whether intact and inhabited or abandoned and tumbledown, were fair game as Ruth gathered logs, old furniture, fixtures, and hardware for her project. When Ruth traded new items for old, the mountain folk puzzled as to why such a nice, tidy lady would want their old junk. Frist sometimes thought that sellers should have paid Ruth for hauling the stuff away.

Ruth and Betty paid around twenty-five dollars for each one-room cabin, had the logs numbered, then had the cabins disassembled for use in their own projects. (Frist used five individual cabins for the bedrooms in her own home.) As her friend saw it, Ruth found "something very special about these old logs which seem to almost pulsate with life." They had "absorbed" a century's flavors and smells — "frying country ham and red eye gravy, freshly baked bread, and bracing hot coffee brewed from newly ground coffee beans." The logs also "plucked from the air" the sounds of life lived within their walls — sounds of rest, love, birth, death, music, and dancing. "Laughter and prayer also penetrated these walls," Frist wrote, "all of which adds up to a host of memory flashbacks."

During construction, Bill again experienced the caution of workmen who took Ruth's wishes more seriously than his. One episode involved stone fireplaces — whether the house would have them and how many. Ruth insisted on five. Bill wanted none. But she bargained him into allowing her two. Then, while Bill was on another evangelizing mission, she told the construction crew, "You build fireplaces faster than you ever have in your life." They built five. She directed the stonemasons and carpenters to keep all their work old-timey looking. Some of these artisans, the stories go, resisted this instruction, too proud to let their work look unskilled. One rock mason grew so frustrated that he quit, huffing as he left, "A man can't take no pride in his work up here." But what Ruth wanted was a home that looked as if it had been on the side of this mountain, tucked away in this cove, for generations. The style, materials, and features she chose helped her remember her childhood at home.

As she had when remodeling the Assembly Drive house, Ruth still treasured handmade things that showed imperfection and wear. Bill's preference, however, was for the plush, even the luxurious. He liked (and, admittedly, needed) pampering. Bill's workspace at Little Piney Cove was not part of the house Ruth built; the office was converted from the existing pole shack on the property. The accommodation of this separate space fit with Ruth's willingness, even insistence, to protect Bill's work. After all, she had given up her own missionary ambition in order to support his call. If the seclusion of a separate office would prosper his crusade preparations, then she would make it happen. Not that she necessarily approved of his taste: Ruth described lovingly to Lois Ferm the "old fashioned furniture" that the office had contained. That was her kind of furniture. When those items were "replaced with modern plush stuff," she groused to Ferm, it "just ruined it." Ruth observed more than once that Bill was not one to rough it.

Eventually, in addition to items that Ruth collected, the décor inside Little Piney Cove included some furnishings and accessories given to the Grahams by their many admirers, famous and otherwise. The rocking chairs out back were a gift from President Lyndon Johnson. (Similar chairs now adorn guest rooms at the Cove training center.) The dining room included at least one ladder-back chair with a cane bottom; it was built by a North Carolina man and caned by his wife. In the spacious living room — made cozy by the timbered ceiling, log walls, and large fireplace and hearth — a giant hand-carved oak plank formed the header under the fireplace mantel and displayed the opening of Martin Luther's famous sixteenth-century hymn, "Ein feste Burg ist unser Gott." (Although that piece is often described as the former diving board from Montreat's Lake Susan, Ruth explained to *Woman's Day* magazine that the "rough oak plank" had come from the now "heated and filtered" swimming pool at Little Piney Cove. Ruth had not really wanted the added flourish of the carved verse but could not bring herself to spoil the excitement of the friend who arranged to have it done.)

Ruth followed the skilled example of Virginia and Nelson in creating Little Piney Cove. Nevertheless, many 1950s news features and press photos depicted Billy Graham the evangelist as a household handyman. Such images reinforced his manly reputation and burnished his credentials as hardworking, frugal, practical, and family-focused but not effeminate. The 1951 account of Billy's early crusades, *America's Hour of Decision*, included "The Billy Graham Family Album," a collection of black and white photos, "informal poses of the Evangelist and his family." Maybe not so informal, though, since Ruth and Bill wear the same clothes in many of the photos, suggesting a more formal photo shoot.

One photo showed "Dr. Billy" looking rugged in flannel shirt and baseball cap. He stood at the base of a precarious wooden scaffold ramp up to the Louisiana Road house's second story, carrying a long two-by-four over his left shoulder. He gazed pensively off to the right, and the toes of his right foot edged over the side of the ramp. The improbable length of the two-by-four, the reflective glance into the distance, the errant footing — all suggest a posed shot rather than an action photo. But showing Billy as a handy homeowner helped ally him with millions of other homeowning husbands. He was just a regular guy.

By contrast, news stories about the Graham family reported somewhat patronizingly on Ruth's work salvaging fixtures and logs and refinishing secondhand furniture. This hobby was reported on as a peculiarity of her character, especially in the early years of Billy's fame. The very existence of Little Piney Cove testified to her hands-on approach to life on the mountain. Ruth was committed to domestic life, but not according to the pattern set by "feminized suburbia."

Did Little Piney Cove accomplish for Ruth what she had hoped? Moving to the mountain enacted her drive for personal privacy and her desire to let the children be themselves. Ruth did not like it when people tried to pigeonhole the children, especially if they tried to coax them toward careers as evangelists. "We believe very deeply in letting them make up their own minds about such things," she told *Woman's Day* in 1969. Ruth (and surely Bill, too) trusted that the Lord would handle the matter of the children's vocations. "As for me," she mused, "as long as my children grow up to be Christians, responsible and well-adjusted adults, I don't care what they do" — although she also wanted them to each have a "trade," a way to support themselves. During that *Woman's Day* interview, Ruth laughed as she recalled Franklin's expressed "ambition" of wanting to "just . . . sit around!" Little Piney Cove was a good place to do just that.

The private world of the cove also allowed Ruth to study. In recent years, the Graham children have described how their mother's Bibles lay open throughout the house, where Ruth could read in an idle moment. She had two dedicated spaces in the house for serious, sit-down reading, studying the Bible, writing, clipping news items, and filing. One desk in her bedroom held Bible study materials. On the wall above it hung a crown of thorns, brought from Jerusalem. Ruth once explained that the "head of the Tourist Police" made the crown for her as they walked the Via Dolorosa. Franklin and Ned had fashioned crosses for her from sticks they found in the yard; those also hung above the desk. Alongside them eventually hung a slave collar given to her by the singer Johnny Cash in 1978, who with his second wife, June Carter Cash, became collaborators and close friends with Ruth and Bill beginning in 1969.

One can only suggest what this gift, from one white privileged southerner to another, meant to either one of them. As critic Leigh Edwards has shown, Cash used his own childhood poverty and marginalization to claim a connection with other poor, marginalized people, "eliding" the privileges he enjoyed of race, gender, and eventually accumulated wealth and cultural influence. Cash's music also reflected a paradoxical racial politics that both celebrated the heroism of the nation's founders and the "True West" of the American cowboy and yet protested mistreatment of Native Americans, past and present, by the US government. Cash, who at one point falsely claimed that he was part Cherokee, highly valued the "authentic" material culture of the nineteenth-century American West, wearing by turns vintage cowboy clothing and Native American accessories. "Relics" from the Old West, he believed, gave him access to past times and peoples he valued — contradictorily, both the brave frontier settler and the dispossessed Native American.

The slave collar may have functioned similarly for Cash. It came from Jamaica, where Cash owned Cinnamon Hill, an eighteenth-century sugar plantation he purchased in the 1970s as a vacation retreat. Cash perhaps imagined that the collar connected him — one of seven children who grew up working on a subsidized cotton farm in Arkansas during the Depression — with the enslaved people of Jamaica's sugar plantations. The collar reminded Ruth of the suffering imposed on enslaved people. But in a short poem she wrote about it, she emphasized that the "evil" of enslavement had ended. Once "snapped" around "some slave's neck," the collar was now "rib-thin, / rigid in rust / as if at last / its own *rigor mortis* / had set in." Enslavement was a dead, desiccated institution. That Ruth hung Cash's gift of the slave collar over her study desk, alongside the thorny crown and the crosses, also suggests that she interpreted it as a useful Christian symbol of human enslavement to sin and Jesus's humble yet redemptive sacrifice on the cross. Her display of the collar allowed Ruth to contain its connection to brutality within triumphant historical and Christian narratives.

Another space where Ruth worked, in the house's attic, held piles of clippings and ephemera that found their way into Bill's sermons and books. Such places and practices fit with Ruth's working style and lifestyle. She prioritized the children's daily needs and activities over quiet seclusion. Yet she was ever on the lookout for relevant biblical, historical, or contemporary sermon illustrations for Bill. She had the space, and occasionally the time, for serious Scripture study, but she also wanted to redeem every possible minute as the day passed.

By building Little Piney Cove where and how she did, Ruth may also have reclaimed the home she longed so desperately for as a young teenager in Pyeng Yang — complete with the parents she preferred to stick close to. That longing for the isolated, mostly safe and self-sufficient community of her own childhood never left her. At Tsingkiangpu, the Bells and their colleagues made do with what supplies they brought with them and occasional shipments received from the States. But they actually lived quite well and enjoyably, even as the occasional sounds of gunfire rang out over the compound walls. Nothing so deadly as armed bandits or warring armies threatened from Assembly Drive (although Billy Graham eventually beefed up security around Little Piney Cove and formalized their security processes, installing a monitored gate, fencing and alarms, and keeping trained guard dogs on the premises). The house satisfied paradoxical urges: Ruth yearned for distance from the clamor of the world, and for a return to the consecrated adventure of her childhood. She wanted a log cabin — the simplest of structures — but one that could accommodate a big family, one that looked plain even as its size, location, décor, and constant activity belied that plainness.

Her parents had been pioneers in the mission field; Ruth would build a pioneer-style home in the North Carolina mountains. Nelson had gloried in the exploits involved in living and working in a more isolated part of the mission field. Ruth, as a homemaker, may have wanted to re-create the feel, if not exactly reproduce the reality, of self-sufficiency in the mountain wilds. The daughter of parents who figured out how to build a swimming pool on the Chinese outback, create new wardrobes from missionary barrel hand-me-downs, devise revolutionary treatments for endemic diseases, and fashion a cereal maker from a mortar shell, Ruth too used what came to hand — mountain streams, forsaken cabins — to make a "nice, comfortable home" for her family. New Urbanism designers Andrés Duany and Elizabeth Plater-Zyberk have interpreted the midcentury rush to the suburbs as a case of mass nostalgia for "the autonomous homestead in the countryside." Ruth did not join that rush. Nostalgia played its part in her move, but she actually came closer to building that autonomous rural homestead. She wanted the outback and built something that looked very much like it — even if she could still drive to the supermarkets and department stores of Asheville. She hungered for security and space — not in the suburbs, but on a mountainside.

Chapter 5

A Christian Mother on the Cusp of a Feminist Era

⟢

1958–1969

Ruth reflected on the Christian vocation of motherhood in one of her poems, published in two collections long after her children were grown and launched, but reflecting a mother deep in the weeds. Casting each child as "a soul / bound for eternity," she felt herself unqualified for guiding them, a "blind leader of the blind — / groping and fumbling, / casual and concerned, / by turns . . . / undisciplined":

> I seek
> by order and command
> to discipline and shape;
> (I who need Thy discipline
> to shape
> my own disordered soul).

Her words reflected her constant sense that her "own disordered soul" prevented her from loving enough, knowing enough, doing enough to lead her children adequately. So she prayed solemnly, in archaic tones,

O Thou
Who seest the heart's true, deep desire,
each shortcoming and
each sad mistake,
supplement
and overrule,
nor let our children be
the victims of our own
unlikeness unto Thee.

The poem's prayerful ending asked God to make up for her (and all parents') deficiencies so that the children would not be scarred by ungodly parents' failings.

At other times when the children were small, Ruth was more lenient on herself and the children. Her neighbor and friend Betty Frist recalled the time when one of the boys, in first grade at the time, brought home a teacher's note. Ruth read the message, which expressed the teacher's concern that the child's clothes were "wrinkled, like he'd slept in them." Frist continued her story: "Ruth penciled on the note, 'They are, and he has,' and sent it back" to the teacher. The little Graham "had gone through a time of being afraid he'd be late to school," Frist explained, "so he'd take his bath, then put on clean clothes and sleep in them." Ruth, Frist observed, must have approved of this rather creative solution. Her friend wrote that "Ruth refused to make a killer whale out of a sardine."

—◇—

Historian Elaine Tyler May locates the "peak of the baby boom" in 1956. Ruth and Bill, therefore, were actually ahead of the postwar curve in expanding their family. As their last child arrived, the older children left home for boarding schools. Soon enough, the Graham girls married. By the end of the 1960s, with an all-but-empty nest, Ruth entered a more public phase of her life, giving interviews and making occasional public appearances without Bill. Interest in her intensified as the wider culture reexamined traditional gender roles. Ruth eschewed "women's liberation" but, along with a cadre of other women in her generation, evinced a stylish, articulate Christian womanhood.

The late 1950s were pivotal for Ruth. Born in May 1958, Nelson Edman ("Ned") took his name from two significant men in the lives of Ruth and Bill — Ruth's father, a significant mentor for Bill, too, and V. Raymond Edman, Wheaton College's president during Ruth and Bill's time there. He oversaw a campus expansion and religious revival and was generally beloved. As this little bird joined the nest, another one flew off, somewhat reluctantly. Eldest daughter Gigi left for boarding school to Hampden Dubose Academy in the central Florida town of Zellwood. Founded in 1934 and named for a storied Presbyterian missionary to China, the school educated the children of white Christian missionaries, pastors, and laypeople. Billy's colleagues T. W. Wilson and Grady Wilson (no relation) sent their children there also. Ruth and Bill were frequent visitors to the school while Gigi and then Anne were students. Billy Graham occasionally preached in chapel services. Students were bused to the Tangerine Bowl in Orlando to attend his 1961 crusade. Gigi never grew to like the place and "cried for four years," she later recalled, although she won a General Excellence Award as a senior and edited the school yearbook, the *Esse*. One thing Gigi later appreciated about her four years at the school was a practice of morning devotions. Hampden Dubose observed a "No Bible, no breakfast" rule.

After visiting Gigi with her family over the years, Anne started at Hampden Dubose in the fall of 1961. She suffered from numbing homesickness. Her misery must have struck Ruth with memories of her own homesickness in Korea when she had begged, wheedled, and connived to stay at home in Tsingkiangpu instead of returning to school in Pyeng Yang or leaving for college in Wheaton. Ruth's efforts had been of no avail. But Anne's unhappiness swayed Ruth and Bill, and they allowed Anne to withdraw from Hampden-Dubose and attend Charles D. Owen High School in Black Mountain instead.

—◇—

In 1959, the year that Gigi departed for Hampden Dubose, the publisher Thomas Nelson issued Ruth's book *Our Christmas Story* — more precisely, the book was "by Mrs. Billy Graham as told to Elizabeth Sherrill," a writer for magazines. The little volume featured simple illustrations by Aldren A. Watson. Billy Graham himself contributed the book's foreword, writing that the idea for the book had been "suggested" to them. We will come to see how Ruth struggled to finish large writing projects. Sherrill's contribution to *Our Christmas Story* was likely as organizer, shaper, and project manager. Writing *Our Christmas Story* with Ruth came at the beginning of Sherrill's career; she and her husband, John, would go on to found Chosen Books in 1970 and coauthor Christian classics like *The Cross & the Switchblade* (with David Wilkerson) and *The Hiding Place* (with Corrie ten Boom).

The narrative of *Our Christmas Story* unfolded as if a young reader were visiting Little Piney Cove. The house, the text reported, "will make you think of a pioneer's cabin in the woods." Ruth reminisced briefly about her own childhood Christmases in China with her mother, father, and siblings, and then introduced the customs the Graham family observed on the mountain in North Carolina. They enjoyed oyster stew for breakfast, a tradition from Virginia Bell's kitchen. They hung stockings by the enormous fireplace in the sitting room, one for each member of their large family plus housekeeper Bea Long and handyman John Rickman. Then came "the moment that's really Christmas," when "the children's father" — unnamed and obscured in the accompanying illustration — read aloud from Luke's Gospel about the birth of Jesus.

This narrative reflected Ruth's research and her thinking about the theological significance of Luke's account. It does not simply focus on child-friendly favorites like the donkey or the crowded inn or the animals in the barn or even the tiny baby. With Sherrill, Ruth constructed a story that taught history, anthropology, and (most significantly for her evangelistic purposes) biblical theology, all on a level she hoped would be comprehensible by adults and children alike. Ruth's distinctive spin on that ancient nativity story — one she would have imbibed during her Presbyterian upbringing — anchored it in the Genesis story of creation and fall. She then developed the meaning of the nativity through the salvation history of the Israelites — through Noah, Abraham, Jacob, and Israel's enslavement in and exodus from Egypt. She vividly described the era of Roman civilization, whose official shared language and technologies of travel over land and sea made it possible for the events of early first-century Palestine to be told widely in the Mediterranean world. *Our Christmas Story* introduced adults and children to the Bible as a cohesive narrative about God saving humanity from its sinfulness. Genesis through Revelation recorded a purposeful and historical account that emphasized and explained Jesus's significance to the celebration of Christmas.

Our Christmas Story made enough of an impression that at least two later editions were published. These editions added a list of Bible references so that readers could explore Scripture on their own. The 1973 edition included new illustrations by a successful artist in Christian publishing circles, David Koechel. It also added a collection of "the family's favorite Christmas carols," including not only sacred Advent and Christmas songs, but also "Jingle Bells" and "The Twelve Days of Christmas." The book presented a joyful domestic setting, lingering over descriptions of the children and Belshazzar, the Great Pyrenees dog, "so big you can ride on his back," as Ruth's children did. In her book as in her life, Ruth did not seek to suck the fun out of a beloved holiday but instead wanted to recapture the fun's deep purpose. Ruth was indeed Nelson's daughter — he of baseball games and swimming pools and costume parties and college pep rallies. The book's strategy reflected Ruth's general approach — that God calls one to believe, embrace God's grace, and live with a sober sense of authentic joy in Christ's redeeming power. Fun is allowed and made all the more enjoyable by knowing, in Ruth's view, the cosmic love that made it possible.

—◇—

Ruth and the children spent the summer of 1960 in Montreux, Switzerland, while Billy Graham crusaded in other Swiss cities and West Germany. Franklin, in his 1995 memoir, recalled that "Daddy" had begun thinking about moving the family to Europe, but his mother's "heart remained in Little Piney Cove" and she unequivocally resisted any of his overtures about relocating. Their host in Switzerland was a wealthy Armenian expatriate named Ara Tchividjian, a businessman who had embraced evangelical Christianity as a result of reading *Peace with God*. Like many powerful men touched by Billy Graham's message, Tchividjian publicly credited Billy for his conversion to Christianity. He looked for ways to show appreciation to the evangelist and to spend personal time with him.

Ara Tchividjian had a dashing twenty-one-year-old son, Stephan, who happened to be engaged. Gigi was herself in love with longtime friend and fellow Hampden Dubose student Jim Wilson, the son of BGEA associate T. W. Wilson. Yet Bill latched onto the idea that his daughter and Stephan should fall in love and marry. Ruth liked Stephan well enough but could not see how the age difference and geographical distance, not to mention the couple's respective commitments, could be negotiated. "Let's pray" instead, Ruth counseled Bill, "that she finds someone like Stephan."

The Grahams returned to the United States, and a year passed. Seventeen-year-old Gigi and boyfriend Jim graduated from high school in spring 1962 and left together for college at Wheaton. Meanwhile, Stephan's marriage plans dissolved. The thought of Gigi Graham came to him. Stephan wrote to Ruth and Bill, asking to marry Gigi apparently out of the blue, having had no contact with her since the Grahams' sojourn in Montreux. Ruth and Bill kept his request from Gigi for fear that it would distract her from her college work and from her relationship to Jim, to whom she was now engaged. Yet such is the power of young love — or more accurately, young dreams of love — that when Gigi came home to Montreat for the Christmas holidays, she somehow knew that Stephan wanted to marry her. Gigi asked for permission to invite Stephan to Montreat for Christmas. Ruth said no, fearing Gigi might "make the wrong decision" and jilt Jim. Ever persistent, Gigi turned to her father and asked him to invite Stephan, which he did. When the young man arrived, Gigi recalled knowing instantly that the Lord had told her "to say yes" to the marriage proposal. She broke things off with Jim and made plans to leave Wheaton. She would marry Stephan in Switzerland that May. (Gigi and Stephan eventually divorced in the early 2000s. She was married briefly and unhappily to a private investigator named Chad Foreman. She and Jim Wilson, the boyfriend of her teenage years, married in 2012 and divorced three years later.)

Just a few years later, Dan Lotz, a captain in the US Air Force, asked Anne Graham to marry him; Bill had engineered their meeting and encouraged his daughter to marry him. Twelve years Anne's senior, Lotz had been a basketball standout at the University of North Carolina and graduated from UNC's dental school. He and Anne wed in fall 1966. Bunny followed her sisters' example and soon married Ted Dienert, the son of another BGEA employee. Gigi, Anne, and Bunny all married at the age of 18, about two years shy of the average age for US women marrying for the first time in the 1960s. Ruth found reassuring the large age differences between the Graham girls and their respective spouses, although Danny Lotz was the outlier. Stephan and Ted were both 24 years old, slightly older than the average of 23.1 years for a first-time US groom in those years.

From a twenty-first-century perspective, these youthful marriages may seem unusual. Yet the Graham daughters were not dramatically far from cultural trends for white middle-class women in the 1960s. These marriages, as young women marrying older men, also reflect ideas that Ruth encountered in one of her favorite child-rearing references, *A Parent's Guide to the Emotional Needs of Children*, published in 1959 and authored by Dr. David Goodman (not a medical doctor or a psychiatrist, but a PhD in education and a family counselor who authored a syndicated column, "What's Best for Your Child"). Ruth apparently passed the book on to at least one child, since Gigi quoted from it in her 1993 book, *Passing It On*. Goodman's book included his extended advice about sexuality, perhaps significantly, in one of the final sections of the 300-page volume. Titled "Faith," the section focused on developing children's moral character. Goodman expressed a clear preference that children marry young rather than engage in promiscuous experimentation. He blamed the latter for what he labeled, in an atypically strident tone, the current "mass orgy of loose sexual indulgence."

The chapter in Goodman's book titled "Only You Can Give Your Child a Sound Sex Ideal" included counsel on the importance of parents' healthy and active sex lives as a foundation for children's security and self-esteem. All of Ruth and Bill's children uniformly recall the warm physical relationship their parents shared. As David Aikman reported, all the Graham children remembered Ruth and Bill as "constantly affectionate" toward one another, "hugging, kissing, and holding hands." Goodman was not a prude, and approached sex talk with the latest research, citing the Kinsey reports from 1948 and 1953, the Chesser report from 1957, and other midcentury research into human sexuality. The good doctor was not averse to sex education or honest talk about sex between parents and children. He did hold to standards of monogamy and fidelity (and assumed, as a man of his time, that heterosexuality was the norm).

"Heavy petting" among young people had become a fixture of dating in the 1950s, according to historian Stephanie Coontz. The strategy of "sexual containment" — which girls were expected to deploy against boys' "natural" sexual advances — did not work very well because it arose from and depended on a disingenuous inequality. Girls were expected to be asexual and "save themselves" for marriage; boys were expected to try their best to overcome girls' resistance. Teen pregnancy rates skyrocketed. The proportion of white women who were pregnant when they married more than doubled.

"Sexual restraint" took effort, Goodman acknowledged, and he doubted that, in the heat of the moment, a young person would be able to muster the will for it. Hence the recommendation for marrying earlier. Goodman suggested that if one knew that such restraint need only be practiced for a little while, sexual activity might reasonably be resisted until after marriage. Under the auspices of marriage, pretty much any mutually satisfying intimacy would be allowed between spouses.

Goodman also assumed that girls did not need higher education, since they were fitted and destined for homemaking. They could and should therefore marry "at a much earlier age than boys," who, as future breadwinners, would need more education or training. With supports such as government grants for men's education and veterans' home ownership loans, the "former assumption that a man should be able to support a family [independently] before embarking on marriage" softened.

Ruth reassured her daughters that if they kept reading, they would become sufficiently educated for the task of marriage and motherhood. Given the importance with which they viewed their own sexual relationship, Ruth and Bill both may have believed that Gigi, Anne, and Bunny would be better off forgoing college diplomas and marrying almost anyone in their circle than if they waited until they were older, more educated, or more experienced. In keeping with the tendencies of evangelical sex advice through the late 1960s, traced by historian Amy DeRogatis, Ruth and Bill saw sexual expression as yet another good part of God's creation for which careful stewardship was required. Evangelicals recommended avoiding pre- or extramarital intimacy, not to mention same-sex intimacy. The counselor-columnist Goodman, who did not identify himself as an evangelical Christian but wrote approvingly of the Bible as a source for good parenting and marriage advice, dispensed advice that Ruth embraced; delaying marriage made no sense if it served only to inflame sexual temptations: "No sex without love," he proclaimed, but "if it's love, it might as well be marriage."

In a profile that appeared in *Woman's Day* in 1969, Ruth reflected on her daughters' early marriages, contrasting her daughters' youth with her own relative age (and college degree) at the time she married Bill. "I'm not as opposed to teen-age marriage as some people," Ruth explained. She might have had more reservations about her own daughters' marriages, she said, "if the boys were also teen-agers, but all three girls chose men at least six years older." For her, the age difference became a positive feature of each match, rather than a bug to worry about. "And they're all such terrific young men," Ruth enthused, "it would've been very foolish to say no." That Ruth focused on the "foolishness" of passing on these marriage proposals reflected again her agreement with Dr. Goodman's perspective: "If it's love," even young love, "it might as well be marriage." Ruth's opinion also spoke volumes about her view of her girls' life purpose and how they should "follow" a husband's lead, just as she had. Gigi, Anne, and Bunny could depend on their older and presumably wiser husbands to guide, provide for, and protect them. The only regret Ruth expressed about her daughters' marriages was that her girls no longer lived at home with her.

—◇—

Franklin was about eight years old during that Montreux summer when Gigi and Stephan first met. With her oldest daughter trying out more serious relationships, and the other girls growing up, Ruth wrote in her journal with concern about her older son and his apparent indifference to building a relationship with God. "Little Franklin," she wrote, "has never, to my knowledge, put his trust in Christ." He had not actively pushed Christ away, but he had not given his mother even the slightest impression that he gave God much thought. In her private writing, Ruth worried over a dream she recalled from the year before in which her little boy had grown into a handsome young man. In her dream, he was full of life but heedless of "his spiritual welfare. Unreachable." She comforted herself with the fact that Franklin "was still a boy at home with us. There is still time." She would not insist outright on his committing to Christ, but she would watch for signs of interest and try to nurture those.

Franklin was a tough customer; in particular, he enjoyed bossing little brother Ned around. Bea Long reported to Ruth the following conversation between the two brothers:

Franklin asked, "Ned, do you love me?"

"Yes, Nock," Ned replied, using his nickname for Franklin. "My love you."

"Well," Nock answered sharply. "I don't love you."

Bea told Ruth that after a moment, Ned answered, "Well, I love you."

"Well," Franklin reinforced the point: "I don't love you."

Ned tried to counter: "The Bible says — "

"The Bible doesn't say I have to love you, does it?" Franklin argued.

"Well," the little one replied, "the Bible says some nice things."

Franklin could mercilessly tease his brother and sisters, testing Ruth's patience terribly. Well-known is the story of a fed-up Ruth stopping in the middle of driving the five children to Asheville for hamburgers, taking the little pest from his seat and locking him in the trunk of the car. Releasing Franklin on arrival, she deadpanned to the surprised carhop, "Don't worry. He enjoyed it."

As Franklin grew older, his rebellions expanded to include speeding — almost baiting the area police — and a blaring devotion to rock music. "All right, Franklin," Ruth had told him one particular day. She would be hosting an afternoon gathering at Little Piney Cove for visiting missionaries, and she sought a compromise with her son: "you can listen to your rock music, but in your bedroom with the door closed. Please don't have it blaring all over the house."

As Gigi wrote of the episode in her 1979 family memoir, Ruth entered the house, missionaries in tow, while Franklin's music indeed blasted through the whole house. Gigi recalled that her mother "was furious, so she went flying up the stairs, two at a time." Franklin was nowhere to be found. Ruth turned off the music, took the records, and returned to her hosting duties. Gigi said that her mother's "conscience" troubled her afterward, not because she felt responsible for Franklin's disobedience but because of her own angry reaction. So the next day, Ruth drove to Asheville and purchased a new album for Franklin's collection. Mother and son listened to it together and talked about it. Practical and prayerful, Ruth went a mile with her son and then two. She wanted to understand his passion for this music even though she did not like it and even feared what she saw as its destructive potential.

This episode illustrated Franklin's later observation that his mother "always took the unorthodox approach to solving problems." He went on, "And with me she gained plenty of experience." He chalked up his many clashes with her as testimony to his "spunk" and her loving and sometimes "unpredictable" style of discipline. Unpredictable, yes, and Ruth chastised herself frequently for being petulant and snappish. But then she would do what she could to demonstrate her abiding mother-love. She tried not to value being right over being present. Gigi remembered Ruth often saying that "anything that is imposed upon . . . children will be discarded with relief when they get old enough." Gigi also credited her parents' openness to their children: "We were always free to talk to our parents about anything, and we were always permitted to disagree respectfully." Ruth tried to hear her children even as they grew into their distinctive adult lives.

—◇—

From the late 1950s on, Billy Graham reigned supreme in the world of Christian evangelism. He realized unprecedented success as a preacher of the gospel — the very work that Ruth had surrendered her own missionary vocation to. While Billy Graham achieved this renown, however, Ruth did her own kind of work. She managed her own and her family's private, day-to-day doings. She immersed herself in the local Montreat community, becoming a quiet and beloved compassionate friend to many mountain folk, Montreat College students, and many others who came into her ambit.

One person recounted to me the deep impact that Ruth made on his young life sometime in 1969 or 1970, when he was about eleven years old. The young boy lived in Georgia; his family attended the church pastored in those years by Ruth's brother, Clayton. He and Clayton's two boys were friends. This boy's father took ill and needed to travel out of state for specialized testing. Clayton's family brought him along on a planned visit to family in Montreat. Nelson and Virginia's home could not accommodate everyone, so the three boys — Clayton's sons and their buddy — stayed with Aunt Ruth at Little Piney Cove. "That week," he remembered, "is one I will never forget," understandably, given "the worry and uncertainty attending my father's condition." But just as powerful in his memory is "how Mrs. Graham overcame" that worry "with her light spirit, her whimsy, her broad and inviting smile, and her infectious laughter." She did not push him to discuss his father's health but prayed for him when they sat down for meals. Moreover, he recalled, "she made me feel better and secure," allowing "the fun we had that week in that very simple, warm, and inviting mountain house to supplant any worries that might otherwise have consumed me." Ruth was for him "a beautiful angel." Similar stories abound of Ruth's angelic, unassuming presence for people in need.

—◇—

Ruth developed a more public profile during these years of Billy Graham's increasing impact. The second wave of feminist activism in the United States stirred new interest among Americans about women's experiences — even among and about women like Ruth who did not align with the movement for "women's liberation." For the first time, several extended magazine profiles focused on Ruth in her own right. Her public role as a speaker and writer also grew, albeit slowly. Ruth rejected the midcentury women's rights crusade but also resisted definition by anyone else's expectations of her, including those of other Christians. In this part of her life, Ruth worked her way toward a new understanding of what it meant for one person to be a wife, mother, and Christian disciple.

Ruth did not self-identify as a feminist; indeed, to the contrary, she redeployed the term "liberation" to describe what she understood as the effects of her Christian faith on her life as a wife and mother. In doing so, Ruth presented an exemplary case of what historian Marie Griffith cites as the "internal challenges and debates over whom feminism can claim to speak for," debates that "have perpetually tested the limits of feminist solidarity and inclusion." Liberal, individualistic notions of feminism did not fit the life Ruth had shaped. Indeed, those notions struck her as illusory. Yet she did not campaign against second-wave feminism. Rather, she lived as close as she could to the mountain, its people, and the children — her own and those of others — she mothered. Doing so demonstrated her own agency.

Through the 1960s, then, Ruth was not only Billy Graham's "pretty" wife that people wanted to read *about* — for she still aroused such admiration — but also a figure that the American public wanted to hear *from*, just as other women's voices became more prominent. Along with the wider culture, in the 1960s, evangelicals began to grapple with new ideas about civil rights, women's rights, and roles for women and men at home and in the workplace. The very fact that Ruth had opinions about women's rights and expressed them for others to hear signaled that both the times and Ruth were changing. In one of history's ironies, Ruth benefited from the women's liberation movement that she opposed. Although engaging this cultural debate was not ever Ruth's first order of business, she occasionally used speaking opportunities to voice her opposition and publicly to express political sentiments on other matters that ran counter to second-wave feminism's message.

Historian Emily Suzanne Johnson has explained how the 1960s began a boom time for Christian evangelical women — both those who wanted to place Christianity within the burgeoning feminist movement and those who used Christian commitments to construct a bulwark against it. Responding in part to the growing number of "secular" feminist writings hitting the market, such as Betty Friedan's *Feminine Mystique* and *Ms.* magazine, women like Marabel Morgan and Anita Bryant found audiences among women readers who wanted to push against the secular feminist vision but also wanted to voice their own views about the freedoms, as they saw it, inherent in Christian womanhood. Many of these female Christian authors wrote in the burgeoning self-help vein.

In later years, Ruth would speak explicitly to the phenomenon of women's liberation, but during one of her first major appearances, she indicated her position by simply dispensing advice to mothers and wives. It was early yet: the occasion, convened in early February 1964, was the Congressional Wives Prayer Breakfast (Ruth called it the "First Lady Prayer Breakfast"). The event complemented the National Prayer Breakfast, popularly known as the Presidential Prayer Breakfast. Her comments were published under the headline "Love Begins at Home." Aiming to comfort the possibly overburdened mothers in her audience, Ruth spoke about the determinative quality of mother-love in forming children's good character, creatively interpreting Luke's Gospel to do so. She suggested that Mary's husband, Joseph, "not mentioned after the episode in the Temple" (Luke 2), had died during Jesus's adolescence. Ruth then focused on Jesus's experience as the child of "a widowed mother." Jesus was, Ruth surmised, "left the chief breadwinner for a family of seven children" and their mother.

Ruth drew her lesson for mothers not from Mary but from Jesus: "there is not a problem which we, as mothers, face, that He did not understand — *particularly we who have to bring up a family for the most part alone*" (emphasis added). This last phrase struck a poignant note, given Ruth's role as primary parent to her and Bill's five offspring. For her remarks to the congressional wives, Ruth found support for mothers not in Mary's example but in Jesus as father figure and breadwinner. Jesus not only redeemed Ruth Graham from sin and guilt — "I couldn't cope with my own" guilt, she confessed to the breakfast attendees — but also kept her company through motherhood's many lonely moments.

Oddly, the photograph that accompanied the news report about Ruth's comments did not show her speaking to the gathered congressmen's wives. Instead, the photo reinforced the point that Ruth mothered a large family for the most part on her own. She posed "outside her home," as the caption read, "with her family and their pets." Billy Graham was not with them. Gigi, recently married — "Mrs. S. Tchividjian" — wore heels, pearls, and ear-bobs, and looked for all the world very much like her mother, who stood beside her. Anne looked too young to be headed for marriage herself in the next two years. Bunny still wore a young girl's ankle socks and flats in this picture. Franklin and Ned stood farthest from Ruth, holding onto the leashed dogs.

Ruth's comments to the gathered women anticipated some of the sentiments of later evangelical feminists Letha Scanzoni and Nancy Hardesty. These scholars published their important evangelical feminist text *All We're Meant to Be* in 1974, affirming women's "far-reaching influence" and their responsibility, even burden, for rearing the next generation of Christians and citizens. In that sense, they aligned with Ruth's own views about mothers' essential work. In contrast to Ruth, however, Scanzoni and Hardesty made their affirmations about mothers as a stepping-stone to insisting that evangelicals undervalued such motherly work. They argued that for two centuries evangelicalism in the United States had been hobbled by deep-seated habits of Western patriarchal culture that denied women credit for power commensurate with their indispensable efforts on behalf of Christ's kingdom.

Ruth did not sound an explicitly antipatriarchal note in her breakfast address; any antipatriarchalism on her part came out with a hefty side of humor. She was not completely comfortable asserting herself. Even in these comments at the prayer breakfast, she reinserted a patriarch back into a central position, positioning Jesus as a mother's companion rather than the more expected figure of mother Mary herself. If American culture, including Christian culture, downplayed the centrality of mothers to a vibrant and productive society, the problem was not, in Ruth's view, remedied by rejection of traditional motherhood, but by the culture renewing its recognition and valuation of traditional motherhood's goodness. Mothers had Jesus's sacrificial example to follow. Ruth was a great one for updating traditions, as she did here. She did not discard her Christian inheritance. Instead she tried to embody and encourage other women to embody Christian commitment to motherhood.

—◇—

When the time came for Bunny and Franklin to enter high school, Ruth and Bill sent them to the Stony Brook Schools on Long Island in New York (Bunny attended the affiliated girls' school since Stony Brook did not become coeducational until 1971). The Christian school, founded by Presbyterians in 1922, appealed to the Grahams for its academic rigor but also for its strong evangelical roots and ethos. Its atmosphere, suffused with spiritual and academic rigors, felt to Ruth like the kind of place Franklin needed.

At one point during his time there, Ruth sent her son some discreet advice about an unnamed quandary he faced. (Her message sounded so opaque perhaps because she worried for his privacy as well as the family's. Any scandal large or small could reflect negatively on Bill's work.) Franklin felt pressure on some unnamed moral issue: "Listen, old boy," she wrote in her letter to him, "you've always had real good taste in selecting your friends." No stranger by now in gaining a teenager's ear, she complimented him, then gave an allusive instruction — perhaps following up on a previous, more direct conversation — "I'm not telling you what to do. I'm telling you the facts." Then the wise mother returned to complimenting mode: "You have excellent judgement, so you can decide for yourself what to do." Finally, she closed with what was surely always her final word on things: "We pray God will help you all along." The indirectness of the brief note — which never named the problem or gave exact advice but made a strong appeal to Franklin to hold firm and use his own good sense — showcased Ruth's practiced ability to give encouraging guidance while trusting in God's real providence in her children's lives.

In the end, Franklin did not graduate from Stony Brook, where he never felt at home. His parents let him come home midway through his junior year; because of the advanced curriculum at Stony Brook, he returned to school in North Carolina as a senior but did not actually graduate for lack of one missed credit. Nevertheless, even Franklin admitted later that the principal, teachers, and his parents were glad to call him "done" that spring. Ruth later recalled that during Franklin's teenage years, "There were calls from school principals, headmasters, irate teachers," and after one occasion when the young man "slammed the gate" to their property in a local police officer's face, an "indignant" call from local law enforcement. In that case, and true to form, Ruth invited the policeman up to Little Piney Cove, "assuring him that the gate would be open and [she] would have a pot of coffee ready." Franklin had been speeding — or so the officer thought "from force of habit." A pursuit ensued up the mountain to the Graham property. Ruth's later account resounded with sympathy for the policeman and with frustration toward Franklin, "totally unrepentant and grinning like a possum." Ruth made sure that Franklin apologized to him, however insincerely his words were delivered. This brush with the law certainly did not bring an end to Franklin's troublemaking. And it revealed Ruth's soft spot for law enforcement. "I'm not sure teenagers always appreciate the value of the police," she wrote in summarizing Franklin's hijinks. As we shall see, Ruth bridled at any show of disrespect for authority, even when her children were not involved.

Bill intervened to secure Franklin's admission to Le Tourneau College, east of Dallas, which had been founded right after World War II as a technical school for returning veterans. But there, too, Franklin ran afoul of campus rules, this time violating curfew with a female student. The incident echoed Ruth's own early Wheaton curfew violation — except that while her date had escaped sanction, Le Tourneau officials expelled Franklin. When he got back to Little Piney Cove, he said, "Mama wrapped her arms around me and, with a smile, kissed me like always, welcoming me back home." Franklin eventually graduated with an associates' degree from Montreat College (then known as Montreat-Anderson College). MaiMai's son John graduated at the same time, with honors. Ruth joked that Franklin graduated "with relief!" (Four years later, he graduated from Appalachian State University.)

As a boy, Ned too tested his mother's limits. He had what Ruth described as "a quick, violent temper" — perhaps a natural defense against a bullying older brother — but to her relief also evidenced a healthy conscience. During one episode, he lashed out at Ruth at bedtime, and she spanked him. He hit her again, and she spanked him again. Climbing into his bed, he pinched her and Ruth ignored it, letting Ned get in that last lick. They said his prayers together, and she left him to sleep. A few minutes later, Ned called his mother back into his bedroom to say, "My sorry my hit you." She left, then once more, he called her back to add, "My just sorry my hit you. My not sorry my pinched your finger." She again left his bedroom. Finally, a third time he called Ruth back: "My sorry my pinched your finger, too. My love you, Mom."

—◇—

Ruth persistently emphasized the critical place mothers held in influencing their children. A 1967 feature story picked up by *Christian Times for a Changing World* quoted Ruth: "a mother has the most enviable position in the world," namely, "training children," which she described for the reporter as "a tremendous responsibility and an enjoyable job." The story's headline — "Mrs. Billy Graham: Rears Family with Switch in One Hand, Bible in Other" — seemed to promise juicy details about Ruth's tough but just discipline style. By this time, however, the nest was practically empty. Franklin was in his first year at Stony Brook. And nine-year-old Ned did not yet pose the same kinds of challenges that his brother had. Nevertheless, Ruth wrestled between maternal and wifely duties. "Now that only Ned is home," Ruth told the reporter, "I still think twice about leaving [home to travel with Bill]. Somehow, one child needs even more care and affection than five." Readers learned that Ruth's strategy for coping when her husband was gone so much was to "keep busy." "You get used to it," she allowed. (Perhaps that distancing "you" signaled that she herself had never really gotten used to it.) She kept busy "running the home, [answering] correspondence, reading, sewing, and working in the yard," as well as teaching a college Sunday school class at Montreat Presbyterian Church. Detailing those activities, the profile story maintained its focus squarely on Ruth's work on behalf of others — children, husband, home, community. Any interest of hers beyond domestic ones, such as her poetry or book writing, seemed to have died with what the story called her "old-maid missionary" dreams.

Ruth did not enjoy public speaking and was once quoted as saying that "one speaker in the family is enough." So the times when she did address a gathering stand out. One such rare occasion: on September 15, 1969, Ruth addressed a crowd of thousands as a prelude to Billy's crusade in Anaheim, California. The *Christian Times*, which featured Ruth's comments in its 1970 Mother's Day issue, fairly swooned about the event, reporting on the day "as one of the greatest public tributes ever accorded any woman anywhere." Over a ladylike lunch of fruit and cottage cheese — "the largest assemblage west of the Rockies that has ever been served such a luncheon at one time" —

eleven thousand women listened (some through closed-circuit television) as Ruth dispensed "practical advice on marriage and child rearing."

Featured on the dais with Ruth was Nancy Reagan, first lady of California at the time; Clara Jane Nixon, sister-in-law of President Richard Nixon; author Helen Kooiman; plus Bunny and her new mother-in-law, Mildred "Millie" Dienert, who introduced Ruth that day. Not too many years before this event, Ruth had determinedly steered Bill away from direct involvement in (Democratic) US electoral politics as a candidate and even as an endorser. Yet here she was, honored by and speaking to the wives of significant Republican Party men. Partisan spirit differed then from our own time, but Ruth's participation in this luncheon still merits attention. Did she consider this women's gathering to be strictly an opportunity to share her message of motherly love and acceptance? Contrary to the budding second-wave feminist movement, Ruth understood women as utterly apolitical. Perhaps Ruth proceeded on that basis, but others — in the BGEA or in Nixon's camp or both — may have orchestrated the occasion to signal the political neutrality, at least, of Ruth's husband, given his previous closeness to Democrat Lyndon Johnson. The BGEA employed Millie's and Bunny's husbands, after all, to widen the reach of Billy's crusades. In spite of the breathless newspaper coverage, given the presence of the political wives, there was probably more to this event than cantaloupe and cottage cheese.

In December 1969, *Woman's Day* magazine featured Ruth in a profile titled "The Two Sides of Mrs. Billy Graham." This issue's Christmas focus meant that Ruth once again detailed her family's holiday preparations and traditions. Christmas celebration may have returned again and again as a topic of Ruth's public disclosures, in print and in person, because it did not require her to disclose too much detail about herself, her family, or their personal lives — particularly in these years of Franklin's various scrapes, run-ins, and rebellions.

The *Woman's Day* profile reported Ruth's comic take on an especially hilarious Christmas tree outing led by Bill. One year, motivated by idealized visions of a tree cut on Christmas Eve from Little Piney Cove's property — what Ruth pooh-poohed as "tradition and all that" — Bill and the children brought home a tree so toweringly tall that it would not fit in the living room. He sawed a few inches from the bottom, then a few from the top, then a few more from the bottom, with the result that by the end, Ruth mordantly reported, "only the middle [was] left." Ruth went to town, shelled out a dollar, and brought home a tree. That was "tradition" enough for her.

Although the story ran in 1969, the interview probably happened the year before. Ruth mentioned that Billy Graham had been invited to visit the troops in Vietnam over the holiday — a trip he made during Christmas week 1968. "I don't know whether he'll be home this Christmas or not," she had told *Woman's Day.* "I'm really torn," Ruth lamented. "It means a lot to the children to have him here, but I know it means a lot to the troops, too." She was still "following" Bill even if it meant they missed spending the holiday together. His absence at significant moments was part of what Ruth had tried to adjust to. Fortunately, Bill rarely missed a Christmas at home with Ruth. The crusade team tended to plan events closer to home in the weeks before Christmas. A 1952 trip to Korea and Japan and two trips to Vietnam (in 1966 and the above-mentioned 1968 visit) were Bill's rare Christmas Day commitments.

But as Ruth disclosed to *Woman's Day*, Bill's presence did not necessarily result in lavish gift giving between the two. It had always been Ruth herself and not Bill who had filled her Christmas stocking. She enjoyed the holiday excuse for "buying perfume, lipstick and things" she'd been wanting for herself. Now that Gigi, Anne, and Bunny were on their own, they took over stuffing their mother's stocking with the things she loved. The *Woman's Day* writer intimated that Ruth and Bill exchanged the kinds of gifts that husbands and wives anywhere would give, "often pretty lingerie for her and carefully chosen books with fine bindings for him." Did Bill give what he valued (lingerie) and Ruth give what she valued (antique books)? Over the years, Ruth did amass a serious collection of valuable books. Like stumped spouses the world over, the magazine reported, the Grahams were not above giving gifts that they wanted for themselves. "One Christmas Bill gave me a plow. I returned the favor by giving him a trundle bed and that spinning wheel in the hall. I knew it was just what he'd always wanted," Ruth explained, grinning.

Ruth's captivating appearance — her physical beauty and sense of style — had always been a focus of media coverage, and of course, *Woman's Day* focused on it as well. The reporter described Ruth as having a "dusting" of gray hair and wearing "a tailored white pantsuit setting off her golden tan." Echoing decades-earlier reports, the article gushed that the evangelist's wife would have looked "more at home in a country club than in a Sunday-school class" — crystallizing in modern lingo the ancient dilemma of women in Western Christianity. What has the Sunday school to do with the country club? Can a woman who appears at ease in the world also be a Christian? These bifurcated role expectations only intensified for women married to (or parented by) clergymen. The profile's title, too, "The Two Sides of Mrs. Billy Graham," reinforced the idea that the "two sides" — the stylishly dressed hostess and the preacher's wife — had to be distinct, separable, mutually exclusive. "The wife of the world's most famous evangelist is a fascinating blend of piety and worldliness . . . who believes 'It's no credit to Christ to be drab.'" Of course, in the genre of women's magazines, "fascination" is never enough, so the story also promises to reveal "some surprising details about [Ruth's] family, her life, her personal philosophy."

The title and subhead epitomized one perennial challenge that Ruth faced. She had by this time in her life encountered many "strangers" following her husband's work who had imagined her as a "prudish churchwoman" but were surprised (sometimes abashed, as we have seen) to discover this beautiful, sharp-witted, up-to-date woman instead. *Woman's Day* enthused: "She has a youthfully slim figure that she dresses with a marked sense of taste and style." (Ruth was forty-nine years old at the time.) That description and the (admittedly stunning) candid photograph that accompanied the write-up — Ruth laughing and smiling broadly — evidenced the dissonance that the writer and possibly readers felt about Ruth. They admired her Christian commitments (however they understood them) and her "warm witty worldly" ways that only intensified her "strikingly attractive" appearance. But how to admire all of it in the same woman? Part of Ruth's appeal was that she lived the embodied reality of Christian womanhood that patriarchy had for centuries tried to render impossible, paradoxical, even demonic. Like her husband — who faced similar criticisms for being too modern, compromising his Christian essentials for the sake of broader reach — Ruth could lure a curious public into at least giving her rigorous Christian message a listen.

Woman's Day included a description of the Sunday school class that Ruth had begun teaching in recent years at Montreat-Anderson College. It attracted "a hundred or so students . . . every week," and had led several of them to make confessions of faith. One such student hailed from Puerto Rico and had what Ruth called a "rather distinctive accent." She described him giving his testimony — his personal story of Christian conversion — "with a cigarette in one hand and a New Testament in the other." Earlier that year, Ruth had visited the student's family in the Bronx. She remembered the "terribly rough neighborhood, with a lot of trash and a totally dismantled car on the street in front of the building — I guess," she concluded, "you'd call it a tenement." She told *Woman's Day*, however, that everything in the family's apartment "was faultlessly clean." Echoing the rather Victorian attitude of the *Woman's Day* editors who could not reconcile Ruth's stylish exterior with her deeply Christian interior, Ruth herself tended to equate outward appearance and behaviors with inward moral dispositions — at least in the abstract. She had to work to make sense of her student-friend's tidy home, in the middle of a "tenement" neighborhood.

The contrast also allowed Ruth to diagnose the underlying causes of difference between her student and his family and their neighbors: they knew better and did better. Ruth had learned from her parents to draw a clear line between the ways of Christian living, which they had followed at Tsingkiangpu, and the ways of the world beyond the mission compound's walls. The nine-year-old who decried Chinese women's smoking habits was now in middle-age decrying rock-and-roll music, boys' shaggy haircuts, girls' skimpy skirts, and permissive sexual and language standards on television and in the movies.

And yet the contrast between Christian and worldly living held more force for Ruth in the abstract than in the concrete circumstance. From the beginning of Billy Graham's crusading work, Ruth had engaged in conversation and prayer with "inquirers," as those who came forward at crusade invitations were called. She had even embraced some who rejected Billy Graham's invitation, connecting with them on the street corners outside arenas where he appeared. She especially felt for those in dire straits. In the turbulent 1960s, Ruth condemned the emptiness of popular culture, the temptations of urban life, alcohol and substance abuse, what she saw as lax sexual mores. Yet if she met an individual floating precariously on those tides, condemnation for that individual dissolved into compassion and a desire to connect.

One of those floundering individuals was a young mother of three, Marilyn Daniels, who sought out Bill and Ruth at Christmastime in 1965. A few years before, Marilyn's husband had abandoned the children and his wife, who suffered from depression. She had moved the family to Montreat and scraped by until this desperate Christmas, when, as her daughter (and now best-selling crime novelist) Patricia Cornwell later remembered, "We'd been snowed in and out of school for weeks and were short of groceries, fuel oil, and our car was stranded down at the gate hill." Marilyn and the three children struggled up the steep slope to Little Piney Cove when Graham handyman John Rickman came driving up in his Jeep, fitted for mountain winters with its snowplow.

"What are you doing? Where are you going?" he asked her.

"We're going up to see the Grahams, and they're expecting us," Marilyn answered.

Cornwell recalled, "Of course, Ruth wasn't expecting us; she didn't even know us."

Rickman loaded the family into the Jeep, and up they went. Cornwell remembered that Ruth stood in the door of her home "with this long skirt on and a shawl wrapped around her with her hair up in a French twist. Ruth was the most beautiful, warm person I'd ever seen," she continued. "It was like something out of a fairy tale." Ruth invited the little family into her home for a spaghetti lunch. So began a relationship between Ruth and Cornwell that endured until Ruth's death.

—◇—

Ruth's compassion for people in dire straits came from an outlook she shared with Bill, a sense that social problems had both their roots and their potential resolutions in individual lives. Changing the world, therefore, began with transforming individual spiritual lives. As historian Curtis Evans has demonstrated, Billy Graham preached a "politics of conversion" in which Christ-filled individuals worked for social transformation. Ruth's engagement with the lost sheep who crossed her path reflected the same conviction. Ruth could live out her Christian commitment on the small scale of those in Montreat and environs who were abandoned, or grieving, or ill. (And sometimes literally a domestic scale: Cornwell recalled another time when Ruth delivered a pot roast to a recently widowed neighbor while the woman was out; noticing that her oven was dirty, Ruth cleaned it and then placed the dish inside.) And even though he sometimes clambered into political controversy, Billy preached that social transformation grew from spiritual transformation.

Ruth's grace, however, was not cheap. For example, regarding the student from Puerto Rico, she expressed approval that he "was working in order to pay back some money that he and a friend stole from a filling station." She expected the young man to make things right. Redress was up to him. Consistent with her focus on individual sins rather than structural inequities, Ruth did not address possible motives for his theft — to buy food, to pay for tuition or books, to relieve pressure from other people.

The *Woman's Day* profile, with its focus on the "two sides" of Ruth's personality, naturally included mention of Ruth's local crusade against the controversial eighteenth-century novel *Fanny Hill* (or *Memoirs of a Woman of Pleasure*), the subject of a 1966 US Supreme Court ruling that found "redeeming social value" in the book and therefore placed it outside the legal bounds of obscenity and censorship. Ruth confessed: "[I] read as much of the book as I could stomach . . . before I burned it page by page" — echoing rumors that her own mother had burned Pearl Buck's novel *The Good Earth* years before. In fact, Virginia had rather liked Buck's novel. She did think Buck had included too much tawdry material but saw it as a commercial decision driven by Buck's need to support her disabled daughter. Considering Virginia's example, Ruth came honestly by her willingness to accommodate abstract moralism to personal realities. But *Fanny Hill* received no such indulgence from her. *Woman's Day* reported that Ruth had spoken publicly against the book and its promoters (one, a local clergyman) and had exerted pressure to have the novel taken out of three Asheville bookstores. Mrs. Billy Graham's less "worldly" side let her opinion be known on this matter.

Woman's Day ended its feature with an appreciation of Ruth's ability to run the household during her husband's travels. "She's had to learn to make many decisions alone" — as if Ruth had not already known how to make decisions before she met Bill. This emphasis reflected expectations from earlier decades that wives depend on and defer to their husbands' direction. But it also reflected some awareness that other wives, too, were "learning" to make decisions — and that their husbands were "learning" to let them. Second-wave feminists insisted that women needed to become aware of their patriarchal subjection and then free themselves and each other from it. According to *Woman's Day*, Ruth had triumphed admirably over what its editors imagined to be learned helplessness, a psychological concept that scientists had just begun to explore. Their findings resonated with feminist activists. Ruth's apparently newfound agency shone as yet another aspect of her multidimensional character, the magazine told its readers. If she could do it — and still look alluring — anyone could! Ruth provided a fitting template on which the magazine, like all women's magazines, could make the extraordinary seem accessible.

Nevertheless, Ruth's positions as a parent and effective head of household, the story reported, brought great anxiety and stress. *Woman's Day* described Ruth's procedure for handling "distress": reading her Bible, "especially the Proverbs." Ruth had learned from Nelson the practice of reading daily from a chapter of that Old Testament book. Bill had adopted the practice as well. Sometimes, though, Ruth needed more than that somewhat passive exercise. She explained: "When I have something really big that I can't cope with . . . I go into my bedroom, close the door and talk to God. I talk over everything that's troubling me, then I ask, 'God, what is it You want me to learn from this? What are You trying to teach me this time?'"

The questions revealed Ruth's understanding of God's intimacy with her. She saw an active God engaged in continued training of a woman then almost fifty years old, with children and grandchildren and five decades of rich life experience. Ruth understood God as a shepherd guiding her into and through trials for her own good. She described the typical outcome of these conversations with God: "I nearly always get the right answer." Presumably she meant that she received divine direction that, in the end, created a good result for those involved — her children, her husband, her grandchildren, her friends, and her "prodigals," as she was beginning to call wayward ones. But the claim almost sounds like another one of Ruth's famous one-liners. She loved to tweak the mighty, be it Bill or the good Lord above. "I *nearly* always get the right answer." Why not always? "I nearly always get the *right* answer." She has in mind what she thinks ought to happen, and "nearly always," God agrees.

The *Woman's Day* story closed with an arresting but somewhat puzzling sentence, given the serious Christian devotion of its subject: "With . . . faith, it's said, you can move mountains," the author intoned. "Ruth Graham is content to *merely* live on one" (emphasis added). While Ruth appeared as an appealing mixture of the "pious" and "worldly," this final sentence tamps all of that texture back down so that she becomes a quiet, contented homebody, "merely" living in her mountain aerie. Her home, the reporter swooned, "reflect[ed] its mistress" in its "worldly and devout qualities" combined "in the same tasteful manner" in which Ruth herself combined them. What does that mean, exactly — in describing a person, much less a house? The breathless quality of empty magazine-speak fails to capture human reality, much less Ruth Graham's dimensions. Perhaps the observation aimed to capture what often surprised popular chroniclers and other observers who met Ruth: that the devoted Christian, daughter of conservative Nelson Bell, wife of world-famous evangelist Billy Graham, did not come off in person as a stuffy rule-obsessed dogmatist, but instead held her own, in her appealing appearance and in personal kindness, with "regular" white women everywhere.

Chapter 6

Poems and Prodigals

—◇—

1970–1975

Two of Ruth's poems frame a period of transition for her and her daughters, all three of whom had married by the time she wrote them. They show her distilling her philosophy of marriage into a few carefully selected words. The poems' context is not clear, but Ruth gave a small hint about the earlier one in a note mentioning "a young bride" in need of advice. All three stanzas of the 1967 poem began this way:

> Love
> without clinging;
> cry
> if you must —
> but privately cry;
> the heart will adjust . . .

The "young bride" in question needed to avoid letting her sadness or frustration show. After some practice, her heart would "adjust" to the unglamorous duties of homemaking:

. . . the heart will adjust
to the newness of loving
in practical ways:
cleaning
and cooking
and sorting out clothes
all say, "I love you,"
when lovingly done.

These ordinary tasks, in the poet's view, demonstrated the most important thing: the bride loved her husband and her family.

In the second stanza, the poem focused on a husband's concerns:

. . . the heart will adjust
to the length of his stride,
the song he is singing,
the trail he must ride,
the tensions that make him
the man that he is,
the world he must face,
the life that is his.

The bride must love her husband selflessly and allow him to set the trajectory and tempo of their life together. The poet expressed confidence that the "heart will adjust," almost in spite of itself, to his pace and direction. As Ruth had said in a recent interview, "You get used to it."

The poem concluded with a final stanza, unflinchingly restating the young wife's duty:

. . . the heart will adjust
to being the heart,
not the forefront of life;
a part of himself

not the object —
his wife.

Ruth forced the lines to make the meter work in order to emphasize her point. The young bride should not expect to be the only focus of her husband's attention — "the forefront" or "the object" of his life. She should instead embrace being "a part of himself." The poem reflected Ruth's experience of almost twenty-five years as the wife of a constantly busy public man. She had repeatedly insisted that Bill remain faithful to his vocation to evangelism, even as she rued the separations and loneliness that his work brought. She had indeed tried to be "a part of himself / not the object."

Embrace the role as background player, Ruth wrote. It is the part you signed on for. Do your work at home, even if it bores or frustrates you. Keep those feelings to yourself. Eventually, you'll get used to it. Love means accepting and coming to embrace the banal everyday "practical" work of running a home well so that your husband can live "the life that is his." The poem's last two lines — "So — / love!" — constituted the poet's final counsel. In light of the way marriage brought women and men together, where women were to follow men's lead, the solution for women who found such an arrangement challenging was to "love!" The poet could not explain or argue the merits of her case. Instead, she exhorted the young bride to her calling.

Ruth had thoughts for young husbands, too, perhaps for one of her three sons-in-law. A 1971 poem dispensed "advice to a new husband." (Franklin did not marry until 1974.) In the short piece she counseled him, "Never turn your back / on tears." Ruth continued by advising him not to stop the tears, even if he could not understand what they were about. She concluded: "Let her cry / — but kindly — / with a kiss." Taken alongside the 1967 advice to the young wife, these lines conjure a somewhat humorous image of a wife trying to cry privately while the young husband insists on being by her side. Yet the poems did reveal Ruth's distillation of what young wives and husbands needed to know about each other. Wives must be stoic and keep the home running smoothly, without expecting much in the way of romance or even appreciation; however, if the mask of wifely reserve slipped and tears fell, husbands must respond with sensitive gestures, not words or questions. The poems offered a model for rather quiet marriages.

This advice ran counter to the kinds of gender-role shifts taking place by the early 1970s. A march of more than fifty thousand women took place in Central Park in late August 1970 — the largest such demonstration since the early twentieth-century movement for woman suffrage, and ten times larger than anticipated. The event signaled a new surge of energy in the women's movement.

On the heels of her appearance in *Woman's Day* at the end of 1969, Ruth found herself on the cover of the March 9, 1970, issue of *Parade* magazine, with Bill, the focus of a story titled "Rev. & Mrs. Billy Graham — How It Feels to Be a Crusader's Wife." The profile asked, "What sort of woman is Billy Graham married to?" His fame continued to broaden: one of the Gallup poll's perennially admired men, a broadcasting juggernaut, friend to presidents. *Parade*'s description of his mate began, as usual, with her appearance. Echoing appraisals from decades past, the story described Ruth's "sort" as a "slim, strikingly pretty woman, 5 feet 5 and 118 lbs." She was fashionable and still anything but "drab." *Parade* set the "obviously intelligent, articulate, independent," and opinionated Ruth Graham against a roiling social backdrop, "a day when many Washington wives are boiling over with opinions, and many women are loudly questioning their traditional role." Comparing Ruth to a political wife, the profile explored the possibility that she might launch her own public career, but then pulled back to assert that a woman can be smart and engaged without affiliating with either the secular or the evangelical women's movement. That relatively nuanced (and perhaps now forgotten) view captured Ruth's attitude precisely.

Parade correspondent Viviane Peter described Ruth: "with a Bible and a firm hand, [Ruth] tackled the job of being both father and mother, general handyman and spiritual guide." She presented Ruth as still domestically focused but certainly not all petticoats and tea parties. Ruth had "chosen" to be a wife and mother, in Peter's words, and had resisted a more public role in both Bill's work — at its zenith — and the women's movement, for or against. The word "chosen" was not unconsidered. Having decided in 1943 to "follow" Bill, Ruth would not now go her own way, even as an empty nester.

Franklin was eighteen, Ned twelve at the time of this profile. "I probably won't speak out more" when the boys are gone, Ruth declared. "I think one speaker in the family is enough."

Ruth's rationale for her "choice" of continued domestic focus included her belief that men and women occupied distinct fields of activity, by divine design. In that view, she anticipated the conservative evangelical marriage model of complementarity propounded by John Piper and Wayne Grudem, among others involved in the Consultation on Biblical Manhood and Womanhood, founded in 1987. Her views reflected a gendered division of labor that had roots in eighteenth- and nineteenth-century cultural norms but experienced new growth in the US postwar period. Men were suited for public work and leadership; women, for marriage and motherhood. Indeed, "we mothers are homemakers by divine appointment," Ruth declared in the *Parade* profile. "We have our field and our role to play," Ruth said, "so why compete with men?" Her abiding role as Bill's wife, she said, "is the part any wife plays in her husband's life — just to try to be the wife that he needs." Indeed, *Parade* noted, "as Reverend Graham puts it, 'The wife is to fit into the life of the husband.'" Even in *Parade* magazine in 1970, Ruth continued to offer to women readers the advice she had poetically expressed to the young bride in 1967 — "adjust."

Reflecting Ruth's own openness to hosting her sons' friends or Montreat-Anderson students (at least when Bill was away), the story also featured her criticism of parents who did not welcome their children's friends. Young people needed places to gather for wholesome fellowship, Ruth opined. If young people could not gather in each other's homes, under parents' watchful eyes, they would seek entertainment or connection elsewhere — presumably even in premarital sex. The outside world, she warned, exposed young people "to so much filth" — she meant sexualized media content — "that they [do not] have a chance to learn that love is beautiful and magical." Ruth worried aloud about the "really serious times" confronting parents and children. She saw the distortion of moral norms all around her. "I don't think a young person has a chance of growing up really normally . . . apart from the lordship of Christ." She elaborated on what she meant by growing up "normally," interrupting herself: "I use that [word] in the broadest sense." She therefore exhorted readers not only to "conversion" but also to "discipleship, following Christ's way of life." For Ruth, that "way of life" included purity, service, honesty, hard work, orderliness, humility, and perhaps most of all, obedience.

Ruth's exhortations may have sounded harsh, even square (to borrow 1970s language). Her comments could sound indifferent to suffering, even cruel. Yet from her perspective, things were bad in the world because human sin was real. The antidote was just as real, though: Ruth reminded *Parade*'s readers that, while "God never promised it would be easy" to follow Christ, "God loves [people] just as they are." Paradoxically, her message was at once uncompromising — "We are spiritually dead until we accept the life He has to offer" — and full of love, compassion, and acceptance. She saw clearly certain demands made of those following a Christian path. To individuals in need, however, she did not operationalize that clarity as the first word spoken to non-Christians. Just as Ruth believed that Christians bent on evangelism need not be "drab," she insisted that they not be doctrinaire. People in pain first needed to hear a word of welcome from Christians. They needed to see something attractive in Christianity in order to come closer. After they did so, of course, Ruth thought it was fine to smash the hammer of righteousness down, not on a suffering person, but on the person's sin.

—◇—

Later in the spring of 1970, in connection with the East Tennessee Crusade held in Knoxville in late May, the local newspaper ran "A Conversation with Mrs. Graham" surrounded by candid pictures of her with "Mrs. Danny Lotz" (Anne) and of Bill with "Mr. and Mrs. Ted Dienert" (Bunny and her husband). This story requisitely acknowledged the rarity of Ruth's crusade appearances, her onetime missionary aspirations, and, quoting Ruth, the "vicarious thrill" she got from Bill's adventures. Her life, readers were told, focused on her "first duty": the remaining two children at home in Montreat, the rambunctious Franklin and the preteen Ned. Ruth also "kept busy with . . . friends and students of Montreat-Anderson College. 'Our house is open at all times, except when Billy's home. Then it's understood he needs his rest.'"

Ruth's concern in this piece focused on young people, her sons' peer groups, which was appropriate given the social and cultural unrest of the late 1960s and early 1970s. This Knoxville profile, however, also featured Ruth's consistent advice about women's need to adjust to the demands of marriage and motherhood. Ruth advised women to marry men they would not mind adapting to. "The primary goal in a woman's life is to make her husband happy, not make him good. Only God can make him good." Ruth's accommodating posture toward her husband grew from her understanding of God's will for her and all women. Yet her attitude toward children and youth seemed to depart from a strict biblical pattern. She was a firm and loving disciplinarian as a mother of young children, but more open to discussion as her children developed distinct personalities and viewpoints. Adjusting, for Ruth, grew to include forbearance toward teenage and college-age children; "Listen to what they say. . . . They're not always right, but sometimes they are."

Ruth thought the stakes in parenting young adults were particularly high. Based on her years of parenting, of meeting and working with them at crusades and at Montreat-Anderson College, she believed that drug use and suicide had increased among young people "because parents aren't listening" to their children. By contrast, she and Bill allowed their children to argue with them as long as they did so with respect. She told the reporter that this freedom, she and Bill thought, gave the Graham children all "better sense" than young people who protested by throwing rocks.

This rock-throwing comment might seem out of place to later readers. In fact, Ruth may have been referring obliquely to the antiwar protests at Kent State University, which had occurred several weeks before, on May 4, 1970. The final deadly clash that day, which left four students dead and nine others injured, included several groups of heavily armed National Guard troops facing off against rock-throwing student protestors. Ruth did not mention the event explicitly, but her dismissive comment seemed to indict the student protestors. She appeared to think they had gotten what they asked for by not following the National Guard's orders to disperse. Just as when Ruth had visited the Puerto Rican student in New York and found the slum conditions in his Bronx neighborhood to be the natural outcome of the neighbors' moral lassitude, so did she apparently find the response of the National Guard troops an expected outcome of what she saw as the student protestors' "disrespect" for authority.

Her own children had been "brought up with a profound respect for law." Protesting was fine, Ruth noted, "but I don't think rock-throwing or abusive language is respectful or shows good sense." Incidentally, "good sense" is a kind of motif in her comments reported at the end of the story. The reporter recognized that being married to "one of the world's foremost voices of Christianity" put a lot of pressure on Ruth Graham. Ruth neutralized those assumptions: "Do people expect perfection from me? Not people with good sense!" The "good sense" that would keep a young person from throwing bottles, rocks, or tear gas canisters at National Guardsmen would also keep her public from expecting her to be an ideal mother or wife. Good sense served as a protective virtue — it kept authority in place, preserved one from physical harm, and protected one from disappointment in the face of human frailty.

—◇—

Away from the glare of celebrity profiles, Ruth continued her poetry writing. She had always dated her poems inconsistently. The poems that do bear dates allow readers to appreciate the breadth of Ruth's concerns. She wrote one piece on October 8, 1971, "for the P.O.W. and M.I.A. wives" — that is, for women married to prisoners of war and soldiers missing in action, presumably in Vietnam. The date marked two national milestones and revealed Ruth's close attention to the country's involvement in the Vietnam War. First, the date marked the end of Operation Jefferson Glenn. A military campaign lasting more than a year, the maneuver brought together US airborne forces and South Vietnamese infantrymen. President Nixon highlighted this cooperation as a showpiece of his "Vietnamization" plan to turn control of the war gradually over to South Vietnam. According to the *World Almanac of the Vietnam War*, Jefferson Glenn marked the "final major operation in which U.S. ground forces" participated. Ruth took time that day to reflect on a significant shift in the long and increasingly unpopular conflict.

The other significant news of October 8, 1971, also related to Vietnam. A military spokesman revealed that of 1,618 American soldiers missing in action there, more than one thousand of them were "assumed to be dead." The staggering number reinforced the doubts of many about US goals in Vietnam. Ruth cannily avoided explicitly offering either political critiques or defenses of the war. Yet this poem showed her on one significant date as she ruminated on those several hundred souls whose fate still eluded sure knowledge. She tried to inhabit the thoughts of someone waiting to hear solid information about the fate of a loved one. The poem opened with a claim that the difficult knowledge of a soldier's death presented his family with a solidity that they could "deal with, adjust to." By contrast, she wrote,

> It's the
> not knowing
> that destroys
> interminably . . . [ellipsis in original]
> This
> being suspended
> in suspense;
> waiting — weightless.

The unknown fate of missing soldiers left open the slim hope that they somewhere survived. Someone mourning a soldier's death might eventually pick up and keep going with life; Christians expect to "outlive" such earthly losses eternally with God through Jesus's conquest of death on the cross. Yet in the absence of clear information, the poem asked, "How does one . . . adjust to nothing?" Will that waiting ever be rewarded by anything — by the return of soldiers or at least their remains?

Significantly, Ruth again employed a treasured concept here — "adjust" — that she had used in her advice to the young bride a few years earlier. Adjustment had dominated Ruth's attention and energy and had become a posture she could recommend to others. She recognized in herself, at least in her poetic explorations, her own ability to empathize and adjust. "Adjusting" was not only the newlywed wife's explicit job, but it was also the implied task of those Stateside military families — wives and mothers especially — who lost soldiers in combat. The "waiting — weightless" indeterminacy of a soldier MIA, however, posed a greater challenge than either marriage or even death in battle. Ruth took care to represent its intensity on the page: the line "interminably . . ." used ellipses to illustrate the word's denotation and suggest a trailing thread of anticipation. With the Stateside families, Ruth asked, will our waiting ever be rewarded? Will adjustment ever be possible? Will it bring satisfaction? The poem ended without providing reassuring answers. It left readers with the insistent questions of devastating, untethered unknowing.

Another poem from this period shows Ruth reflecting on a different deadly circumstance, one from the eighteenth century rather than from her own time. Writing in Vero Beach, Florida, Ruth was stirred by looking out at the ocean, where, she explained in a note, "Spanish Galleons sank off the coast."

> Theirs
> is a still-less,
> restless grave —
> dismantled
> by each churning wave,
> each tugging tide,
> and pried
> by treasure seekers, till
> they know no rest
> — who should be still.

Ruth dolefully observed the natural pull of ocean tides and the invasiveness of diving treasure-hunters. Natural and human forces alike disturbed the graves of those who went down with the ships. As protective of their solitude as she was of her own, Ruth wrote in the poem's second stanza of her refusal to buy a coin salvaged from one of these wrecks. Her careful observations, and then her exploration of what existed literally beneath the surface of what she saw, combined in this melancholy meditation to defend the right to rest of the dutiful dead.

One more poem from 1972 again drew on ships and seas, this time metaphorical ones. These symbols lent themselves to sorrowful musing about death and the pain of not knowing. Ruth dedicated this poem to "W.S.," whom she described in a note as "a street kid" when she first met her in a large city, apparently some years before. The girl, Ruth explained, had suffered from drug addiction but had embraced Christianity. "She was a baby Christian learning to walk," Ruth explained, "and like any baby learning to walk, she fell. And fell frequently." She and Ruth "wrote regularly" to one another and had connected in person with each other over the years. Ruth mourned in 1972 that the girl she first met had aged into a "drawn . . . tired" woman. The poem Ruth wrote "for her" evinced worry for the woman's fate.

> Perhaps
> she will land
> upon That Shore,
> not in full sail,
> but rather,
> a bit of broken wreckage
> for Him
> to gather.

The poem's concluding lines echoed the end of chapter 7 in Luke's Gospel. While breaking bread at a Pharisee's home, Jesus was interrupted by a "woman in the city, who was a sinner." She washed Jesus's feet with her tears and dried them with her hair. Jesus calmed the Pharisee's alarm at the apparent impropriety by telling a story about forgiveness. He wanted the Pharisee to see how God's unexpected mercy inspired worshipers' extravagant love. Ruth translated the point into poetry:

Perhaps
of all the souls redeemed
they most
adore.

Examining her own pharisaic tendencies, Ruth tried to see W.S. as a modern-day incarnation of Jesus's reproof of doctrinaire religious authority. Ruth's poem elevated W.S. as a deeply grateful recipient of Christ's grace, exemplifying true Christian love.

A playful poem in November 1971 commemorated special visitors to Little Piney Cove — Charles Massey and his wife, the former Emily Cavanaugh, to whom Bill had been engaged before arriving at Wheaton College in 1940. Ruth wrote her "Ode to Emily and Charles" to mark the "first get-together of the two families." The comical, rambling piece went like this: "The night / Bill told me / he loved me, / what / did we discuss? / Us? / No. / Emily!" Guilelessly, Bill had gushed about his former fiancée: "Beautiful. / Sweet. / Talented. / Spiritual. / (And second cousin to / Herbert Hoover!)" — probably an added plus for Ruth, since Nelson had detested FDR. Ruth was not above poking fun at Bill. Nor would she spare herself: "I got madder, / (not sadder), / just madder and madder, till *blam!*" Had she exploded in jealous rage? No — the crash was literal, as a distracted Bill drove into a truck — "(what luck!)" Ruth joked.

What saved Bill and Ruth from further heated discussions about Emily was the latter's own love interest: "there were no quarrels," Ruth rhymed, *"thanks to Charles!"* Emily's attention had turned toward a more suitable mate. Years passed, and the opportunity arose for the couples to meet. Of course, Ruth had confidence in the strength of her marriage, but she nevertheless admitted in her poem, "I hoped / (how I hoped!) / by now" that Emily had "become / fat and dumb." She had not. After meeting her, Ruth confessed, "I liked her!" Yet she remained grateful for Emily's husband, who had supplanted Bill all those years ago. "This is the moral / of my ode / (if this is an ode, / and if odes have morals): / *Thank you, Charles!*"

CHAPTER 6

◇

In the fall of 1972, Ruth accompanied her youngest child, Ned, to London, where he would begin his high school years at Felsted, a boys' school in Essex. Founded in 1564, the school aligned with Puritan reformers and counted Oliver Cromwell's sons among its alumni. As Ned arrived, the school, having recently marked its four hundredth anniversary, was in a period of capital expansion, renovating its chapel, adding a concert hall with practice spaces, classrooms, and a "sports hall."

For all the school's splendor and tradition, Ruth mourned the separation. In a poem titled "Parting," Ruth confessed, "Perhaps I wouldn't feel / this way / if school were near." She returned home to Little Piney Cove, to a mostly bare nest. Years afterward, Ruth described the experience of returning to the empty house. She recalled being "greeted by a living Presence." Quoting the risen Jesus's words from the end of Matthew's Gospel, Ruth remembered grasping in a novel way his assurance: "Lo, I am with you." As it turned out, Felsted did not agree with Ned. He wrote home, Ruth later reported, "about the bad language and certain undesirable things going on." She later learned that Ned was actually another "prodigal" son, like Franklin, "enthusiastically . . . entering into the life of the far country." But in the moment, she thought he simply needed to be in a different environment. So Ned left Felsted, returned to the States, and went to Stony Brook. A poem dated January 19–20, 1977, "for Ned," indicates that his time there was not without difficulties. Some "storm" related to her youngest vexed Ruth.

> My soul was drenched
> in wind and rain
> frozen in fear
> that fell like snow.

"Then," suddenly, "all was still." Ruth wondered about the "peace" that had broken in upon her distress. "Had someone" — Ned — "prayed? / I do not know." In any event, he graduated from Stony Brook that spring.

Even though Ned was no longer an ocean away from her, Ruth's moment-to-moment task of mothering a child at home was really over.

Rather than shepherding each of them from dawn to dusk, she now started each day with coffee and prayer, sitting on the porch at Little Piney Cove, praying "for each of our children, and for each of theirs." She had an acute sense of God's companionship but still grieved the absence of her children, their constant activity and presence. During this period, she wrote a poem titled "Then, and Now." Bill quoted it in one of his last books:

> The house was full of living then
> And there was need to view
> the quiet contours of the hills,
> heaven's vast expanse of blue.

Back "then," the calming view of the mountain landscape gave Ruth what she needed — exemplary stillness, reassuring peace. "Now," however, she needed something different.

> This old house is empty now
> with mostly only me,
> the trees are crowding up the hill
> as if for company.

Without any children around, she needed the companionship of the mountains' innumerable trees. She recognized a new emptiness not connected to Bill's absence, which had been a fixture of their marriage since the late 1940s. She had adjusted to that. The house was "empty now," after almost thirty years of the children's daily comings and goings. Ned's departure for school signaled the end of Ruth's life as a mother with children at home to schedule, monitor, feed, clothe, console, and love up close. Another poem, composed in January 1978, ended by trying to turn that moment-by-moment shepherding task — protecting her flock from "wolves and leopards / hungry and clever" — over to God:

> Lord, still
> my anxious heart

to calm delight —
for the Great Shepherd
watches with me
over my flock
by night.

Ruth wrote and revisited another poem during these years in which she recommitted to trusting in God's care for her loved ones:

I find my leaden spirit
lifted from the dust
confident that You
Who've brought them
thus far on the way,
will see them through.

Ruth dated this poem 1977 and 1980, years marking both Ned's graduation from Stony Brook and his first marriage.

Ruth did derive satisfaction from the realization that her children had done what all children do. They had become independent adults. "I would not have them back for good — / My birds have learned to fly," she wrote. But she hoped that at least one of them would settle close enough to Little Piney Cove for her to spend time with. Indeed, after his expulsion from LeTourneau College just weeks before graduation, Franklin returned home and at last graduated from Montreat-Anderson. He married in 1974 and settled near his wife's family in Boone, less than two hours from Montreat. The town was home to Appalachian State University, where Franklin earned a bachelor's degree in 1978. Perhaps Ruth alluded to him in the poem's concluding lines: "But I find lovely comfort when / A wild bird nests close by." The natural world continued to bring Ruth comfort, perspective, and the language she needed for expressing her feelings.

Ruth reimagined her house in those years as her "business address" in one poem, or "base of operations," in another description that drew on a concept that she had probably heard from Bill and his team countless times over the decades. She tried traveling at Bill's side for a couple of years, making two worldwide swings with him in 1977 and 1978. The result, Ruth confessed later, was not a positive one: "I wound up a zombie. I cannot keep up with the man." She compared Bill taking her with him to a "general taking his wife to battle" — she felt out of place and unnecessary. Hers was the home front in this battle for souls. She felt that she did her part best by staying at Little Piney Cove, continuing to make it a restful place for her and Bill to share. She also hosted the children and a growing roster of grandchildren, or visited them in their own homes. Jonathan Lotz remembered staying at the Montreat home as a little boy of six or seven years old, finding Bibles open throughout the house during the day and his grandmother on her knees praying in the middle of the night. Even as her world and family changed around her, Ruth held to her lifelong devotional practices.

Ruth devoted many personal resources to Montreat-Anderson College in those years, too. The college's new library was named for Nelson Bell and dedicated in 1972 on his birthday, July 30. In the fall of that year, Ruth began serving on the college's Board of Trustees, first as a member of the Buildings and Grounds Committee and then, the following spring, moving to the Academic Affairs Committee. She eventually served three terms before rolling off in April 1981, when the board awarded her the title of honorary trustee. The resolution that recognized her service to the institution praised her work as "a staunch advocate" of the school who "encourag[ed] students to enroll" and "work[ed] to gain financial support for the ongoing program in ministry." She had been "an encouraging friend whose presence and activity have consistently reinforced [the college's] Christian ministry."

During the early 1970s, Ruth also confronted more immediately the physical frailties of her aging parents. Nelson had suffered a series of heart attacks and a mild stroke in 1965 and 1966. Prediabetes also left him with circulation problems. Virginia had survived strokes and had struggled with mobility and speech difficulties since late 1968. In 1972, which turned out to be the last year of his life, Nelson was elected to serve a one-year term as moderator of the PCUS. Given his failing health, his election more than anything honored his lifelong service to the denomination as a mission doctor and a leading layman of the conservative old guard. Nelson still insisted on getting up well before dawn every day for Bible reading and prayer. Energized by his devotions, he was then prepared to help Virginia for the rest of the day. When Ruth popped in one morning to see them, she came upon Nelson, kneeling to help Virginia put her stockings on. "You know," Ruth reported Nelson saying, "these are the happiest days of our lives. Caring for your mother is the greatest privilege of my life" — language and sentiments that echoed Ruth's somewhat heedless prayer after her first date with Bill some thirty years before. If Nelson traveled, as he sometimes did in the role of moderator, Virginia waited anxiously for his return. They would kiss, Ruth declared, "long and tenderly" upon his return. Virginia actually intervened to prevent one trip that he hoped to take with Ruth back to China. While in Switzerland with Bill, Ruth had personally petitioned the Chinese consul for permission to travel to China with Nelson. She returned to Montreat with the appropriate forms for him to complete. Virginia expressed her opposition by hiding the forms, which were only discovered after her death.

Ruth admired the sweet closeness of her parents' fifty-one-year marriage. She penned a poem in 1973 that reflected her reverence. As usual, a natural scene had stirred her attention:

> Atop the ridge
> against the sky
> where clouds,
> windwhipped,
> sail free, sail high,
> a tree uprooted,
> fell and lodged
> in the forks of an oak tree
> standing by.

She explained in a later note that this pair of trees — one "uprooted" on the windy peak, the other acting as support — "reminded [her] of how Daddy cared for Mother after her stroke." Even with his own significant health struggles, Nelson continued to dote on his wife and take primary responsibility for her care.

Ruth tried to capture this fragile strength in the subsequent lines:

> There they stood —
> felled,
> upheld,
> in the windswept wood.
> Atop the ridge
> I found them there
> one cold Spring day;
> and stopped
> to stare;
>
> and stayed
> to pray.

She saw her parents' faithfulness — and especially her father's caring support — as a holy thing. For Ruth, Nelson embodied adjusting, unselfishly setting his own schedule around Virginia. This fidelity and sacrifice moved Ruth to pray, perhaps for her own steadfastness as she and Bill aged. Nelson died late that summer, on August 2, 1973.

—◇—

Another relationship from the early 1970s left traces in Ruth's writing. Richard and Pat Nixon had known the Grahams since 1952 when Bill first met Senator Nixon and his family in Washington during a crusade. Ruth commemorated Nixon's second inauguration in a poem; Bill did not participate formally, as he had at Nixon's first ceremony, but the Grahams did attend. The poem is classic Ruth Graham style: only fourteen words, arranged into seven brief lines, reflecting one moment in terse description.

> Low gray skies,
> clouds
> moving fast,

crowds . . .
one man,
and a flag
half mast.

Instead of sounding a bombastic celebratory tone, the poem zeroed in on the occasion's somber natural and visual aspects. January 20, 1973, was a cold day, cloudy and windy with temperatures in the low forties. The darkened sky dominated the scene, as it dominated the poem's shape on the page. Underneath the clouds' gloomy presence, the "crowds . . ." — stretched and vaguely defined by Ruth's perennial ellipses — spread across the landscape. The flag at half-staff recognized the passing of former president Harry Truman less than a month before, on December 26, 1972.

It seems strange, perhaps, that Ruth would have focused so somberly on the death of a figure who had shut her husband out. Decades before, in July 1950, a young, inexperienced (and starstruck) Billy Graham made the mistake of talking to the press on the White House lawn after an awkward meeting with Truman. The prickly president responded by blackballing the evangelist until the late 1960s. Yet for Ruth, the convergence of Nixon's second electoral victory, signs of a still-mourning nation, and gloomy, cold weather that dominated the scene led her to ruminate on the inconsequence of human action, represented in the moment by "one man," Nixon. The large antiwar and anti-Nixon demonstrations that marked the day may also have added to Ruth's melancholy. Against the tableau of the natural world, human life seemed brief and combative.

Only two days after Nixon's second inauguration, former president Lyndon Johnson died. Nancy Gibbs and Michael Duffy observed that Billy Graham had ministered not just to LBJ but to the entire Johnson family. The Grahams and the Johnsons had, in fact, formed a close bond, in part because they were of the same generation and because their experiences in work and life shared deep similarities. Ruth and Lady Bird lived comparable experiences of putting their husbands' all-consuming careers first. As Lady Bird described their connection, "Both of us married very strong men and grew into the wife of someone who belongs to the world." They both endured those husbands' long absences from home and tried to protect their children from prying eyes, wagging tongues, or worse. Lady Bird knew that Billy Graham's life, like her husband's, had "been filled with needful people." She and Ruth labored so that these titans could relax when they needed to. Lady Bird probably also understood and felt Ruth's gravitation toward solitude. In the late 1970s, when Ruth's volume of poems was published, Lady Bird commented of the title poem, "I understood 'Sitting by My Laughing Fire' so well, because it is the best company in the world."

Johnson's January 25 burial at his Texas ranch, held after the official Washington funeral, prompted Ruth to pen a poem whose length ran in inverse proportion to the legendary breadth of LBJ's spirit:

> Of this historic moment
> two things I kept:
> that earth was gray
> and cold,
> and heaven wept.

As it had at Nixon's second inauguration, the weather again pressed in on Ruth. It insisted on what mattered: the very cosmos grieved over the passing of her friend. His personal dynamism was as mythic as his undoing by the inherited conflict in Vietnam. Another poem dated January 25 showed Ruth reflecting on the hill country grandeur of Johnson's ranch, where he had been born and now was laid to rest. This place fit his "larger than life" way in the world even as, in death, Johnson lay "smaller than death . . . under the spreading oak trees" and expansive Texas sky. In the second stanza, Ruth's perspective filtered through her Christian faith:

> If mercy is for sinners,
> (which God
> in mercy gives)
> smaller than Life
> he lived here,

larger than death
he lives.

Death's victory over LBJ's body became God's resurrecting power over his eternal soul. Using her characteristic capitalization — earthly life contrasted with Life in eternity with God — Ruth tried to signal transcendent meaning to readers.

In the early 1970s, however, Ruth's poems were not yet circulating publicly. Some women's writing was finding a new place on the cultural landscape. But Ruth did not affiliate with the cause espoused by Betty Friedan, Gloria Steinem, Germaine Greer, and other white feminists whose writings and speeches captured much popular attention beginning in the early 1960s. The claims of second-wave feminists did not strike everyone, or even every woman, as liberating. If Ruth belonged to any literary tribe, it included women like her favorites, Holiness evangelist Hannah Whitall Smith, missionary-poet Amy Carmichael, and disabled poet Jane Merchant — women whose Christian service found expression at least in part through their writings.

One such contemporary female voice sounded in 1973 with the publication of Marabel Morgan's *The Total Woman* by the evangelical house Fleming H. Revell. The text collected material from a series of workshops Morgan taught for married homemakers. Morgan had forged the principles of "Total Womanhood" herself, she claimed, as she tried to improve her own marriage. Indeed, Morgan dedicated the book to her husband, Charlie. This chipper marriage and sex-advice manual for women was one of several such books published for married men and women by evangelical presses in the mid-twentieth century. The slim volume's chapters concluded with homework assignments aimed at having readers practice what Morgan preached.

The Total Woman exhorted women to pay careful attention to appearance — of self, of home, of children — all for the sake of pleasing their husbands. A happy husband would become putty in a wife's hands. Chapters titled "Accept Him," "Admire Him," "Adapt to Him," "Appreciate Him" indicated the direction and weight of a wife's responsibility toward her mate.

If she did these things, by an act of will, a wife would enjoy greater financial security, closer emotional ties, and better sexual intimacy — what Morgan called "Super Sex" — with her husband. The book combined wily feminine strategies and (for its time) frank sexual advice, all warranted with biblical texts. As one current in the growing tide of Christian self-help, *The Total Woman* was an unusual book for its time.

Ruth read and approved of Morgan's advice to wives. In Ruth's view, women needed to adjust to their husbands; so for Morgan, women needed to forgive, adjust, even "protect" their husbands from their own "complex" feelings — such as tears. "Privately cry," Ruth had written to "the young bride." "A Total Woman," Morgan wrote with emphasis, "*chooses* to go the second mile." Ruth found Morgan's book so compelling that she gave each of her daughters a copy, with varying results: One daughter loved its advice. Another decidedly did not. The third thought her mother's present was a typical Ruth-style practical joke.

In 1973 a Dallas lawyer using several million dollars from a BGEA-adjacent fund and acting apparently on behalf of the organization purchased more than a thousand acres of mountain property outside of Asheville known as Porter's Cove. The arrangement only came to light later, in 1977, as part of a *Charlotte Observer* investigation of Graham's finances, personal and organizational. Billy Graham justified the circuitous and secretive purchase by characterizing it as a strategy to protect the BGEA from appearing to have limitless resources. He did not want his evangelistic operation being overwhelmed by either criticism or appeals for aid. A series of miscommunications — furthered by Graham's more or less innocent but unwise failure to mention the fund's existence — led to the very censure Billy had hoped to avoid. According to Billy Graham biographer Bill Martin, even after more than a decade had passed, Ruth still held a grudge against one of the *Observer* reporters who had discovered the fund's existence. He had made innuendos about Billy's brother Melvin profiting illicitly from the land purchase. The evangelist chalked the whole thing up to lessons learned, but a salty Ruth told Martin, "My husband is more gracious than I am."

The property was destined to become the site of the Billy Graham Training Center at the Cove, which began in the late 1980s offering workshops and retreats for laypeople, encouraging them in personal faith and honing their skills in evangelistic outreach (see chapter 7 for more on the Cove). Where Montreat Conference Center operated under the aegis of the PCUS and later the reunited Presbyterian Church USA, the Cove would follow the BGEA's nondenominational evangelical lead. This planning signaled a new desire among the organization's leadership to institutionalize its work for future generations.

Another move, in late July 1974, signaled a similar desire to ensure Billy Graham's legacy of worldwide evangelization. Gathering Christian evangelists from around the globe, he convened an International Congress on World Evangelization in Lausanne, Switzerland. Ruth accompanied Bill to Lausanne and participated in some of the congress's discussions. The various sessions elaborated on the conference theme, "Let the Earth Hear His Voice." Those gathered aimed to chart a path for bringing the gospel to the modern world, around the world. One outcome of the meeting was the Lausanne Covenant, a fifteen-part statement that offered a kind of systematic theology in miniature for mission-minded evangelical laypeople. The statement clarified its signatories' understanding of God, Scripture, Jesus Christ and his expected return, the Holy Spirit, and the church worldwide and its cooperative mission to evangelize and show compassion to the world regardless of risks or consequences.

Section 9 of the Lausanne Covenant, titled "The Urgency of the Evangelistic Task," confessed the church's guilt in not yet spreading the gospel to all the world. "The goal," the statement asserted, "should be, by all available means and at the earliest possible time, that every person will have the opportunity to hear, to understand, and to receive the good news." In the view of participants, the urgency of this project could hardly be overstated. Some congress attendees proposed hastening the work of world evangelization by making material sacrifices in the face of global poverty and related injustices: "Those of us who live in affluent circumstances *accept our duty to develop a simple life-style* in order to contribute more generously to both relief and evangelism" (emphasis added).

This section of the Lausanne Covenant, included at the insistence of the covenant's author, Anglican priest and evangelical theologian John Stott, rubbed Ruth the wrong way. (It would become for many others the foundation of a simple lifestyle movement in the early 1980s.) Ruth recognized that her own material circumstances might have looked extravagant. Yet she and Bill had contributed their financial and personal support to causes beyond his crusade work. They founded the Ruth and Billy Graham Children's Health Center and foundation in Asheville in the mid-1960s. Ruth had donated to a Mexican orphanage almost all of the inheritance she had received after Nelson's death. She gave material aid regularly to distressed folk in Montreat and beyond. Her life with Bill had many moving parts — the house on the mountain, the various staff needed to maintain it, the entourage of associates and assistants, and Bill's requisite tropical vacations. Ruth justified it all by declaring it necessary for Bill's calling. In Bill Martin's account of Ruth's refusal to sign on to the Lausanne Covenant, she rejected Stott's formula as "too confining." Ruth declared to Stott, "If it said 'simpler,' . . . I would sign it. But what is 'simple'?" Highlighting the differences between the unmarried and childless Stott and her and Bill, Ruth tried to explain: "You live in two rooms; I have a bigger home. You have no children; I have five. You say your life is simple and mine isn't." Ruth implied that where Stott saw distracting encumbrances, she and Bill saw many needed tools that helped them to accomplish his evangelism.

Anytime rumors reached Ruth about Billy Graham's apparent wealth, her protective instincts reacted. The episode at Lausanne helped explain her defensiveness; in her view, Billy's work — whose scope impressed even those who were lukewarm about his style and methods — justified accommodations made to his convenience and comfort, such as sunny beach vacations and flights in acquaintances' private planes. The regular sunny holidays that Bill more or less required in order to regain strength and release stress appeared somewhat posh. Gigi later said her father loved sunshine and did not enjoy spartan surroundings. Ruth teased him about his inability to rough it. Yet even she defended the winter escapes to Florida or the Caribbean that fueled Bill for carrying on the exhausting work of the crusades. On these grounds, Ruth took umbrage at the uniformity of Stott's simple-living standard. In a 1978 oral history interview with Lois Ferm, Ruth also pushed back against mischaracterizations of Little Piney Cove's size and opulence. What wags and critics imagined as luxurious living was, in Ruth's view, the product of her efforts to make simple materials shine, to guard her family's privacy, and to keep Bill at his best. They had all needed the mountaintop retreat Ruth created. It allowed Bill to do the work God had called him to and that Ruth had kept him focused on.

Bill Martin also linked Ruth's Lausanne objection to another refusal she had made early and often: in spite of her husband's pleas, Ruth never agreed to join her husband in becoming a Baptist. Martin wrote that Ruth knew "she could be a quite acceptable Christian," thank you very much, without embracing requirements such as particular forms of Christian practice — immersion baptism, ascetic living — that "she regarded as a bit self-righteous and precious." Demanding a "simple life-style" from evangelists struck her as unduly autocratic, overly doctrinaire, a denial of individuals' ability to discern and address wisely their own needs.

In early October 1974, Ruth visited Gigi and her family, who were living outside of Milwaukee, while Bill and his team prepared for a crusade in Rio de Janeiro, Brazil. Ruth was helping the Tchividjian children set up a "pipe slide" or zipline like one they had played on during a European visit. Ruth's granddaughter Berdjette, eight years old at the time, later remembered that she and her siblings were intimidated by the line's height. So they turned to Ruth — whom they called "Teh-Teh," meaning Great One — telling their fearless grandmother, "You do it, you do it first."

Even under the negligible weight of the petite Ruth, the line immediately collapsed. She slammed fifteen feet to the ground. At first, Gigi and her children thought that their ever-playful Ruth, who lay motionless on the ground, was pretending. "Oh come on, Teh-Teh," Berdjette remembered them saying to her. After the family Doberman pinscher approached and licked Ruth's face, they realized that Teh-Teh was not playing around this time. Stephan, Gigi's husband, carried Ruth's limp body into their house and called a doctor-friend. (Ruth later derived great amusement from the fact that this doctor happened to be a psychiatrist.) The doctor in turn summoned an ambulance, which transported Ruth to the hospital.

Ruth was unconscious for a week after the accident. She suffered a severe concussion and multiple broken and crushed bones — her left heel, one rib, a neck vertebra — and exhibited severe memory loss even after coming-to. This troubling sign, consistent with her concussion, disturbed Ruth the most. She grieved her inability to remember a lifetime's worth of memorized Bible passages, many learned during breaks in busy days at home with the children. She later recalled feeling as ruined "as a man must feel who learns the bank has failed and he has lost his life savings." She prayed to God, "You can have anything I've got, but please give me back my Bible verses." Words from Jeremiah 31 came immediately: "I have loved thee with an everlasting love: therefore with lovingkindness have I drawn thee" (KJV). Surprisingly, this verse had not been among Ruth's memorized store — not that she recalled, anyway. But the verse signaled the eventual return of the other treasured verses. Physical effects of the accident continued to bedevil her, some for the rest of her life. Ruth eventually had one wrist joint and a hip joint replaced; Bill Martin surmised that the fall caused joint damage requiring these surgeries. He also noted that the accident was "possibly related" to a later surgery on her esophagus, which may in turn have caused the cough that vexed Ruth from then on. She dealt for years with nerve disorders also possibly related to this trauma. Ruth later quipped, "Now a properly built pipe slide can be great fun, but I'm not going to tell you how to build one, for fear you might."

But at the time, Ruth lay unconscious in the hospital while Bill put the finishing touches on preparations for the Brazil crusade. Gigi contacted her father to inform him of Ruth's accident and some of her injuries, but tried to be reassuring. Bill vacillated: Should he return immediately to Ruth's hospital bedside, or remain in Brazil to complete the crusade? His indecision confirmed his family nickname, Puddleglum, wielded by Ruth and the children to tease him about his gloomy outlook. Puddleglum, a character from C. S. Lewis's novel *The Silver Chair*, lived and fretted away in the bogs. Bill had a tendency toward fretfulness, so Gigi tried to assure him that Ruth was receiving the best of care. Satisfied, he carried on with the crusade, then came to the hospital in Wisconsin afterward. Bill was with her for a couple of weeks before leaving for another far-flung crusade late that month in Hawaii.

As she recovered, Ruth suffered yet another blow. Virginia Bell had been hospitalized in North Carolina with another stroke. After Nelson Bell's death, Ruth and her siblings prioritized keeping Virginia "as happy as possible" over "keeping her well." Ruth explained that that meant letting "her do exactly what she wanted, whether it was good for her or not." Ruth observed, somewhat prophetically given the controversy that roiled her own final weeks, "I've seen too many old people whose lives were made miserable because of bossy children."

The widowed Virginia had lived alone in the Assembly Drive house since Nelson's death. Ruth tried bringing her up to live at Little Piney Cove, which had a downstairs guest suite designed for the eventuality that one or both Bells would live there. Yet that arrangement did not last. Ruth found that what Bill and she needed was what her mother did not need. "We need quiet and privacy," she said. "Mother needed people." Virginia had wanted to move back to her familiar and centrally located home, and with the addition of a housekeeper and live-in companion, she did just that. As it had been for thirty years, the Bell home remained a center of activity, a gathering place for Montreat-Anderson students, who would come with guitars and sing "till the house bulged with music," Ruth remembered. "Mother knew she was surrounded by love."

Upon the news of Virginia's stroke, Gigi flew with Ruth to North Carolina on a friend's private plane. The contrasts between their immediate trip to her side and Billy Graham staying to get the Brazil crusade done highlight much that was different about Ruth and her husband. He had professional obligations; she had personal ones. He worried and freely expressed those worries so that others could reassure him; she worried but kept things to herself. He knew that Gigi would watch over her mother; Ruth felt that no one could watch over Virginia but her. These contrasts suggest no right or wrong way to behave during a spouse or parent's health crisis. At almost the same time under similar circumstances, however, the contrasts do show Bill and Ruth making very different choices. For Billy Graham, work almost always came first; for Ruth, her family, especially her parents, almost always came first.

Arriving at the hospital, Ruth found Virginia terribly agitated, hooked up to all kinds of medical paraphernalia and enraged at having had her rings "forcibly" removed. She had resisted having her partial plate removed by attempting to bite the nurse. Fresh from her own hospitalization, Ruth bristled at what she saw as the nurses' officious treatment of her beloved mother. She could feel Virginia's frustration at not being able to make herself understood to a staff that seemed indifferent to her wishes. Ruth granted that Virginia, now without the ability to communicate verbally but "with her old spunk," could be difficult to manage. But Ruth's recollection of seeing her mother "helpless and furious" stuck with her.

Ruth did not want to see her vibrant, creative, strong mother reduced to this state. She saw the doctors "postpon[ing] death" but not usefully "prolong[ing] life." She talked with Virginia's physician, who had also cared for Nelson and knew the Bells well. Could we take Virginia home? Ruth asked. We might risk shortening her life, Ruth admitted, but we can more fully guarantee that her death would be a happy one.

"If all you children agree," the doctor replied, "you have my permission."

So they took Virginia back to Montreat. Ruth's sister Rosa, a nurse, rode along in the transport ambulance. Virginia initially feared that she was being moved to a long-term care facility, "a thing she dreaded." Rosa reported to Ruth that Virginia looked concerned "till they passed through the arched stone Montreat Gate. Then her face lit up." With Rosa assisting in her medical care, Virginia spent her final months at home on Assembly Drive, listening to favorite hymns. The family had pulled together their Christian record albums, marking the songs that seemed appropriate for someone facing death. The local Christian radio station made cassette tapes of the selections, so that Virginia could listen when she wanted to, which she did by the hour.

Virginia died in early November 1974. Ruth, all the while still recovering from her fall at Gigi's, attended the funeral on crutches. She memorialized her mother's passing in a poem titled "Not Easy, but Precious." The family had prayed that Virginia pass peacefully. "But days stretched year-like /

and when death came, God / it was not easy." Implicit in these lines was Ruth's question: Why did her mother have to linger and suffer? What role had God played in Virginia's declining health and difficult death? From her perspective, prayers for an "easy" death went unanswered. She concluded by reminding herself to trust God's plan.

> Forgive my complaints;
> for precious to You
> is the death of Your saints.

Friend and biographer Patricia Cornwell gave a sobering account of Ruth's losses in this period: her father's and then mother's deaths "blended into a single hazy event" punctuated by her accident and hospitalization, "and it seemed," Cornwell wrote, that Ruth "had endured one interminable suffering." As time passed, Ruth "missed her parents more, not less." Her grief and pain echoed all around her.

Ruth continued to feel her mother's absence deeply, but she also treasured many memories of the life they had shared, especially during Ruth's adulthood in Montreat. The following May, Ruth composed a poem on Mother's Day 1975, inspired by the white flowers traditionally honoring mothers who have passed on. Expecting to feel the acute loss of her mother all over again, Ruth expressed surprise that she instead experienced "a flood of memories / with which / my life / is full." She treasured these recollections: "Because of her / I'm rich."

In another poem, titled "Empty," written in the fall of 1976, Ruth's tone took on a more somber note as she described the Bells' old house on Assembly Drive. Although the physical appearance of the home had not changed, without Virginia it was "not the same"; "she / who made it home / is gone," and "an emptiness / within, / a silence," had replaced "her chuckle." The empty house betokened how bereft Ruth felt, as the last lines of the poem reveal: "From now on / it is me alone / who once was 'us.'" The desolate tone of the poem might lead a reader to believe that Ruth alone survived her parents. Her sisters, Rosa and Virginia (the adorable MaiMai of yore), and brother, Clayton, were alive and well. Rosa lived in Los Alamos, New

Mexico, with her husband, Don Montgomery, and their daughter Robyn. Don, an electrical engineer, worked at what is now the National Laboratory there. Rosa had a Bible study ministry, and Don was active in Gideons International. Virginia, a nurse, had already served for twenty years as a missionary in South Korea with her husband, John Sommerville, and would serve twenty more before retiring to Montreat to live in the Bells' former home. Clayton, a PCUS pastor, by 1976 lived with wife, Peggy, and their children in Dallas, where he pastored the Highland Park Presbyterian Church. Despite fierce divisions in the 1980s that Clayton worked to mediate, Highland Park eventually became one of the largest Presbyterian churches in the United States.

It had, however, been Ruth's daily experience that had revolved around Virginia and Nelson Bell and their Assembly Drive home for thirty years, and their absence that seemed to leave her particularly alone. Perhaps typical for families formed and tested in overseas service — especially in missionary service — the Bells, parents and children, had shared more common challenges and triumphs than the average white family in the United States. For twenty-five years, Nelson and Virginia, then Rosa, Ruth, MaiMai, and Clayton, had created in China an enclave of Christian devotion, family fun and togetherness, and hard work. Over the miles in countless letters they had poured out to each other news and jokes and troubles and prayers. When Bill dove into his calling and Ruth needed to feel like she belonged somewhere, she alone made her way back to Nelson and Virginia in Montreat to settle her family and build their home. Now without either of her parents, Ruth — a lover of solitude — felt a new aloneness.

—◇—

Meanwhile, the nation had moved through the final stages of the Watergate break-in scandal. Just a few days after the Lausanne conference had adjourned, the US House Judiciary Committee had voted articles of impeachment against President Richard Nixon. He left office on August 9, 1974, under threat of a Senate conviction. Nixon fled to his native California and isolated himself, humiliated and physically broken. After his pardon on September 8 by President Gerald Ford, Nixon continued to rebuff visitors.

He refused even a personal visit from Billy Graham, who had to settle for a mid-September telephone call with the disgraced ex-president. This period of Nixon's withdrawal and despondency intensified through a series of hospitalizations that he endured in September and October. He had suffered from a blood clot earlier in 1974; the clot returned with a vengeance once he settled back home in California.

In late October, Nixon underwent surgery in Long Beach. Some feared he would not survive the procedure. Before his release from the hospital in mid-November, Ruth, still on the mend from her own injuries and mourning Virginia's death, acted covertly — perhaps mindful of Stott's exhortation to avoid extravagance — to convey a grand, public message of compassion to the beleaguered man. With friends, she hired a plane to fly in sight of Nixon's hospital room window, pulling behind it a banner that read, "Nixon, God Loves You & So Do We." The extravagance of the effort reflected her own immediate awareness of what it meant to be alone, in physical agony, and afraid.

Nixon wrote of the exploit and the profound effect it had on him in his 1990 memoir, *In the Arena*. He had confessed despair to his wife, Pat. Physically, he felt spent; professionally, he saw nothing he could live for. In these depths, he was wheeled by a nurse from his windowless hospital room to an adjacent area where he could see the small airplane and its encouraging public declaration of love. The disgraced former president wrote that he "learned later that Ruth Graham and some of her friends had arranged it." He credited it and similar signs of support for helping him climb out of despondency. Without such expressions of love, Nixon wrote, "I would not have made it." In Ruth's judgment, Nixon's circumstances warranted more than a card or telephone call. Nixon's despair warranted a lavish, even zany, display of love.

The desolate Nixon called forth Ruth's compassionate instincts. Only a few months later, however, in another public display, Ruth's disciplinarian side took a turn onstage, almost literally. It was May 1975, in Charlotte. Ruth likely still felt the effects of her October 1974 accident. President Gerald Ford paid a visit to North Carolina's "Queen City" to help in celebrating the two-hundredth anniversary of the storied "Meck Dec," Mecklenburg

County's declaration of independence from Britain. (The celebration anticipated the nation's bicentennial celebrations to come in 1976; the Mecklenburg Declaration is said to be the American colonists' first move to sever
ties with the mother country.) Not only was Ford in attendance, but also the
governor, one state representative, and native son Billy Graham, all on the
dais. Ruth sat in the audience and observed from the front row. The setting,
a hot early-summer day in Charlotte's downtown Freedom Park, became
what one observer described as "the world's largest church picnic, or maybe
a giant patriotic rally."

The singularly American occasion, melding politics, commerce, and
Christianity, struck several notes that might sound familiar to twenty-
first-century observers. Billy's sermon rang one of them: "Our nation in
1975 is in deep trouble," he intoned. Sounding less like the elder religious
statesman that he became in the 1990s and early 2000s and more like a
patriotic firebrand, Billy declared, "I would die for my faith in God, and I
would die for that flag." Another curious moment came after the religious
portion of the program concluded. Billy received the honor of "Man of
the South" from a Georgia-based magazine titled *Dixie Business*. The pre-
senter, W. H. Barnhardt, a previous winner himself, noted that Graham
merited the award because "religion is the greatest business in the South."
Although the comment might sound like a discounting of "religion's" seriousness, in classic evangelical fashion, Barnhardt's collapse of distinctions between the Lord's work and the workaday world actually argued for
the heightened significance of religion. Just as Nelson Bell had cultivated
wealthy Texans in order to expand the hospital in Tsingkiangpu, so had
Billy and the BGEA built hundreds of successful crusades on a foundation
of business support.

The day took an unexpected turn during President Ford's remarks. His
presence had attracted a number of protestors who rejected this public celebration of business, religion, and politics. Stationed at some distance from
the main stage, demonstrators displayed signs reading "Eat the Rich" and
"Ford Is a Tory." What happened next might have arisen from some lingering discomfort from Ruth's zipline injuries combined with the broiling
heat and her readiness to police the bounds of respect for authority. In any

event, Ruth's calm soured when a sign-carrying protestor approached the stage. A news account reported that "Mrs. Billy Graham, on what she said was an instinctive impulse, pulled one of the 'Eat the Rich' signs from the hands of Don Pollock, 28, a woodcarver, as he stood near her." (The reverse of Pollock's sign read, "Don't Tread on Me." The *Observer* account quoted Ruth as describing the sign's message as "rather stupid.")

Pollock was about Anne Lotz's age, and Ruth clearly proceeded as if she were dealing with one of her own children. Refusing to return the sign, she placed it under her "white pump shoes" whence he could not gracefully retrieve it. Her move demonstrated that this occasion was not her first go-round with what she saw as an insubordinate young man. Unaware of Ruth's identity, Pollock knelt to ask for the sign back. "He looked rather helpless and harmless," Ruth reported. "I just patted him on the shoulder" — a gesture that would later become significant — "and shook my head." She treated him as she would have treated Franklin or Ned in the aftermath of one of their irresponsible exploits. "I am the mother of five children, and disrespect has never been tolerated," she later explained; "what he did [by displaying the sign and blocking others' view of the stage] was disrespectful." Police did not arrest Pollock but moved him away from the stage, encircling him and ordering him to stay back under threat of imprisonment.

Pollock had aroused not only Ruth's parental impatience but also her commitment to good order and love of country. Pollock, she noted, "had every right to his opinion, but when the President of the United States is speaking, it is definitely not the place to express his opinion." (One with a different view of authority might rather say that it is the ideal time.) Pollock had created a distraction, she complained, noting that audience members around her had turned to see his sign as he stood up in the row behind her. Pollock later issued a statement protesting his treatment and pointing out that he had committed no wrongdoing. The *Observer* story noted that even Ruth "wished the whole affair had not been reported."

As the Associated Press recounted in the succeeding days, however, Pollock ended up filing simple assault charges against Ruth. He accused her not only of taking his sign but also of "pushing him away" from her — exaggerating her motherly pat on his shoulder. The AP informed readers that police intended to notify "Mrs. Graham" by letter or phone call about the charge against her. The police certainly knew who this accused assailant was.

It took the entire summer of 1975 for the case to make it to Mecklenburg District Court. Ruth appeared, a United Press International story recounted, wearing a suit in shades of pink and green. (The story omitted mention of other participants' dress that day; interest in Ruth's wardrobe and appearance was evergreen.) In a bit of courtroom overkill, two attorneys represented Ruth, lawyers with the Charlotte firm that represented her husband, including one of the firm's principals. She had vowed to accept the thirty-day jail sentence if convicted. These men perhaps hoped to double-team their client into silence, in the event that she tried to make good on that vow.

This strange episode concluded when plaintiff Pollock backed away from his assault accusations. According to the news account, Pollock's counsel clarified that "the person who took his sign did not strike him even though the warrant stated that Mrs. Graham took his sign and pushed him." Judge William G. Robinson summarily dismissed the charge, agreeing with Ruth's defense team that the prosecution had "failed to show" evidence of assault. Ruth Graham and Don Pollock walked out of the courtroom side by side. "As they neared the door," the news account said, "Mrs. Graham pulled a brown Bible from her pocketbook and tried to hand it to him." Pollock "smiled but refused to take it." Ruth responded by saying, "I'll be praying for you."

The friendly offer of the Bible and Ruth's promise to pray for Pollock showed that she had moved beyond her previous judgments about his "stupid" sign and disrespectful behavior. In making this gesture, Ruth followed her familiar pattern. Ruth thought young people under the influence of popular culture generally appeared callow and loutish. But once Ruth made a personal connection with someone, she insisted on trying to love that person as best she knew how — even if her approach was rebuffed. Ruth's attempt to give Pollock a Bible, a typical evangelical strategy, showed her determination to connect with an individual who had needs she imagined she could meet. Pollock had brought a frivolous charge against her, dragging her into court and possibly hoping to embarrass one of the "Tories" he despised. She saw Pollock as the one who needed loving correction, much as one of her own children might. When she disciplined her children, she started with the Bible as guidebook and bridge-builder. She had grabbed Pollock's sign and prevented him from reclaiming it. At the time, she declared she would have acted the same way if a Graham child had been holding the protest sign — except, she added, "I'd have given him a resounding whack on the bottom." After her case was dismissed, she tried to build a bridge, just as she had with her own children, Bible in hand.

Chapter 7

Poetry and Politics

⟡

1976–1987

Ruth accompanied Bill to Texas at the end of April 1976; he was speaking at the Southern Baptist seminary in Fort Worth, and both were giving talks at her brother Clayton's church, Highland Park Presbyterian in Dallas. During this trip, a reporter conducting an interview for the Associated Press asked Ruth about the "women's liberation movement," eliciting perhaps Ruth's most pointed public comments on midcentury feminism. The resulting news item carried the jazzily terse headline, "Graham's Wife No Libber Fan." Unlike some better-known evangelical women such as Anita Bryant and the Catholic anti-ERA crusader Phyllis Schlafly, Ruth did not make a career of publicly criticizing the women's movement. But when asked, she voiced objections in line with previous public comments about marriage and women's most important roles of wife and mother.

Ruth sometimes theorized in her poetry, but it was theory based on observations, and rarely if ever about being a woman in a man's world. She thought of herself as a broken sinner in God's world. She simply did not think about "oppression" in gendered terms. She rather understood oppression as a matter of human subjection to sin. Sinfulness was a universal problem that individuals needed to address in their own lives, by confessing it to God and embracing God's salvation.

In the AP interview, therefore, Ruth relabeled the women's movement as "men's lib," decrying its effect of "freeing [men] from their responsibilities." Ruth warned, "I think we [women] are being taken for a ride." In the abstract, Ruth thought women needed men's protection and provision. Feminism, in her view, rejected men's safekeeping and put women at risk. Moreover, in line with antifeminist crusaders such as Schlafly, Ruth believed that traditional gender roles protected men, too, by keeping them accountable. Ruth feared that men who no longer felt an essential calling to shelter women — metaphorically and literally — would sacrifice a duty that humanized them. God made women and men with needs and abilities that answered to each other. Feminism took women "for a ride," but also ran roughshod over men by allowing them a dangerous freedom that they could not be trusted with.

In criticizing the midcentury women's liberation movement, Ruth drew deeply on the evidence of her missionary childhood. Nelson and Virginia had lived out their belief that only Christianity (as interpreted by southern whites) would bring true freedom to the Chinese people. Virginia's leadership in the women's clinic demonstrated to Ruth how Christian service and the gospel message could relieve missionized women's physical and spiritual miseries — the classic nineteenth- and early twentieth-century mission ideology of "woman's work for woman." Ruth also witnessed the fierce purpose and satisfaction that such work gave to her mother and many other women who worked in Tsingkiangpu. Hence Ruth's declaration to the AP reporter in Texas that a woman engaged in even menial Christian service was "the most truly liberated": "She can be liberated behind a sinkfull [sic] of dirty dishes or a load of dirty clothes. She is free to do what God has called her to do" (emphasis added). A woman's freedom, for Ruth, came through adjusting to her God-ordained duty to love husband, children, neighbors — while men experienced true freedom by adjusting to the "responsibility" of their own divinely ordained family leadership role.

Popular books such as Betty Friedan's The Feminine Mystique and Germaine Greer's The Female Eunuch had diagnosed, described, and proposed remedies for white middle-class women's experience of patriarchal oppression. Friedan argued that these women suffered a malaise — the "problem

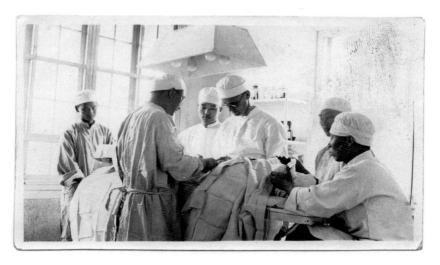

Dr. Nelson Bell operating

Virginia Bell and women nurses

Virginia Bell in Tsingkiangpu

Nelson Bell (front row, fourth from right, seated) with Tsingkiangpu staff

Tsingkiangpu Hospital

Portrait of Virginia Bell, c. 1917

Ruth and Billy in front of her childhood home in Huayin

Nelson and Virginia Bell with their children Rosa (standing, right), Ruth
(standing, left), Virginia "MaiMai" (seated), and Clayton

Ruth Bell and Harold Lindsell

Ruth's Tower yearbook senior class photo, 1944

Billy and Ruth with Raymond and Edith Edman

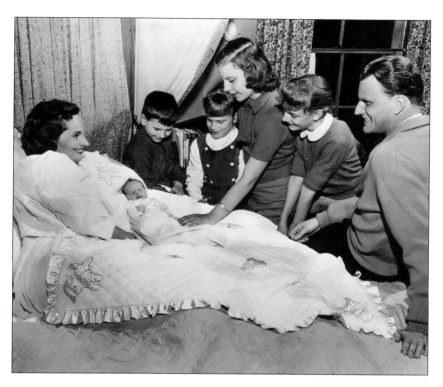

Billy says goodbye to Ruth and their five children Jan. 15, 1958, before departing on a crusade tour that will take him to eight Latin American countries. The children are (from left): Nelson, four days old, Franklin, 5, Ruth, 7, Virginia, 12, and Anne, 9.

Ruth in 1957, reading *Through Gates of Splendor* by missionary
Elisabeth Elliot in New York City during Billy's crusade at
Madison Square Gardens

Ruth and Billy and their children in the 1960s

Ruth speaking at a women's luncheon held during the US Congress
on Evangelism in Minneapolis

Billy and Ruth wave goodbye to media following a press conference at their home in Montreat in 1996

Ruth's grave

that has no name" — rooted in the sacrifice of energies to others' needs, goals, and cares. Husbands and children outranked a woman's own care for self. By contrast, Ruth told the AP reporter that her other-directed life had not produced in her any such "identity crisis" (the reporter's phrase). "I am known as Billy's wife," Ruth asserted. "But when I was growing up I was Dr. Nelson Bell's daughter, and then I was Gigi's mother, Anne's mother, Bunny's mother, Franklin and Ned's mother." She claimed to have always known who she was, at least *whose* she was "known as."

Ruth's demurral is worth pondering. On one hand, it legitimated Friedan's argument. Ruth described herself as Nelson's daughter, Billy's wife, and the children's mother, rather than as Ruth the poet, the philanthropist, the community servant, the lover of practical jokes. On the other hand, her other-directed self-description did not constitute a "problem" for her. If she had a problem that she could not name — but experienced as loneliness, indecision, anxiety — she framed it as a symptom of incomplete adjustment. It rose from the sacrifice she had chosen to make in order to follow both Jesus's teachings and, through them, Bill's lead. Feminist historian Joan Scott has pointed out that the characterization of "women as wounded subjects" typified much of second-wave feminism. Ruth did not experience herself as having been wounded by patriarchy, but by her own human sinfulness.

The way Ruth expressed her self-understanding also bears examination for its subtle demonstration of the distinctions she made between public persona and private circumstances. She acknowledged that being "known as Billy's wife" arose from the connection to her famous husband in his public role. To the public, she was married to Billy Graham the evangelist, not to Bill the husband only she knew. As a child and young woman, before Bill bounded into her life, Ruth Bell "was" Nelson's daughter. In Montreat, away from the glare of crusade publicity and the nosiness of tour bus passengers, she "was" the mother of five children. She *was*, therefore, more than what the public knew her as. Living the daily life of a daughter and a mother was, for her, more genuine and essential than her being "known as" the wife of a world-famous figure, even the evangelist she had fought so hard to support and guide. Friedan and her sisters (and maybe even later observers) may have preferred that Ruth see herself as an autonomous agent, rather than be so defined by connections to others. (Indeed, why did Ruth not at least identify herself here with Virginia instead of Nelson?) While she clearly did not object to defining herself in terms of a father or a husband, or in terms of a traditional female role, she did distinguish between her public and private identities in an agentive way. Significantly, the AP writer reported, "Being married to [Billy] Graham, [Ruth] said, has required a lot of *adjustment*" (emphasis added), using the very term that Ruth herself had embraced years before.

—◇—

In 1977, Ruth published her first collection of poems, titled *Sitting by My Laughing Fire . . .*, a title that reflected one of her favorite locations as well as her frequent resort to ellipses (I will refer to the book as *SLF*). The book's appearance signaled Ruth's new willingness to share a mostly hidden dimension of her private, isolated life. Like *Our Christmas Story*, the material for the book arose from Ruth's experiences — as a daughter in China and Korea, as a married woman, a mother, the daughter of aging parents. The poems voiced Ruth's desire to find the meaning in those experiences as well as in her encounters with the people and natural world around her. Her daughter Bunny said that Ruth wanted the book to be something "just like Amy Carmichael" would have published. Ruth's poems, like Carmichael's, reflected on day-to-day occurrences through the lens of Christian faith and sought encouragement, solace, wisdom.

The book's design also emphasized how much Ruth valued her carefully created domestic environment. *SLF* came in a large, square format and featured a cloth binding with a homespun look and feel. The typeface on the book's cover and interior dividers mimicked handwriting. All of these features contributed to the folksy handmade aura of the volume. Its inclusion of dozens of pictures featuring Little Piney Cove and its mountain setting added an intimate quality. Even if one did not read the poems, the artifact of the book itself appeared to be a memento straight from Ruth's own hand.

The book differed in other ways from her earlier book, *Our Christmas Story*, which was clearly intended as an evangelistic tool issued by the publishing arm of the BGEA. The author of the Christmas book, "Mrs. Billy

Graham," received the imprimatur of her famous husband, who contributed the foreword. *SLF*, on the other hand, showed its author, "Ruth Bell Graham," occupying a new space even as she wrote about the same household. In these pages, she emerged from the backdrop that constituted Billy Graham's "brand." Admittedly, Ruth put her poems forward somewhat reluctantly, confessing in the foreword she wrote herself that she was "obviously, not a true poet and these poems were never written for publication." She had written them originally for herself, in her own private confessional, healing, even playful space. Occasionally, as we have already seen, she wrote poems for specific occasions and people. Some of these found a place in *SLF*. Generally, though, Ruth explained, "I wrote because, at times, I had to. It was write, or develop an ulcer — or forget. I chose to write. At times I even wrote for sheer fun." Her rejection of forgetting as an option betokened both her desire to hold onto past moments — of joy, sadness, even irritation — and to honor and especially redeem her feelings in those moments. Ruth ever wanted to wring a lesson from what she saw and felt.

Having accomplished those private purposes over the years, Ruth turned them into an offering to others who might find them useful. She concluded *SLF*'s introductory "explanation" by writing of her hope that "each one who may read [the poems] will find in them that which 'speaks to their condition.'" The book's dedication read, "These are for YOU" (emphasis in original). Indeed, according to both her literary mentor Stephen Griffith and her daughter Gigi, editors wanted Ruth to include dates and other information alongside the poems and started the process of helping her compile notes. Ruth soon changed her mind, though, and ripped up the annotations, insisting that readers should be free to encounter each poem as if it had been written for them. She may have wanted to protect her own privacy as much as she wanted to free the reader from her intentions. If the publication signaled a new openness or budding confidence about sharing her work publicly, omitting annotations hedged against too much openness.

One poem, however, clearly drew from Ruth's worries about Franklin during his years in what she called "the far country," that untethered place of struggle where the prodigal son had wandered, in a parable Jesus told in Luke's Gospel. Waiting for Franklin's "return" gave Ruth special compassion for young people who rebelled against parents and church. Her heart especially went out to those parents who, like her, had dedicated themselves to following Proverbs 22:6: "Train up a child in the way he should go: and when he is old, he will not depart from it." Ruth felt a connection to these parents, who watched as children careered off "the way" and seemed destined never to make it back. Her experience of others' unkind, self-righteous judgment inspired a tart poem about "good parents" with "good children" who looked askance at others' "wandering one."

> The good folk never meant
> to act smug or condemn,
> but having prodigals
> just "wasn't done" with them.

Closing the poem with a bit of theological anthropology, Ruth took gentle but direct aim at the well-meaning self-righteousness of folk who judged parents of "wandering" children:

> Remind them gently, Lord,
> how You
> have trouble with Your children,
> too.

Unwittingly, Franklin had planted in Ruth the seed of compassion for parents of such children. The poem would reappear in Ruth's 1991 book, *Prodigals and Those Who Love Them*.

—◇—

One poem Ruth wrote after the publication of *SLF* showed her brooding on right and wrong, violence, justice, and forgiveness. Dated April 5, 1977, "The Murderer's Prayer" may have been inspired by a long-delayed murder confession Ruth learned about in the local newspaper. (This poem should not be confused with "Prayer for the Murderer," which appeared some years later in *Prodigals*.) She may have asked herself, Can God really forgive such a person? and constructed the poem as a way of feeling her way to an answer.

Edgar Smith, convicted of murder in 1957 and sentenced to death in New Jersey, had insisted on his innocence for twenty years. He won his freedom and national fame in 1971. He published books and won the support of notables such as William F. Buckley, appearing on his program *Firing Line* as a critic of the criminal justice system. But in the spring of 1977, on trial for another assault, he confessed to the 1957 murder. News accounts reported his comment: "I recognized that the devil I had been looking at in the mirror for 43 years was me." Ruth's poem opened with an invocation of God's truth and grace:

> Beyond all custom
> all tradition,
> Lord, I would see
> Your truth revealed;
> then could I come,
> in my condition,
> to see Your face,
> and by Your grace
> be healed.

"What I confess / You long have known," the poem continued. "'Just as I am' / to me confirms / that none but You / would take one on such terms." In the poet's view, God was able to forgive even this sinner because the price incurred had already been paid. Death and sin were "defeated" by Jesus. Even though Smith's acknowledgment of his crimes meant losing his freedom, he "glor[ied] in . . . loss / for You [God] have won!" The confessing sinner then asked God to give "special help" to those whom he had victimized.

When one considers Ruth's opinions about criminal justice and the death penalty, one is surprised at her willingness to spend time and energy thinking so empathetically about a killer. In a 1979 interview with *Charlotte Observer* writer Frye Gaillard, the topic of capital punishment — reinstated by a 1976 US Supreme Court ruling — arose out of Ruth's meandering thoughts during a relaxed and rainy afternoon at the Grahams' Montreat home. This gentle and admiring feature story appeared just below the masthead in the Sunday *Charlotte Observer*. It clearly aimed to counteract the excerpt of Marshall Frady's new, edgy biography of Billy included on the front of the paper's Perspective section. Billy's hometown paper would not have wanted to alienate the evangelist or his many friends and admirers in Charlotte.

To Gaillard, Billy regretted that capital punishment made the human "imperfection" of the American criminal justice system "final." He especially mourned the death penalty's disproportionate application to Black people. But Ruth countered, declaring, "I'm for capital punishment. I think it is a deterrent." She continued, "I know in countries where they have it, I feel safer walking down the streets." Her view reflected a Calvinist view of the law inherited from Nelson Bell. This view, historian Aaron Griffith has explained, characterized midcentury evangelical understandings of law and order. Obedience to the law would not save anyone for life in the hereafter; disobedience would condemn no one eternally. Properly enforced, however, the law could restrain wrongdoers and preserve social order in the here and now. Nelson Bell supported capital punishment and said so as columnist and executive editor of *Christianity Today*, which in 1960 had taken a position opposed to Billy Graham and argued for convicted kidnapper and rapist Caryl Chessman to be executed by the state of California.

As Griffith has shown, Ruth had other good company among evangelicals, Bill notwithstanding, in her support for executing convicted criminals. The National Association of Evangelicals had issued a statement in 1972 supportive of capital punishment's appropriateness as a penalty for any premeditated "crime that results in the loss of life." Use of the death penalty could preserve "the value of human life" for society. As Nelson had in his *Christianity Today* columns, Ruth lamented the moral lassitude of American culture and had a lively fear of crime, drugs, and sexual decadence, concerns rooted in her Calvinist anthropology and fed by her news consumption. She was therefore very much in tune with the trend Griffith traces among evangelicals that gained strength from the mid-1960s onward: "More law and order, not the spiritual redemption of criminals," as the "primary" response to lawbreaking.

Ruth's worries about crime and delinquency would appear vividly in the revisions she made for the 1984 reissue of Bill's best-selling book *Peace with*

God, first published in 1953. Punk rock — Ruth labeled it "blasphemous" — evidenced the devil's real activity in the contemporary world. The sexual revolution had brought with it more diseases such as herpes and AIDS, which Ruth felt were consequences of disordered behavior. The margin notes she made in her copy of *Peace with God* mentioned other trends that troubled her: divorce on the rise, increased illegal drug use, easy access to pornography (she included "kiddie porn" in her notes), and Satan worship, as well as "abortions, child abuse, soaring crime[, and] wife abuse."

Coincidentally, during the Grahams' interview with Gaillard, the phone rang. Bill answered, then passed the receiver to Ruth, explaining to the writer that the caller had been convicted in 1977 of a murder she committed while robbing a beauty salon in the nearby Asheville suburb of Biltmore Forest. Bill told Gaillard that Ruth had befriended this woman, named Carol Snow. "Ruth visits a number of people in prison," he continued. "Mental hospitals, too. She does a lot of that sort of thing without seeking any publicity for it." For her part, Ruth explained doing "that sort of thing" as "just what you do."

Ruth's support of capital punishment, expressed so clearly if abstractly during the interview with Frye Gaillard, met a concrete challenge in the person of Velma Barfield, condemned in December 1978 to North Carolina's death row. Margie Velma Bullard was born in South Carolina and grew up near Fayetteville, North Carolina, with an abusive father. As a teenager, Velma married Thomas Burke, had two children, then underwent a hysterectomy that led to a pain medication addiction and a spiral of destruction — failed marriages, broken family relationships, and theft. Thomas Burke died in a suspicious house fire in 1969. Velma married Jennings Barfield in 1970, but he died soon after. Velma's mother also died a couple of years after that.

A bereft and deeply troubled Velma found encouragement in a story she read about Ruth and Billy Graham in the *Raleigh (NC) News & Observer*. She especially admired Ruth's kindness and motherly wisdom. As Jerry Bledsoe recounted in his book about Barfield, she wrote to Ruth about "how she wished her own family could have been" like the Grahams. Ruth wrote back, and a regular correspondence began.

But on May 13, 1978, police arrested Barfield for the death of her boyfriend, Stuart Taylor. Not only was she suspected of having poisoned him with arsenic, but officials' suspicions also led them to accuse her of killing Jennings Barfield. Eventually, Velma Barfield confessed to killing her mother and two elderly people she had taken care of; she was responsible for at least one additional death, for a total of as many as seven victims. In December 1978, a jury convicted Barfield of Stuart Taylor's murder and sentenced her to death.

The sensational case eventually drew international attention. Barfield was the first woman in the United States sentenced to die after the Supreme Court's reinstatement of the death penalty, and the first white woman in North Carolina to be so sentenced in the twentieth century. Barfield's sentence signaled to everyone that the state meant business when it came to capital punishment. This reality alerted and alarmed many death penalty opponents in the state and beyond.

After lawyers initiated her appeal and Barfield began to surface from her drug addiction, deep remorse took hold of her. She experienced a conversion to Christianity. From that point until her execution in November 1984, Barfield earned a reputation as a model prisoner, a dedicated Christian servant, a friend and encourager to both guards and prisoners. In letters, Ruth thanked Velma for her friendship; she also encouraged her to continue sharing her faith with other women prisoners. The BGEA sent books and other materials to Barfield.

The condemned woman corresponded with many who learned of her crimes and her conversion through a lengthy front-page story in the New York City weekly newspaper the *Village Voice* in July 1984, months before her scheduled execution. An odd amalgam of supporters worked to gain commutation for Barfield, including the *Village Voice* reporter, a member of the Wake County (NC) ACLU, and Anne Graham Lotz's brother-in-law, who conducted a prison ministry. Ruth had asked Anne to visit Velma, and she had done so regularly. When Barfield's supporters met with North Carolina governor Jim Hunt in September 1984, their appeal included a letter from Ruth asking for a commutation of Barfield's death sentence. Describing this episode, Bledsoe noted Ruth's continued support of capital punishment even as she called for mercy in this case.

Governor Hunt refused these petitions, at least in part because he faced pressure as a Democrat running for the US Senate against a militantly law-and-order incumbent, Republican Jesse Helms. Ruth later wrote about a visit Anne made to the condemned woman as her execution approached. The "little cubicle" Anne and Velma occupied during their visit, Ruth wrote, "was touched with glory, for there were not two but three there." Anne and Velma, Ruth reported, were visited by "the reality of Jesus' presence." As important as that experience was, however, Ruth recounted the less comforting realization that hit her daughter as she turned to wave good-bye: "there were prisoners," Anne suddenly understood, "sitting in their little cubicles behind their glass partitions whom no one had bothered to visit." They were, Ruth concluded, "ignored."

Ruth's main concern in this retelling was not Velma's fate. In Ruth's view, as a professed Christian, Velma would enter heaven to dwell eternally with God. But other prisoners, "ignored" by family and friends, might be fearful of death, skeptical of Jesus's message, and at risk, she thought, of eternal damnation. In reflecting on their isolation, Ruth drew on a prayer-poem by Tennessee poet Jane Merchant (1919–1972). Ruth offered it up on behalf of Anne, Velma, and the unvisited prisoners. In keeping with her growing mindfulness of those who awaited the return of "prodigals," she even offered the poem to those who did not visit their incarcerated family members:

> God bless and fortify them,
> God hear when they entreat,
> The strong courageous people
> Too brave to own defeat.
>
> And oh, God, bless and help them,
> God answer when they call,
> The tired defeated people
> Who are not brave at all.

Ruth remained vigilant on behalf of the forsaken and those who loved them.

Anne coordinated a phone call between her mother and Barfield about a month before the execution date. It was their only actual conversation in all the years they had known one another. Bledsoe wrote that the two women "chatted like sisters." On the day of the execution, Anne walked with Barfield to the death chamber and served as one of the sixteen official witnesses.

Ruth did not attend Velma Barfield's funeral service in Fayetteville, which the executed woman had carefully planned to include her favorite hymns and Bible passages. She had, however, written a poem for Barfield. She had meant for it to reach the convicted woman before she was put to death. It arrived too late, and so one of the worship leaders (Presbyterian elder Sam Roane) read it as the closing word of the service. In the poem, titled "Welcome Home, Velma," Ruth relayed a comforting message that recognized the reality of suffering and the hope of salvation. Her intensifying focus on parents awaiting "the homing of their child" governed the poem's imagery. In the first stanza, that child returned "from far lands desolate / from living wild" to "home assured." The poem's second stanza shows God as the "eager" parent waiting at home:

> So the Heavenly Father waits
> the homing of His child;
> thrown wide those Heavenly Gates
> in welcome glorious wild!
> His, His the joy by right
> — once crucified, reviled —
> So —
> Precious in God's sight
> is the death of His child.

As was her way, Ruth used the materials of human experience to explore holy truths. Meditating here on Psalm 116:15, reproduced in the poem's last two lines, Ruth asked herself, How can this statement be true? and then wrote herself toward an answer. Ruth drew on her own human experience as an "eager" mother who had so often waited for her own children to sort out their "wounded and wounding" ways. The waiting God welcomed the "homing . . . child" with joy rather than rejection or vengeance. In Ruth's view, God — "once crucified, reviled" — understood the very deepest wounds that human beings could inflict and suffer. Yet God's enduring of such pain, she believed, was part of God's plan to set love once more over every other force — sin, hatred, death. Ruth thought that Velma had, in her conversion to Christianity, come to see that very truth. She had lived it out in prison by loving her fellow inmates and even those who supervised her incarceration.

Ruth had wanted Velma to write a book about her transformation and connected her with editor Victor Oliver and minister and author Cecil Murphey for a possible collaboration. Murphey elicited the whole story from Barfield — even additional confessions to murder, although editors deleted them from the final manuscript. Ruth wrote the book's foreword; daughter Anne contributed the afterword. Ever brief, Ruth wrote a scant half page, and much of it directly quoting Barfield's own writing. Mother and daughter presented the story as one of a sinner redeemed. *Woman on Death Row* was published in 1985 by Thomas Nelson. The BGEA's World Wide Publications also distributed its own free edition.

—◇—

In the spring of 1980, Ruth; her sisters, Rosa and Virginia; and their pastor-brother, Clayton, traveled to China for a two-week, nine-city tour. Hosted by the Chinese government, the Bell siblings met local and national leaders, including Madame Sun Yat-sen, the ailing widow of one of the founders of the People's Republic of China and a prominent Chinese political figure in her own right. The public face of the trip was to be one of reminiscence; Clayton perhaps aimed to assuage Chinese authorities' worries about these Americans' ulterior motives by labeling their visit a "sentimental journey." Yet the siblings' tour of their birthplace did help to prepare the way for a second visit that Ruth made in 1988 with Bill (discussed in the next chapter). Ruth made contact with leaders of house churches and the government-approved "Three-Self Movement," based on the idea that churches in China would be established, governed, and financed by Chinese Christians themselves rather than through foreign intervention. Ruth saw for herself the complicated nature of Chinese religious freedom. The Chinese Christian church was a going concern, but also subject to strict government control. Government authorities described to Ruth a plan to make a limited supply of Bibles available to Chinese folk, but only if recipients agreed to furnish detailed personal information.

The Bell siblings' trip included a visit to their childhood home and the mission compound in Tsingkiangpu, where local residents posted welcome signs. Their former home had been "graciously emptied" by its current inhabitants for their inspection, Ruth recalled. She solemnly likened the once warm and bustling home to "an old woman, no longer loved or cared for." The hospital buildings, *Christianity Today* reported, "were intact, though currently used for quite different purposes" as an industrial school. Ruth spoke to the students there, where so many years before Lucy Fletcher had toiled in earnest to teach the Bell girls and the other missionary children. All the Bells spent time talking with a few Chinese friends from decades past. Even though, like Nelson and Virginia, the older generation of Christian converts had passed away, one woman told the Bells that the younger generation was "carrying on" with their Christian devotion.

After their "pilgrimage" home, Ruth took Rosa, who had never toured Europe, on a return trip through Athens, Paris, and London, while Clayton and Virginia headed back to the States via Hong Kong. Back on American soil, Clayton lamented that the Chinese government was not "open to missionaries . . . particularly [from] the West." But he nevertheless found encouragement in the growth of Christianity among regular Chinese citizens. Ruth, too, seemed hopeful about the future of Christianity in China. Her prayers, she said, would be directed at helping people in China recognize "that Christianity is not a Western religion" and that "the Bible is . . . as old as their written language."

Ruth described the experience of visiting this lost childhood world as "a death and a resurrection." Her own "sentimental feelings" for her girlhood home, "nurtured lovingly over the decades, died." She realized that it was not the buildings — hospital and home now both serving other purposes and people — that really mattered to her. She had cared instead about the "transformed lives" that had met a turning point in those places, the "seed," as a Chinese woman described it, that was "still bearing fruit." The journey helped Ruth identify a certain detachment from the place and her life there. The visit was a watershed moment, an arrival point that gave Ruth a greater acceptance of her own life. Perhaps because Nelson and Virginia were gone, Ruth could more fully embrace her own life in Montreat with Bill and feel less mournful about her Chinese past.

The experience struck one of her sisters — unidentified by Ruth, but likely Rosa — very differently. As a girl, Rosa had typically adjusted to new settings eagerly and easily. Nelson and Virginia's letters described Rosa's un-flagging aplomb as she went from China to Korea to the American Midwest. Ruth had always admired Rosa's self-assurance. In their youth the peren-nially homesick Ruth had depended on her older sister to bolster her. But something about being back in Tsingkiangpu provoked disparate reactions from the two sisters, as Ruth described in a characteristically allusive poem. One sister, "The fledgling / eager to be free," independent, self-confident, returned home "in later years" to find "she came / in tears."

In her typical fashion, Ruth used the poem's second stanza to highlight a contrast. Here, the sister who never wanted to leave returns home:

> The other one,
> nudged from the nest
> (reluctantly,
> to make her fly),
> coming back
> in later years,
> found she could
> not cry.

Rosa had been the pacesetter for Ruth in those early China years. Ruth connected Rosa's apparently tearful response in returning to Tsingkiangpu to her elder sister's youthful "eager[ness] to be free," Rosa's determination and daring. Being back in the land of her childhood made the oldest Bell child feel nostalgic for home, for parents and family and those years of fun and purpose.

The second stanza contrasted Ruth with her generally more confident, self-assured sister. Ruth captured all of those delayed departures that she had prayed for and sometimes received, all of the childhood fretfulness about being away from her parents, all of the homesickness while at school in Pyeng Yang. So why could she, on visiting Tsingkiangpu in her middle age, "not cry"? Was this not where she had longed to be, to stay, all those years of her young life? As on Mother's Day 1975, the poet seemed surprised by her own lack of tears. If one considers that Ruth had re-created in Montreat the experience of growing up in Tsiangkiangpu alongside the Love and Mercy Hospital, her absence of emotion makes some sense. In her beloved childhood home, Ruth had been surrounded by people united by Christian purpose. They prayed, worked, and played together. They faced the adversities of isolation and exhausting work together. Ruth had also been surrounded by adults who carried with them a sense of heroic purpose — blind to what we might now see as the imperialist energies riding alongside the missionary project. Ruth remembered her childhood as an idyll, even amidst the dangers and diseases and discomforts. In establishing her and Bill's home in Montreat, Ruth had laid claim to a place where she could offer their children a similar experience of relative isolation, security, and lofty purpose. Behind the stone gate of Montreat, a community of Presbyterians — clergy, missionaries, and active laypeople — lived and worked, hosted denominational conferences, preserved Southern Presbyterian history, and guided the small college through its ups and downs. It was, like Tsingkiangpu, a place set apart for Christian work, but unlike the mission hospital, whose work manifested in surgeries completed, maladies relieved, and "heathen" evangelized, inhabitants of Montreat enjoyed the "work" of extended Sabbath among kindred Southern Presbyterian souls.

Ruth wanted her children to feel part of a consecrated Christian community. Moreover, being in Montreat was what Ruth needed. She wanted be near her parents, from whom she had never wanted to be separated. She had built an isolated home in a craggy cove so that her family would be protected by and immersed in a natural setting. When she felt little sadness on returning to Tsingkiangpu in 1988, it was not because she had not loved the place. The nostalgia passed Ruth by because she had, in a sense, never left Tsingkiangpu. She still lived there.

—◇—

In the early 1980s, Ruth had more time for her study and writing. She had an old rolltop desk in her bedroom downstairs for her Bible studies. There, she used several different "good" Bible translations plus a Bible dictionary and concordance and some devotional works. She wrote in *It's My Turn* that when she began working on the book, she fixed herself a permanent office "upstairs." "Upstairs" was Little Piney Cove's attic; a photograph on the back cover of Ruth's later book *Legacy of a Pack Rat*, published in 1989 (see chapter 8), revealed a space crowded with boxes, books, furniture, knick-knacks, and toys, but with just enough room for Ruth to perch on a piano stool in front of a table. She wrote out poems and recollections longhand, preferring Rapidograph pens for their sharp point and quick-drying ink. Even though she wrote with her left hand, the ink would not smear.

Published in 1982, *It's My Turn* was written, like *Sitting by My Laughing Fire...*, "For YOU" and included autobiographical sketches. They spanned from Ruth's youth in China and Korea through her time at Wheaton, her marriage, experiences with each child, up to the 1980 siblings' trip to China. As if apologizing for prevailing on her readers' attention, Ruth ended the book by explaining how her daughters "urged" her to write a book about her "different sort of life." They thought she could create a book that would encourage young mothers. The Graham daughters had to do some convincing. They assured Ruth that her writing did not have to be autobiographical — "I should hope not!" the self-effacing Ruth declared, ever watchful over her privacy. Yet the book turned out to be substantially autobiographical. Although the short chapters lack a clear narrative connection, *It's My Turn* remains the closest thing to a memoir that Ruth Bell Graham ever wrote.

Getting the manuscript finished proved to be a trial for her. "How I got myself into this I'll never quite know," she wrote in the book's afterword, "but once in, there was no way out." She drafted the book while sick with the flu. When she received a corrected copy back from her editor at Revell, she joked that it had read to him "just as if it had been written" while she had the flu. After yet another round of illness and bad rewrites, she under-went hip-replacement surgery in 1981 that further delayed her progress. Bill eventually intervened and told Ruth she needed to hand the project over to someone who could compile her jottings into the book that Revell had contracted for. Bill Mead, Dallas businessman and BGEA and World Evangelism and Christian Education Fund (WECEF) board member, along with his wife, Vivian, offered Ruth their island condominium for a two-day book-writing marathon. Ruth, with Victor Oliver — her editor, "inspiration and 'cattle prod'" — dove in for the "final assault," along with Ruth's sec-retary Evelyn Freeland, Bill's longtime secretary Stephanie Wills, and the Meads' housekeeper. Ruth's Bill, meanwhile, took up his beloved post on the sunny beach. The team managed to hammer the manuscript out. Her temperament and attention span were better suited to the solitary produc-tion of pithy poems than to the extended process of constructing a narrative and revising prose.

The title of the book suggests an awareness by Ruth and the BGEA of the tenor of the early 1980s. Never mind Ruth's earlier disavowal of the "libber" movement. A portion of Billy's public, and perhaps even a portion of the general public, was interested in what Ruth Graham had to say. Second-wave feminists had been reshaping understandings of gender and sex roles for years. Ruth's views about women and men reflected her traditional ori-entation, yet by taking "her turn," she evidenced some sympathy with what feminist books had to say about women's value, potential, and equality with men before God. A brief *Library Journal* review featured *It's My Turn* among other "inspirational reading" that included books by Mother Teresa and Pope John Paul II. The reviewer recommended the book for showing a "warm, delightful woman adept at transcending through prayer and laughter." More-over, the stories therein revealed that the "Billy Graham of these pages is no saint, but he is Ruth's man all the way, and she obviously adores him."

—◇—

As Ruth's book hit the shelves, Billy Graham received a long-sought invita-tion to the Soviet Union and a May 1982 conference to be held in Moscow under an earnest but ungainly name: the World Conference of Religious

Workers for Saving the Sacred Gift of Life from Nuclear Catastrophe. Billy had traveled to the USSR previously, in 1959, but had not preached publicly. He saw this invitation as an opportunity to do so. It was the height of the Cold War, and distrust between the United States and the USSR ran high. Since the early 1960s, the world had lived under the shadow of "mutually assured destruction." This deterrence strategy aimed to restrain US and Soviet use of their prodigious stockpiles of intercontinental thermonuclear weapons, but its one-up logic actually fueled the proliferation of those arsenals.

According to President Jimmy Carter's secretary of defense Harold Brown, Carter had been determined to protect Europe from Soviet threat. He had pressed Billy Graham to give public support to his Strategic Arms Limitation Treaty (SALT); according to David Aikman, a "high-ranking Defense Department official" gave Bill and Ruth a hair-raising briefing about the probable results of a nuclear exchange with the USSR. Aikman reported that the Grahams were "appalled" at what they heard. Given their respective temperaments and experiences (and despite Aikman's tendency to lump Ruth and Bill together), this briefing may have affected Ruth and Bill differently. Billy Graham felt more inclined to support disarmament, yet he avoided making public statements on the issue until the spring of 1979. As in the past, Ruth certainly would not have wanted Bill to insert himself into the midst of a politically charged debate by standing openly for arms control or any other position that she saw as political rather than evangelistic. He had to keep his focus on winning souls. But Bill worried about Soviet machinations and about President Carter's ability to withstand them. He also worried about the threat nuclear weapons posed to the survival of the human race. Ruth's heightened mistrust of Soviet power may have led her to support the United States in maintaining its preemptive nuclear capabilities. Consonant with the views she expressed during the Frye Gaillard interview supporting the death penalty as a crime deterrent, Ruth might have seen American nuclear weaponry as an effective check against Soviet evil.

Historians offer various explanations for Billy Graham's shift to support of nuclear disarmament, including his and Ruth's travel in October 1978 to Poland, a nation within striking distance of such weapons. They had toured the site of Auschwitz and been confronted by the senseless reality of state-imposed mass murder. Billy Graham held crusade meetings and met with clergy. Ruth spoke with local women about teaching their children the Christian faith. A Russian woman in the audience came to Ruth with a message from her Christian friends back home: "Will you pray for us?" Mindful of the Soviet regime's long hostility toward Christians and their churches, Ruth replied, "We have not ceased praying for Russian believers."

Carter's successor, Ronald Reagan, opposed SALT. Moreover, Reagan had what Nancy Gibbs and Michael Duffy describe as an "intense interest," bordering on an "obsession," with encouraging religious freedom in the USSR. The president saw encouraging freedom of religion as one way of increasing democratic impulses and checking authoritarianism. Perhaps Reagan's countervailing interests eventually allowed him to support Billy's attendance at the Moscow conference. A growing number of American religious groups, such as the National Association of Evangelicals and the Southern Baptist Convention, appealed to governmental leaders to disarm and suspend further nuclear weapons testing and research. This groundswell and the terrifying threat of nuclear Armageddon reinforced Billy Graham's stance toward arms control. So he considered the Soviet invitation a welcome opportunity to advance the global conversation about a nonnuclear peace. The American ambassador advised against it, and Vice President George H. W. Bush shared others' (if not his own) objections with Billy by telephone. President Reagan gave the evangelist his explicit blessing — albeit privately — and promised to pray for him "every mile of the way." Billy did go on the voyage, after careful and sometimes exasperating negotiations, the results of which mostly evaporated once he arrived in Moscow.

Ruth insisted, as usual, that Bill stick to his evangelistic calling despite temptations or distractions, even one as world-historical as preventing nuclear annihilation. She tried to persuade her husband to decline the conference invitation. In addition to her fears about a Soviet first strike, Ruth's opposition to the trip may have been spurred in part by her reading of Aleksandr Solzhenitsyn's work. Solzhenitsyn, whom she called in 1975 "a writer without fear," had served with distinction in the Red Army during World War II, but when he began to criticize the Soviet hierarchy, he was sentenced to serve eight years in a so-called Corrective Labor Camp. After his release, he lived in enforced exile in the Soviet-controlled Kazakh Republic. Solzhenitsyn became a hero to Christians in the United States during the 1970s for his endurance under Soviet persecution, which was fed in part by his return while imprisoned to the Orthodox faith of his youth.

Ruth read *From under the Rubble*, a collection of essays by Solzhenitsyn and other Soviet dissidents. It was published in 1974 while the contributors were still living in the Soviet Union under various degrees of state scrutiny. Ruth would have found this collection of essays compelling both because of the subject matter — authors protested both antireligious autocracy and secular liberalism — and because the authors risked everything by criticizing the Soviet system. They suffered for conscience's sake, some by imprisonment, others by being denied employment or the freedom to leave the country. Yet they maintained their principles in spite of these hardships, enduring political martyrdom for the sake of truth. Such suffering gave Solzhenitsyn and his colleagues great credibility in Ruth's eyes.

The contrarian Solzhenitsyn may have particularly appealed to Ruth because he did not simply denounce the Russians and trumpet American superiority. He critiqued both the atheistic totalitarianism of the Soviet Union and secular liberal tendencies in the United States; these views jibed with Ruth's own understanding of what was wrong with both nations. She understood Solzhenitsyn as an exponent of what she felt were traditional Christian mores. The world's deepest problem, he declared, was not limited to the Soviet bloc. He claimed (and Ruth would have agreed) that the Western world's spiritual surrender to the desires and demands of power, money, pleasure, and purposeless ease had helped Soviet power flourish. One could witness the effects of this surrender most alarmingly, he wrote, in the destruction of the natural world by pollution. He also saw grave threats to human existence by imminent nuclear annihilation. But mere political interventions would not lead humanity away from destruction. What was needed, in Solzhenitsyn's view, was "repentance." Nations and individuals needed to humble themselves. The Soviet and US hierarchies needed to admit their wrongs against their own people and against peoples around the world.

Another component of Solzhenitsyn's prescription was "self-limitation." In describing his meaning here, Solzhenitsyn drew on Eastern Orthodox faith that he had come to during his imprisonment. Self-limitation constituted "true Christian" freedom. "Freedom," he asserted, "is *self-restriction*! Restriction of the self for the sake of others!" Surprisingly, given her 1974 rejection of John Stott's inclusion of "simple living" in the Lausanne Covenant, Ruth found this message of sacrifice both affirming and admirable. As a wife and mother, she had restricted herself "for the sake of others!," putting her mission vocation aside to be Bill's wife and the mother of their children, and pouring her energies into creating a safe, loving, invigorating home for them and a peaceful retreat for Bill.

She would also have recognized elements of Billy's political vision in Solzhenitsyn's call. As described by historian Curtis Evans, Billy Graham's political program depended on individual transformation to bring about a renewed communal moral and ethical code. Ruth believed that the health of American culture and community would grow from individuals first embracing biblical truths and promises. She therefore found in Solzhenitsyn someone who had been tested terribly by an authoritarian regime who nevertheless believed with fervor in the centrality of individual spiritual transformation to social and political change. One might discern in her interpretation of Solzhenitsyn some version of Southern Presbyterianism's belief in the "spirituality of the church." Like her father, Ruth did not want the church making or even discussing policy about nonchurch matters. Worldly questions about nuclear weapons or poverty lay outside of the church's exclusive bailiwick, an individual sinner's relationship to the saving God. Regenerate sinners could be good neighbors, but the church could only encourage them in that direction, and that, most modestly.

Reading Solzhenitsyn's work fleshed out Ruth's view of the USSR as the United States' nemesis on the world stage and Christianity's opponent on the cosmic stage. It was a regime that she deplored for its suppression of the Christian church and individual Christians, and its brutal repression of any slight opposition. At the end of the day, Ruth worried that in agreeing to attend the Soviet-sponsored conference, Bill would be drawn into a political context beyond his ken — one that might compromise his evangelistic work.

—◇—

While Ruth's objections to Bill's Soviet trip went unheeded, her influence on another project that took shape in the early 1980s visibly endures. The buildings and grounds of what became the Billy Graham Training Center at the Cove, near Asheville, bear Ruth's aesthetic stamp. As noted, some mild controversy dogged the very beginnings of the Cove, built on land purchased in the early 1970s through a secret BGEA-related fund. But in the early 1980s, Billy began assembling a team to design, build, and program a Bible-based training retreat for lay Christians that would inhabit the mountain site.

Ruth and Bill both knew that his evangelistic work prevented him from taking the daily operational helm of such a place. So in 1983, Billy recruited Christian businessman Jerry Miller, a retired Texaco marketing executive, to take the lead in planning and implementation. With his wife, Dee, he moved from Houston to Asheville to begin this work. Jerry and Billy visited conference centers of various parachurch organizations around the country to gather ideas — although, characteristically, Billy also wanted to avoid direct competition with these other organizations. From Jerry's account, Billy was actually too busy, still at the height of his activity and influence, to do much more than glance at an architectural model constructed for potential funders and respond with a quick okay. Ruth had more time to be involved in aspects of the project's design and construction.

Some maintain that the Cove was Ruth's idea. In comments she made at the Cove's dedication ceremony, on a rainy May day in 1993, Ruth described her vision for the place as one of "retreat, rest, relaxation and renewal." (Billy had used another four words to capture his hopes: "impact, intercession, instruction, and inspiration.") Ruth's words and the story of her involvement now appear across the Cove's marketing materials, but this version of the Cove's origins has come almost completely after the fact as a way of burnishing the center's personal connections to Billy and especially Ruth.

Nevertheless, one can see Ruth's role at the Cove as an extension of the construction project she oversaw thirty years earlier, when she collected materials and cajoled architects and contractors to erect Little Piney Cove. That house had been her family's respite from prying eyes on Assembly Drive and her husband's restorative retreat from the hurly-burly of protracted travel and preaching. In the Cove, Ruth saw an opportunity to offer that kind of restoration to people who were not professional evangelists. Gigi described her mother's idea as "Bible college for a week," along the lines of a Christian conference center but providing Bible studies "with a little more depth" — a classic evangelical combination of devotional and scholarly study of the Bible. In that sense, Ruth envisioned something very much like her own Wheaton College experience, filtered through her decades of personal daily Bible study. Her mountaintop home had provided her time and space to read and pray and take in God's creation; she wanted others to have the same opportunities. Her work in developing the Cove focused on creating restful places. No television or daily newspapers intrude on the Cove's atmosphere, dedicated to study and edifying, prayerful conversation.

Ruth brought her salvaging skills and homespun design sensibilities to bear at the Cove, just as she had over in Little Piney Cove. Salvaged and handcrafted materials give the Cove's buildings texture. The Millers reclaimed the chapel's pulpit from an old school for the blind in England. Ruth wanted chairs to match the chapel's pulpit, so she sat on the chapel's floor, sketched what she wanted, then had a local furniture builder work from her drawings. Dee Miller observed that Ruth "loves things that aren't quite perfect"; the chapel's pews were also secondhand, purchased based only on photographs. When they arrived at the Cove, they were not exactly the required dimensions, but Ruth was pleased nevertheless. They added heft and character to the soaring new chapel, which was given by the Florida-based private religious nonprofit organization the Chatlos Foundation.

With the pragmatic Jerry considering both the bottom line and the laws of physics, Ruth also helped create the chapel's towering steeple. She admired steeples with "character" — that is, ones that leaned. Jerry was able to dissuade her from an off-kilter spire, but Ruth held firm to a boundary-pushing height requirement. She dismissed the architect's original specification as not tall enough. In order to find the compromise between Ruth's expectations and the feasibility of engineering and erecting such a structure, they used a crane and suspended a headache ball at the level of the future steeple's point. Ruth gave instructions from the ground about the steeple height she envisioned as the crane operator raised the ball higher and higher. Eventually, Ruth, Jerry, and the architect settled on a style, and a height, everyone could live with.

In matters of steeples and more, Jerry Miller admitted to playing the "bad guy," the intermediary between Ruth and the architect — presumably not only delivering to her news of her ideas' infeasibility, but also delivering to the architect Ruth's quibbles (or worse) with his design. In determining the height of the steeple, Ruth cast aside technical concerns and notions of proper architectural proportion, opting for a narrower, longer shape for the steeple in order to make sure it could be seen. Ruth wanted everything at the chapel to point up — the arched windows, the sharply peaked arches of the building, and of course the steeple. Just as her poems sent readers' attention into woods, into snowy landscapes, and out over the ocean, here in an architectural form, Ruth sent the eyes of the chapel's visitors up to the heavens.

Other touches, less monumental, also abide to this day at the Cove. The antique copper ware that decorates the main lobby's hearth came from Ruth's own home — a teapot and stand, a copper bin filled with wood, other cooking implements. She chose warm, earthy tones for furnishings in public areas and guest rooms and wanted seating arranged for easy conversation. She would not — and could not — invite everyone in the world to her own living room for a Bible lesson and a cup of coffee. But she could help create this place where Christians in need of encouragement and instruction could gather, learn, and be refreshed.

The Cove's plans called for the construction of four guest cabins, separate from the property's main guest building. Ruth wanted to decorate all of them herself — presumably with handpicked and probably salvaged materials from her antiquing expeditions. Jerry and his team resisted this idea as being too time-consuming for everyone and too demanding for Ruth. After all, Jerry had his position because Bill and Ruth both knew they had other work to do. In the end, Ruth personally oversaw the construction and décor of the first cabin only. The other three cabins, and a fifth cabin added later, also reflect Ruth's interior design choices. "Her" cabin is simple and homespun, but comfortable. On the exterior, Ruth wanted steep lines for the metal roof, natural stone and exposed wood, and windows looking out at mountain views. In her customary joshing way, Ruth had a teasing welcome mat framed next to the cabin's front door. It read, "OH, NO. NOT YOU AGAIN!" Handmade baskets hung from the small kitchen's exposed beams over floors of wide planks. The effect is cozy and personal.

The cabin also bears the mark of a comic misunderstanding between Ruth the visionary and the down-to-earth crew that constructed it. As at Little Piney Cove, Ruth insisted on a rugged, antique-looking fireplace and chimney for this guest cabin. Ruth wanted a picturesque chimney that was "half stone, half brick," with the external stone veneer of the chimney broken away to reveal the brick substrate, as if last century's settlers had built it rather than modern-day craftsmen. The masons failed to understand Ruth's instruction, but eager to please her, kept building. The chimney is indeed half stone and half brick — stone to its midpoint, then brick to its top.

Ruth dipped in and out of other aspects of Cove design — at her insistence, all of the tables in the dining hall have lazy Susans in the center. After the design team had narrowed the choice of dining room chairs from a dozen styles to two, they invited Ruth to choose the one they would purchase. Ruth and Dee Miller hunted around in mountain shops for accessories, Ruth gravitating toward old tables with burn marks and handmade quilts. The pair purchased new furniture, too, at a local Black Mountain furniture store and an outlet in nearby Hendersonville.

The handwrought light fixtures in the chapel, dining room, and main lobby also bear Ruth's imprint. She sketched her designs, and they were produced by an Asheville blacksmith, a young pipe-smoking woman named Berry Bate. She adorned the simple design with dogwood blooms, reflecting both the mountain setting and the traditional association of the tree and its flowers with the crucifixion and resurrection of Jesus.

The team's caution about handing major design responsibilities to Ruth was probably justified. Her expectations could outrun pragmatism and safety, as they almost had with the steeple. And she could be demanding in her own way. (Anticipating the words on her irreverent grave marker, discussed in chapter 8, the cheeky sign over her bedroom door read, "Nobody knows the trouble I've been.") For instance, the prayer room in the upper level of the Cove's chapel features in its center a low table surrounded by kneeling cushions. Ruth and Jerry Miller went there one day to inspect the setup and Ruth said, "What about my elbows?"

Jerry replied, puzzled, "What *about* your elbows?"

"They're *bony*," Ruth complained.

The result of this exchange came in the form of soft cushions ringed around the edge of the table, to accommodate bony elbows at prayer.

The back wall of the prayer room bears a hand-painted mural of Philippians 4:6–7. Ruth selected it as a welcome and instruction to those coming to pray. "Be anxious for nothing," it reads, "but in everything by prayer and supplication, with thanksgiving, let your requests be made known unto God. And the peace of God, which passeth all understanding, shall keep your hearts and minds through Christ Jesus" (the mural identifies the translation as the King James Version, although the wording does not correspond exactly). Exiting the room, visitors read the benediction Ruth chose: "Now to him who is able to do exceedingly abundantly above all that we ask or think, according to the power that works in us, unto him be glory in the church by Christ Jesus throughout all ages, world without end" (Ephesians 3:20–21a; again the mural identifies the KJV as the source, although the quotation does not follow that translation exactly).

Elbow cushions were perhaps not the kind of detail that a design team would want to be bothered with, unless the boss — or his wife — is doing the bothering. These kinds of details are not about the process of making something come into existence but are in-the-moment details, details of being. Such minute concerns very much reflected Ruth, much as her poetry reflected her short but focused attention.

Chapter 8

Prodigals

—◇—

1989–2007

After traveling with Bill in 1987 and 1988, Ruth expressed relief about being
back on the mountain in Montreat. In 1989, she published another collection of memories and poems self-effacingly titled *Legacy of a Pack Rat*.
The book collected more of Ruth's memories and observations, which she
had shaped into teaching moments about God's presence in everyday life.
Its sometimes playful combination of Scripture, reflection, and illustrative
stories gave a sense of what Ruth's Sunday school class for Montreat College
students was like. She drew lessons for the Christian life from Ned's rock
climbing, from Franklin's forced airplane landing in Mississippi, from the
pens and ink she preferred when writing.

Much as her design ideas had sometimes challenged convention during
construction of her home and the Cove, Ruth offered some quirky thoughts
for the design of the *Pack Rat* book. She wanted the book to feature a fuzzy
tail as a bookmark — the tail of the pack rat in question. She also felt that the
cover illustration should depict not a cuddly mouse, but a real rat — to the
point where she took to catching rats around Little Piney Cove, capturing
their image on a photocopier, and sending those reproductions to the beleaguered illustrator, Floyd Hosmer. (According to Ruth's literary collaborator
Stephen Griffith, who worked for the BGEA in the late 1980s selecting its

book club reading list, Ruth wanted to execute the illustrations herself, but he dissuaded her.) Meanwhile a young artist in Minnesota, Chris Garborg, was tapped by his firm to generate a cover illustration. He created a chipper, bright-eyed mouse carrying a tiny basket of colorful books. Throughout the volume's pages, Hosmer's pen and ink drawings showed a large-eyed mouse mirroring the circumstances of the accompanying text — looking in on baby mice, carefully spying on a cat, mournfully holding up a length of chain. The final drawing showed the mouse signing her name — Ruth Bell Graham, in her distinctive backward-leaning script. The image left no doubt as to the identity of the real pack rat.

The book had an interactive feel. Some pages featured only a question at the top of an otherwise blank page. "Had any ideas lately?" Ruth asked the reader, atop a page where one might jot those ideas down. She included myriad quotations from some of her favorite authors, including seventeenth-century Christian thinker John Trapp, nineteenth-century poets Amy Carmichael and John Greenleaf Whittier, and twentieth-century authors Frank W. Boreham, Gilbert Beers, and Jane Merchant. Ruth had gathered a lifetime of treasures from Christian authors of the early and mid-twentieth century.

Another source Ruth drew on for *Pack Rat* provides additional texture to what we know about Ruth's life, which through her parents was deeply rooted in the South's beliefs and traditions. In a chapter titled "Spiritual B.O." — a term Ruth attributed to a friend who spoke "with more accuracy than delicacy" — Ruth retold a story from Matthew 25. Jesus blessed his sheep, who had cared for him through other people, and denounced the goats, who had refused to give such care. Neither sheep nor goats had known that "the least of these" had been Jesus's own. To seal this point, Ruth quoted allusively from one "T. Dixon, Jr.," referring to his description of President Abraham Lincoln as "a man who was always doing merciful things stealthily as other men do crimes." T. Dixon Jr. was North Carolina native Thomas Dixon Jr., author of the early twentieth-century novels *The Leopard's Spots*, *The Clansman*, and *The Traitor* — stories that glorified the slave South and anti-Black violence. The best-selling *Clansman*, subtitled *An Historical Romance of the Ku Klux Klan*, came out in 1905 and later inspired a play by the same name and the now-infamous early motion picture *The Birth of a Nation*, directed by D. W. Griffith. Dixon had penned an admiring portrait of Lincoln, including the description Ruth quoted, drawing on the president's rejection of both abolition and US Blacks' equality with whites. Lincoln, rather, supported colonizing the African continent by forcing freed Black people to emigrate.

Did Ruth intentionally finesse Dixon's identity, and her source along with it, when she included the quotation in *Legacy of a Pack Rat*? By the late 1980s, the cadre of people who helped Ruth pull the book together might have included at least one person who thought it unwise for her even to include the quotation, much less the name of its author. But Ruth knew her own mind and, moreover, loved a well-turned phrase, as this one certainly was. The description of Lincoln fit her point about Christian selflessness so perfectly. Ruth's politics, too, were conventionally southern, given her upbringing. Nelson and Virginia likely read and recommended Dixon's novels. Ruth's emphasis would have been on admiring Lincoln rather than tiptoeing around Dixon's work, its violent themes, and the impact it had on reviving the Klan.

Ruth had included in her 1982 quasi memoir *It's My Turn* a chapter addressed to the "prodigal's parents." In 1991, Ruth returned to the subject and published a whole book about the anguish of waiting for the return of a wayward one, titled *Prodigals and Those Who Love Them*. (The book came out in a revised edition in 1999, subtitled *Words of Encouragement for Those Who Wait*. It included new material added by Gigi about her own "prodigal," son Tullian.) *Prodigals* set biographies of famous wanderers against poems and sayings of encouragement "for those who love them" in today's world. According to Stephen Griffith, *Prodigals* pulled together a collection that Ruth had been amassing over the years — "everything" she came across that related to prodigals. These words, according to Griffith, "would give her hope when her kids were in trouble." Ruth explained in the book's brief introduction, "Prodigals are as new as tomorrow's headlines, as old as the Garden of Eden." They can come in any age, sex, or race. "They do have one thing in common," she concluded. "They have left home. And they are missed." When she presented the book's raw materials to Griffith, it was in the form of a "zipped up" notebook with "like 1,000 Post-It notes" held inside. Griffith crafted the book into its final form over the ensuing nine months.

Although Ruth's children were well launched with families of their own by the time of this book's publication, she reflected on her own mothering work in the pages of *Prodigals* almost as if she still had them all at home. The book included a chapter on Saint Augustine, which appreciated his mother Monica's steadfast pursuit of his conversion from heresy and sexual sin to orthodoxy and moral recovery. Ruth followed this account with "a few suggestions for me as a mother," which ranged from the practical — "Permit person-to-person collect phone calls" — to the ethical — "Make a clear distinction between moral and nonmoral issues" — to the emotional — "Encourage." She had wanted so badly to give her children the kind of love that she felt God gave her. They needed limits, but they also needed to know "they are loved and welcome at home," even if they had momentarily wandered. She "condensed" her advice to mothers about how to train up children: "Preteens, teach. Teens, listen."

A piece of wisdom that Ruth shared repeatedly in these years — in *Prodigals*, in a 1991 interview with Canadian Christian broadcaster Moira Brown, and in a later filmed conversation with daughter Anne — was for mothers to "take care of the possible and to trust [God] with the impossible." Under the possible, she catalogued "love — love expressed," along with praying "intelligently / logically / urgently / without ceasing / in faith." She advised audiences to "enjoy being a mother," to "provide a warm, happy home," while "minister[ing] to their physical / and emotional needs," according to their abilities. The "conviction of sin . . . conversion . . . sanctification" was the "impossible" — for humans, at least — and these tasks were left for God. "These are miracles," Ruth wrote, "and miracles are not in our department" as mothers.

Ruth recognized how powerless she could feel when she resigned herself to focusing on only the "possible." Moreover, in a poem inspired by Jacob's wrestling the angel in Genesis 32 and written in early October 1980, perhaps as she reflected on her sons' struggles, she worried that allowing her children the space to fail could be dangerous to them in the short term:

> "Lord,
> with my Jacob," I would pray,
> "wrestle till the break of Day";
> till he, knowing who Thou art,
> tho' asked, will not let Thee depart;
> saying, "I'll not let Thee free
> saving Thou wilt first bless me."
> O God of Jacob, who knew how
> to change supplanters then, so now
> deal, I pray, with this my son,
> though he may limp when Thou art
> done.

Ruth's experience mothering through her sons' rebellion gave deep roots and staying power to her love for "prodigals and those who love them." More recent family crises, however, had created new urgency in Ruth's concern for people who suffered through the errant behavior of loved ones. Bunny's marriage to Ted Dienert had dissolved over his infidelity; their divorce became final in 1991, rocking not only their two lives but the worlds of their three children. Gigi added her substantial contribution to the 1999 revised edition of *Prodigals*, writing a foreword and a chapter detailing her experience mothering a rebellious son. Her marriage to Stephan would soon end in divorce, as would a second hasty and tempestuous marriage. By 1999, Ned's first marriage had also dissolved.

Through these upheavals, Ruth did not focus only or even primarily on whatever errors in judgment the wanderers made. She focused the main energy of her concern instead on the state of those left in their wake, those who blamed themselves, asking, "What did we do wrong?" Ruth's response emphatically did not list possible parental or spousal errors. Her answer to those who wanted their love and concern for others to be reciprocated was to remind them of God's love, God's deep patience, God's presence, and forgiveness. Ruth had encountered such despair during Franklin's turbulent years, with Ned as a young man, now in the late 1990s as Tullian's grandmother, and with some of her other many grandchildren.

Ruth experienced a similar powerlessness as Billy Graham's wife. Of course, her evangelist husband had distinguished himself from the run of evangelists because he avoided the pitfalls that derailed other famed preachers' careers. But, for the sake of his work, Bill had often left Ruth behind. She had indeed pushed him to embrace evangelism over a settled pastorate that would keep him close by. And she frequently insisted that her place was at home and that she preferred "a little bit of Bill over a whole lot of any other man." Ruth, then, lived in a bind of her own making: she wanted Bill, and she wanted him to answer God's call. The fact that "those who wait" on "prodigals" took up such a large part of her concern indicates that being left waiting by anyone in whom she had invested substantially consumed her own thoughts. The girl Ruth Bell had been "sensitive" about being left behind by dutiful parents traveling around China. This sensitivity persisted in Ruth Graham's adulthood, as husband and children came and went, literally and figuratively.

—◇—

Ruth created a new collection of poetry that was published in 1992, titled *Clouds Are the Dust of His Feet*; the title referred to Nahum 1:3. It included certain poems in common with *Sitting by My Laughing Fire* . . . but many more written since that volume's publication fifteen years before. Stephen Griffith invited Christian poet and essayist Luci Shaw to edit Ruth's poems for publication this time. Ruth admired Luci Shaw and her poetry. But Shaw's work as Ruth's editor did not sit well with Ruth, who was accustomed to collecting and writing without extensive critique. Ruth's longtime secretary Evelyn Freeland had only typed and retyped her distinctive handwriting as Ruth recalibrated punctuation and phrasing. But before *Clouds* Ruth had never had a professional editor, not to mention "a *true* poet," as she called Shaw. When the book emerged, Ruth hated it. For her part, Shaw appreciated and understood Ruth's poetic agenda, writing in the book's preface that Ruth's poems expressed an "incarnational theology."

But Ruth just did not want other hands on her poems. Ruth's discomfort with the book may have aroused her son Franklin's protective instincts; he had the book pulled from the market, and he abandoned the contract with publisher Crossway. As a result, Franklin did not want Ruth to work with Griffith on any more publishing projects, since he had negotiated the *Clouds* contract and brought Shaw onboard.

But Griffith persisted in his work with Ruth, who trusted him and, moreover, already had another project under way with him. Griffith had wanted for some time to create a fine children's book, complete with rich illustrations, from Ruth's old Christmas story, which she had first published in 1959. Indeed, this project had been the one to bring Stephen Griffith and Ruth Graham together originally in the mid-1980s. When as a BGEA employee he approached her with the idea, he brought with him an armload of children's books as examples. Among them was James Dickey's narrative poem *Bronwen, the Traw, and the Shape Shifter*. The cover illustration caught Ruth's eye. "That's the artist I want," she declared. Richard Jesse Watson had created the finely detailed image of the little blonde girl Bronwen, standing in her garden under a buttermilk sky, looking into the distance. (A photograph included in daughter Ruth's book *A Legacy of Love*, published in 2005, showed Ruth reading Dickey's book with one of her grandchildren.)

Watson was reluctant to work on the book, having eschewed what he called "biblical artwork." In his view, no one could surpass what Rembrandt had accomplished in portrayals of Moses, Jeremiah, Jacob, or Jesus. But he found Ruth's Christmas story compelling. A collaboration lasting almost a decade ensued. This story, an expansion of the 1959 version, presented the Christmas story according to Reformed theology — that is, with a sovereign God at center stage. For Ruth, the Christmas story did not begin with a star or shepherds or angels, but with the creation events narrated in Genesis.

The project faced myriad obstacles. They struggled to find a publisher, because the length stretched the bounds of a traditional children's book. At one point, the paintings Watson created for the book had to be airlifted from his house, which was under siege by forest fires (flames that reappeared on the page depicting Adam and Eve's banishment from the garden). As was to be expected, Ruth herself sometimes presented less dangerous but still challenging obstacles; when Watson showed her the painting of a lamp and cat that was to stand at the beginning of one chapter, she gave her immediate appraisal: "That's not my cat. . . . That's not Chester." Needless to say, Watson repainted the illustration. Moreover, he included Chester in several other illustrations — an "Easter egg" like those included in many classic children's books. Watson's illustrations were unconventional, even given Ruth's unconventional telling of the Christmas story. According to Ruth's literary collaborator Stephen Griffith, when *One Wintry Night* finally came out, *Publishers Weekly* took the book to task for taking cultural diversity to the extreme by depicting Adam, Eve, and the angel who banished them from Eden as people of color. But the combination of Ruth's narration and Watson's dynamic images was irresistible to many. The book was perfectly timed for Christmas gift giving in 1994, and a large first printing sold out by Halloween.

—◇—

During this period, while Ruth and Stephen Griffith organized her Post-it notes into *Legacy of a Pack Rat*, corralled her collection of prodigal sayings into the manuscript for *Prodigals and Those Who Love Them*, and worked to create the newest version of her Christmas story, *One Wintry Night*, Ruth also worked behind the scenes to connect with a figure enduring his own sojourn in a far country. Evangelist Jim Bakker had blazed a trail for other television preachers. He and his college sweetheart Tammy Faye LaValley met and married, left school, and began producing a children's show featuring Tammy Faye's puppets. They collaborated with Pat Robertson, helping elevate his *700 Club* television program to the top of the Christian broadcast ratings, then moved on to start their own network with Jan and Paul Crouch. With their own popular Christian talk show, *The PTL Club*, Jim and Tammy Faye started a new network headquartered in Fort Mill, South Carolina. It shared the site with the Bakkers' Christian theme park, the wildly successful Heritage USA.

Through a combination of their own malfeasance uncovered by journalistic and federal investigations and their competitors' scheming, the Bakkers lost control of their network and Heritage USA in 1987. Indicted for multiple counts of fraud and conspiracy in 1988, Jim Bakker went to trial and was convicted on every charge. The judge sharply rebuked Bakker, then sentenced him to serve forty-five years in federal prison and pay a fine of $500,000. Bakker reported to the federal prison at Rochester, Minnesota, the city that also was home to the Mayo Clinic, a perennial retreat for Billy Graham.

As Bakker later recalled, one day early in his prison term, he woke up sick with the flu but forced himself to trudge through his assigned work of cleaning the building's toilets. His rounds completed, he had changed into clean but old clothes and crawled back into his bed to relieve his shivering when a guard came to escort him to the warden's office, to meet a visitor.

"My mind raced," Bakker remembered. "It wasn't visiting day."

The guard explained: "Billy Graham is here to meet you." Bakker immediately looked down at his old clothes, his toes sticking through the holes in his sneakers, and remembered that he had interviewed Billy Graham years before on his television show.

"I was embarrassed and almost said no" to the visit, he recounted. "But I thought, He's come to see me, so I better do it because only Billy Graham and the president of the United States can walk into a federal prison when they want to see somebody."

When Bakker walked into the office, Billy Graham hugged him, saying, "Jim, I love you."

After that visit, Ruth and Bill's son Franklin began visiting Bakker and giving talks to the inmates. Franklin and Jim Bakker had first met in 1980 when Franklin appeared on *PTL* to talk about the Samaritan's Purse ministry and an addition to a hospital the group wanted to build in Kenya. Bob Pierce, the founder of Samaritan's Purse, had recently died, and Franklin was on the verge of moving into his position. In the middle of their interview, Bakker appealed to his viewers and his studio audience to give, and within two months, Samaritan's Purse had received more than the $400,000 needed to construct the hospital addition. Franklin returned to announce on Bakker's show the amount received, and to present *PTL* a check for the overage. Franklin later wrote that this return of funds had been a first for Bakker. The two evangelists formed a meaningful bond through this experience.

In 1993, Bakker's attorneys secured a sentence reduction, aiming their argument at the original trial judge, who had revealed his own antireligious biases in his excoriation of the former televangelist. Bakker also received a transfer to a federal prison in Georgia and soon afterward was paroled. The one thing he lacked as he prepared for his release was a sponsor. Franklin Graham insisted on playing that role for Bakker. Although the disgraced evangelist tried to demur, Franklin told him with characteristic swagger, "Jim Bakker, you were my friend before. You helped me build that hospital in Africa when no one else wanted to help me. You were my friend then, and you're my friend now. If anyone doesn't like it, I'm looking for a fight."

Bakker recalled, "I found out later that Ruth Graham was the player behind the scenes" of Billy Graham's initial visit to his prison in Minnesota. "She was," he wrote, "that silent, powerful woman behind the scenes." If Ruth had not directly promoted Franklin's visits to Bakker's prison, she had watched and prayed over Franklin's developing interest in direct-service missions, with his first trip driving a Land Rover across Europe to Jordan, up to his work to expand the Kenyan hospital. Franklin had, with Bakker's help, returned from the "far country" and thrown himself into mission fields around the world — places like the Tibetan wilds that she had imagined as a girl. So Jim Bakker's aid at that critical moment in Franklin's career must have touched Ruth so deeply on so many levels — as an evangelist's wife, as a mother, and as a lover of missions — that she could overlook his failings and flaws.

Upon his release in December 1994 from the federal prison in Georgia, Bakker was dispatched to Asheville, near Montreat, where he would work for the Salvation Army. He felt afraid and alone. Again, a member of the Graham family showed up when Bakker least expected it. Within two days of his settling in, Ruth had called to ask the Salvation Army officers for permission to take him to church the following Sunday. Bakker arrived at the church for a service featuring Franklin preaching. He met the pastor and was seated in the crowded sanctuary. Ruth soon entered; "she walked down the aisle," Bakker recalled, "and sat down next to me. Without saying a word," he continued, "she told the whole world, 'Jim Bakker is my friend.'" Afterward, she hosted Bakker at Little Piney Cove for lunch. When she realized he did not even have a wallet, she gave him one of Bill's. "He doesn't need this," she explained, "it's an extra one."

—◇—

Ruth suffered a bout of spinal meningitis in March 1996 and underwent surgery for the condition in Asheville's Mission Hospital. News reports listed her condition as critical afterward. They also quoted her brother-in-law Leighton Ford, who shared a family joke about Ruth and Billy that contrasted her stoic endurance of pain and his tendency to hypochondria: "We said that when Billy dies, he would say, 'I told you so,' and when Ruth dies, she'll say, 'I never felt better.'" By May, Ruth had recovered enough to attend the Washington, DC, ceremony during which she and Bill received the Congressional Medal of Honor. Bills proposing such an honor must be cosponsored in the US House of Representatives by at least two-thirds of the membership, and by at least sixty-seven senators. On an occasional basis, the Congress has honored a variety of accomplishments since the first recipient, George Washington, was honored by the Continental Congress in 1776. The medal recognized scientific discoveries, global and space exploration, artistic and athletic accomplishment, and in the years around Ruth and Bill's recognition, religious work. Indeed, the Grahams seemed to have participated in a bit of a trend in congressional acclaim for religious leaders. Rabbi Menachem Shneerson received the medal posthumously in 1994, and after the Grahams, in 1997, Mother Teresa (just a few months before she died) and Ecumenical Patriarch Bartholomew, in separate ceremonies; Father Theodore Hesburgh in 1999; and John Cardinal O'Connor and Pope John Paul II, separately (the latter in a much-scaled-down Vatican ceremony), in 2000.

The ceremony to honor the Grahams fell on the National Day of Prayer, May 2, 1996. It also happened to be a presidential election year, with Republican senator Bob Dole challenging the incumbent Democratic president Bill Clinton for the job of chief executive. Perhaps hoping to benefit electorally from proximity to Billy, Republican members of Congress made a strong showing at the ceremony, which played out in the Capitol rotunda before a crowd that included the Grahams' children and many grandchildren. Speaker of the House Newt Gingrich served as the event's emcee; incumbent Republican senators from North Carolina, conservatives Jesse Helms (being challenged by Harvey Gantt) and Lauch Faircloth, awarded the medal to the couple, with the ninety-four-year-old senator Strom Thurmond of South Carolina very briefly lending a hand.

Senator Dole was one of the occasion's few speakers who made specific mention of Ruth's accomplishments. Most other speakers simply made vague passing reference to her writing and her community service or characterized Billy's evangelizing work as the couple's shared effort. But Dole, whose wife hailed from North Carolina, spoke about their long friendship with Ruth and Billy. He painted a picture of Ruth not only as "Billy's remarkable partner of 53 years" but also as "a distinguished communicator of God's power and peace in her own right." Moreover, he revealed the subject and title of the new book she was working on at the time — a project that both Gigi and Stephen Griffith were involved in. Dole clearly relished telling about Ruth's book, whose title brought raucous laughter from the crowd: *How to Marry a Preacher and Remain a Christian*. (Unfortunately, this manuscript remains unpublished.)

When the time came for Ruth and Bill to receive the medal, she moved gingerly from her front-row seat among her family to the platform where Gingrich, Helms, and Faircloth stood. All but hidden from the television camera's view by Bill and these other men, Ruth struggled to suppress a cough. She stood unsteadily, prompting Vice President Al Gore to supply a chair for her; seated on the stage, she was even harder to spot on camera. Awkwardly, Faircloth and Helms alternated reading each line of the strangely worded, uneven commendation, Faircloth ad-libbing at points in variance with the wording of the law passed by Congress approving the medal. The junior senator extemporized, "Ruth and Billy Graham have been the driving force for many things in this country." Then he continued with the official text, noting that they "have made outstanding and lasting contributions to morality, racial equality, family, philanthropy, and religion." One section recognized that "his 52-year marriage to Ruth Graham . . . exemplified the highest ideals of teaching, counseling, ethics, charity, faith, and family." And the commendation's final section, specifying the "philanthropy" trumpeted earlier, credited the couple as the "driving force" behind the Children's Health Center at Asheville's Memorial Mission Hospital. The other two sections of the declaration extolled Billy's accomplishment of reaching billions of people through his preaching, in person, on television, and in print.

So the recognition landed primarily on Billy Graham — for his fine qualities and his unparalleled outreach. Ruth appeared largely in the declaration as Billy's sidecar. The ceremony amounted to a public recognition of Billy Graham's two-person career. The occasion featured Ruth as an essential accessory to Billy, necessary but not sufficient. Except for the mention of the hospital — an image of which appeared on the reverse side of the commemorative medal — the ceremony and recognition appended Ruth to Billy Graham's lifework. The hospital for children was a notable exception, as a local community project that Ruth took the lead on. Given the political energies and ambitions that, in an election year, brought everyone running in an effort to draw close to Billy Graham for his imprimatur, Ruth might have preferred not to attend at all. She had always tried to fend off political entanglements that would have obligated Bill to one party or another. She still wanted his evangelist's vision unshadowed by naked political calculations.

Having read the commendation, Senators Helms and Faircloth were joined at the podium by Thurmond, who presented the medal to the Grahams. Perhaps the strangest feature of the event was the gold medal itself; on one face are the Grahams, and on the other, an image of the Asheville children's hospital. The depiction has Billy in almost three-quarter profile and looking leonine as ever. Ruth's image appeared in full profile, flashing that magical smile. But her hair looks like a helmet, pulled back in a large flat bun; with the large-collared blouse, the figure looks like it could be on a coin from the 1800s rather than from the turn of the second millennium. Ruth's shoulders share the same plane as Billy's, but her face remained in full profile. It is an awkward effect that further heightens her consignment to accessory status.

After an ovation, with Ned's help, Ruth made haste back to her front-row seat, and the evangelist began to speak. In opening his remarks, Billy said that he was "especially grateful" to Ruth. "We're both being given this honor," he insisted. "No one has sacrificed more than Ruth has to God's calling for the two of us." From those words, he shifted immediately to the story of his conversion under evangelist Mordecai Ham in Charlotte in 1934.

In the remarks he made during the dinner that evening honoring the Grahams, President Bill Clinton paid homage primarily to Billy. Like the majority of the day's speakers, Clinton mentioned Ruth only in conjunction with Billy's accomplishments — the children's hospital, ministering to poor and wounded people worldwide, befriending and guiding presidents, setting an example for married couples and families everywhere. The bulk of his comments recounted Billy's insistence on desegregating the 1959 Little Rock crusade, which a preteen Bill Clinton attended, and Billy's message at a service after the Oklahoma City bombing, just one year before. But he did not address Ruth's individual accomplishments as a poet and storyteller or even individually as a mother. The president left in place the picture of Ruth as a supporting player in the show that starred Billy Graham.

—◇—

Bill published his autobiography, *Just as I Am*, in the spring of 1997, after working on it for ten years. He and Ruth asked Mel Lorentzen, a Wheaton College professor of journalism, to research and oversee the creation of a first draft. Other writers, including Jerry Jenkins — whose Left Behind book series, coauthored with Tim LaHaye, began appearing in the mid-1990s — contributed to later drafts. The ocean of raw material at hand convinced Ruth that the work would become a multivolume project. But Bill joked that he wanted the book to come out while they were all still alive to see it hit the shelves. He gave Ruth sizable credit for developing much of the archive he depended on to fill out his story. "Over the years," Bill observed, "Ruth has kept diaries, and she always wrote long letters home to her parents when she was traveling with me." These missives contained "a gold mine of stories and descriptions." Moreover, Ruth had kept the letters, notes, and reports that he wrote to her. In a tender tribute — a far cry from the vague dedication of his first book from 1947, *Calling Youth to Christ*, to "My Life's Companion" — he wrote, "Most of all, without my wife, Ruth, there would have been no autobiography to write, for she has been vital to my life and an integral part of our ministry." Billy recognized and declared Ruth's determination for him to do the work he had been called to do.

After the book came out, Ruth traveled with Gigi and Ned in fall 1997 to China and then North Korea, where they met with government officials, visited schools, and met with North Korean Christians. Ruth remembered the "experience as one of the true highlights" of her life, visiting Pyeng Yang, where many years before she had at first been so desperately home-sick. Everything from those years was transformed, Ruth reported. "Almost nothing remains from my school days," she said at the time, except for "the beauty of the two rivers that flow through the city" — she could see the natu-ral beauty of any place — "and the warmth and hospitality of the people."

The trip punctuated a crescendo of reflection on her many years of life. Working to set her story in place produced *Footprints of a Pilgrim*, another project drawn from Ruth's life and writings that Stephen Griffith and Gigi midwifed. A reader's theater piece, *Footprints* unfolded Ruth's life story as actors read "poems and snippets" from her writings. The five players — three women and two men — represented different parts of Ruth's voice at dif-ferent times in her life, as well as a select group of other figures in her life. The show was to play before a small invitation-only audience in Asheville's Diana Wortham Theater on April 5, 1998, to benefit the Children's Health Center. With Chinese food catered from Ruth's favorite restaurant and an exhibit of Richard Jesse Watson's illustrations for *One Wintry Night* and other books, they planned a gala night. Griffith and Gigi both put great stock in Ruth's poems; Gigi wrote that she "always thought that Mother reveals her personality in her prose, but she reveals her heart and soul in her poetry."

This celebratory production almost did not happen. Just days before the show, Bill and Franklin tried to intervene with Gigi and get her to call everything off. Apparently unaware of the efforts already expended to send invitations and confirm attendance, the Graham men feared Ruth's embar-rassment if no one showed up. Gigi dismissed their worries — "Daddy didn't have a clue as to what this was all about," she recalled, and Franklin could not "understand or grasp the idea behind this unusual event." Ruth could not understand their fears; sneaking to her bedroom to call Gigi, she refused to cancel, and Bill eventually agreed. Gigi reported that, in the end, Bill was "very moved" by the production.

The source material for the show appeared as a new volume published in 2001. The play and the book made explicit for the first time the connections between Ruth's poems and her life experiences. The theatrical setting and the live audience, with the shaping of the story by Kerry Meads, brought a narrative thread to Ruth's life story that even her published books of poems had not included. Indeed, Ruth had heretofore resisted the inclusion of that connecting thread, wanting her poems to stand on their own and reach the reader's heart on terms that only the reader would grasp.

The extraordinary nature of the *Footprints* production extended to the fact that it was fully mounted only that one time, in April 1998. To celebrate Ruth's eightieth birthday in 2000, the piece was again presented, but more informally. This time, the venue was Asheville's Grove Park Inn, a landmark of arts and crafts design that opened in 1913, site of the Grahams' honeymoon in 1943, and the place where Bill's ninety-fifth birthday would be celebrated in 2013.

—◇—

Ruth traveled to her parents' hometown of Waynesboro, Virginia, in early May 1998, where local and state officials honored her by declaring Saturday, May 2, 1998, "Ruth Bell Graham Day." The occasion was front-page news in Waynesboro, which at the time had a population of about twenty thousand people. The celebration took place at the historic Fishburne Military School in Waynesboro, founded in 1879 by a protégé of Confederate general Robert E. Lee. During his comments at the ceremony, Franklin recounted a story Ruth told him about a Civil War–era ancestor who resisted Union encroachments, both by putting out fires they set and by delivering a blow to a Union soldier who demanded the pin she wore. She gave it to him, stabbing the sharp point into his hand. Pulling it out and handing it back to her, the soldier said, "Ma'am, I admire your spunk."

The ceremony was an offshoot of Franklin's "Festival 98," his revival occurring the same weekend in Charlottesville, thirty miles to the east. The spokesman for the revival emceed the recognition ceremony, describing Ruth as a "confidante [and] a spiritual mentor" to Billy. He quoted from Proverbs 31, that paradigmatic biblical description of "a virtuous woman," to capture her accomplishments of "strength and dignity . . . wisdom . . . kindness." Mayor Charles Ricketts III presented Ruth with a key to the city, mounted on a plaque that declared the city "her true home town." The label was justified; Ruth noted at the time that Waynesboro was where Bill first met Nelson and Virginia, when he asked permission to marry her.

This flurry of recognition perhaps reflected Ruth's and others' awareness that her physical frailty was only intensifying. By this time in his career, Billy Graham's crusading work had slowed in response to both his own and Ruth's health demands. He had been diagnosed with Parkinson's disease in the late 1980s. Ruth suffered a broken hip in 1999. His appearances at crusades became less frequent; after 1998, he committed only to two four-night events annually. Otherwise, he remained stationed at Little Piney Cove for the most part, with Ruth. In 2001, Franklin was elected to succeed his father as the leader of the BGEA. By the end of the year 2000, Ruth had undergone two hip-replacement surgeries. She suffered pain constantly, and movement was not easy for her.

Even as her own health deteriorated, Ruth suffered a series of losses over the next several years. Her brother, Clayton Bell, died suddenly from a heart attack on July 4, 2000, while in Montreat visiting Ruth, Bill, and other family, including their sister Virginia and her husband, John Sommerville, retired from the Korean mission field and living in Nelson and Virginia's old house on Assembly Drive. Clayton was relatively young at his death, twelve years younger than Ruth and only recently retired from pastoring Highland Park Presbyterian Church in Dallas. But he had long borne the physical stress of leading that congregation through a tumultuous period that culminated in the 1991 departure of thousands of members to start a new church affiliated with the conservative Presbyterian Church in America. Although Clayton tried to put the best face on the outcome, commenting that the split left "those of us who are in Highland Park Presbyterian Church now united in a renewed effort to serve the Lord in, with, and through the PCUSA," the long-running battle cost him dearly, professionally and personally. A *Chris-*

tianity Today obituary claimed that the division "nearly killed" him in the late 1980s, when his effort to keep the congregation in the PCUSA precipitated a heart attack back then.

—◇—

Ned and his second wife, Christina, moved to Montreat in 2002 to help care for his parents, working especially to improve Ruth's nutritional intake, personal care, and hygiene and making changes to Little Piney Cove to facilitate his father's mobility. (Ned also supervised interior updates to the Grahams' first Montreat home, across Louisiana Road from the Bells' house.)

A new series of losses began in 2003 with the death of Bill's brother Melvin, who was killed by a heart attack at the age of seventy-nine. He had continued the dairy business of their father and had also served on the BGEA board. When former president Ronald Reagan passed away the following summer, in June 2004, Nancy Reagan called family members first and Ruth and Bill next. Billy had been one of the only non–family members who was welcomed to visit the ailing president during the years of his steepest decline into Alzheimer's-related dementia. In the summer of 2006, Ruth's sister Virginia — the adorable little sister MaiMai — died at the age of seventy-nine.

This cycle of losses, accompanied by other trials involving Gigi and Bunny and their families, challenged Ruth's endurance. At the end of 2006, moreover, as her strength dramatically decreased and she was in pain from degeneration of her spine, a conflict that had been brewing inside the family broke into the open. At Ned's invitation, Laura Sessions Stepp, a reporter for the *Washington Post*, revealed the schism. The Billy Graham Library, the latest project of the BGEA and part of Franklin's new vision for the organization, neared completion in Charlotte. Its function belied its name. One of the Graham daughters told Ned the complex reminded her of a Cracker Barrel restaurant. More a religious tourist attraction than a library, the site included Billy Frank's childhood home, moved from Park Road, rebuilt, and filled with photos and memorabilia from his early years. The "library" itself was to be housed in a new monumental barnlike structure. An animatronic dairy cow greeted entering guests; "Bessie's" voice had the tone and cadence of an African American woman. The talking cow's presence hinted at the designers' previous work for the Walt Disney Company. The barn also included a book shop ("Ruth's Attic"), a café ("Graham Brothers Dairy Bar"), and a self-guided tour through Billy Graham's evangelistic triumphs. Exiting the tour and the barn, visitors would walk a path to the shaded area set aside, according to Franklin's plan, for Billy and Ruth's graves.

The effect of the tour, which placed visitors in the midst of a crusade audience, was ostensibly to continue Billy Graham's evangelistic work beyond his active career, indeed, beyond his death. In that light, Ruth might have been supportive of the effort. What she did not want, and what prompted the family scuffle, was to be buried in the library's memorial garden, even if it was next to Bill. She had planned decades before to be buried on the grounds of the Cove. Ned felt that his parents' impact and memory had already been captured by the historical exhibits housed at and the mission pursued at the Cove. But Franklin, who had begun consolidating all of BGEA's Minneapolis and Cove operations in Charlotte, did not want the memorabilia, exhibits, and grave sites at the Cove to compete with the library.

According to Stepp's reporting, at the end of 2006 Ned had dispatched Ruth and Bill's longtime friend Patricia Cornwell to tour the almost completed library grounds and report back her thoughts. Ned had already helped Ruth prepare a legal document, "My Final Wishes concerning My Burial Site," which declared, "Under no circumstances am I to be buried in Charlotte, North Carolina." She actually would have loved a final resting place "at my 'first home' in China," she stated. Failing that, however, her "next choice is the beautiful mountains of Western North Carolina which I have loved and where I have lived for the past 60 years." Ned gathered six witnesses (including someone described as a neuroscientist) and a notary to attend the document's preparation.

Cornwell visited the library; her guide, a BGEA board member, told her rather dismissively that "Billy was working on" Ruth to convince her to accept the idea of being buried there. Back at Little Piney Cove, Cornwell minced no words for her audience: Bill, Ruth, Ned, and Christina. "I was horrified by what I saw," the novelist told them. She was particularly disturbed by the focus on gathering visitors' personal information for the purposes of fund-raising — a practice that Billy Graham had always treated gingerly. "I know who you are," Cornwell told Bill, "and you are not that place. It's a mockery," she continued. "People are going to laugh." Cornwell surely knew Bill's aversion to being publicly embarrassed or allowing Ruth or his ministry to be objects of ridicule. "Please don't be buried there," Cornwell pleaded.

From the hospital bed where she lay, Ruth quietly sighed in response, "It's a circus. A tourist attraction."

Billy demurred, perhaps acutely aware of Stepp's presence in the room. (Stepp later quoted two Graham daughters who described him as "deeply conflicted" about the disagreement.) Cornwell poked him: "I tell you, if you're buried there I'll dig you up and move you here."

Ruth chimed in from her hospital bed, "I'll be one of the pallbearers." Even in duress, she maintained her unmistakable wit.

That wit had sustained her through almost nine decades. Through the frights of childhood, the despair of homesick adolescence, the aridity of college academics, the frustrations of early marriage, the long separations imposed by a two-person career, Ruth had wielded her sense of humor to lift her mood, prick inflated egos, and entertain young charges. Even as she trained Bill's focus relentlessly on his evangelism, she used her wit also to deflect the glare of spotlights and repel the attention of crowds. She had treasured her ability to disappear into a crowd, to sing and pray alongside other crusade worshipers, to listen in on the criticisms and crises of regular folks.

Her wit was not her only tool. Hard-won ties to family and place also sustained her. Back in the 1940s, she had not moved to Charlotte to build a home, but to the enclave of Montreat and the reassuring presence of her parents. In the 1980s, she had latched on to various projects at the Cove, where the BGEA created its own "mountain retreat" — the phrase for which Montreat served as portmanteau — but one not subject to denominational wrangles, as Montreat, its church, and its college sometimes were. The Cove's relative remoteness, the rugged terrain, the abundance of wildlife — these things Ruth loved. There, she could rest.

What she had not anticipated was Franklin's assertion of control over not only the BGEA but also the Cove, which suffered the loss of endowment funds and personnel to the library as that project moved forward. By the time Ruth slipped into a coma in mid-June 2007, Bill announced his decision: he and his beloved Ruth would be buried at the library in Charlotte. Bill's statement, released by the BGEA, explained that he and Ruth had prayed about and talked through the subject. "Ruth and I made the decision to be buried beside each other at the Billy Graham Library in my home town of Charlotte, N.C.," the announcement said, further explaining that their decision came earlier that spring and was recorded in yet another document that they both signed in the presence of an attorney and a physician. "Now that she is close to going to heaven," Billy explained, they wanted to make the announcement publicly. Several close advisers, plus Ned and Anne, indicated to Stepp that they had only learned of the change in burial plans the night before Billy's statement became public.

Ruth Bell Graham died on June 14, 2007, at Little Piney Cove, with Bill and their five children surrounding her. She had just days before marked her eighty-seventh birthday. Stepp's remembrance quoted from the statement that Billy Graham issued in anticipation of Ruth's death: "Ruth was my life partner, and we were called by God as a team." He took the measure of Ruth's role in his career: "No one else could have borne the load that she carried." Declaring what others would claim for years after her death, Billy gave credit to Ruth for her distinctive contribution: "My work through the years would have been impossible without her encouragement and support." As the children's "spiritual teacher," and his own source for "spiritual guidance," he called Ruth "the greatest Christian I ever knew."

Ruth's faith was great, marking her life daily, shaping her decisions and guiding her thoughts, including her approach to death. Several decades before she died, she wrote a poem about how she hoped her soul's approach to heaven would go.

> And when I die
> I hope my soul ascends
> slowly, so that I

may watch the earth receding
out of sight,
its vastness growing smaller
as I rise,
savoring its recession
with delight.

Imagining the process as something like a flight into space, Ruth hoped to "savor" her passage from earthly to heavenly life. She also wanted to feel the anticipatory joy of moving heavenward. So the poem voiced Ruth's mild complaint about the description of resurrection given by Paul in his first letter to the church in Corinth (1 Corinthians 15:52):

. . . joy unspeakable
and full of glory
needs more
than "in the twinkling of an eye,"
more than "in a moment."

Paul's words depicted an instantaneous transformation — too quick for Ruth. She realized the absurdity of her gripe, however. "Lord, who am I / to disagree?" The poem ended with Ruth's profession that, while she had "much [on earth] / to leave behind," she also wanted "time / to adore" God, presumably in the way she had during her life. The poem poses a bit of a logical puzzle but does provide readers another example of Ruth's wide curiosity. She had an imagination that made space for possibilities and questions. What is lost if Christian believers make an instant shift from earthly to eternal life? Her reliance on biblical guidance did not stop her from engaging in a little poetic play here, teasing but still adoring God.

—◇—

Ruth's last — and lasting public — words on her own death, famously, also sounded a teasing note, a gentle rebuff both to Billy's superlative characterization of her Christian faith and to Franklin's insistence that she be buried at the Billy Graham Library in Charlotte. On her massive grave marker there, Ruth tweaked them both.

Franklin had engaged his mother in a lifelong battle of obstinate wits. They enjoyed calling each other's bluff — little Franklin eagerly smoking all of a workman's cigarettes when Ruth had intended the sentence as a punishment for his theft; Ruth nonchalantly stowing a stubbornly vexatious Franklin in the car trunk on a drive from Montreat to Asheville. They shared a love of mischief. One can place the odd inscription on Ruth's rough stone grave marker in this context. On the bottom third of the large slab, below Ruth's name and dates, this message appears:

> End of Construction —
> Thank you for your patience.

She had read the words on a road sign some decades before and saw them as an apt description of her own journey as a human being. She was flawed by sinfulness, as she believed all humans were, but she was also called by God to live as a redeemed sinner — under construction. Over the decades of her life, Ruth had extended patient compassion to family, friends, and complete strangers who had wandered, like the prodigal son, into the far country. Here, she offered this final note of appreciation to those who had been patient with her. As she often had during her life, she expressed profound ideas with a wink. Her resting place was not to be a site for the morose. Do not take my passing too seriously. Do not make too big of a deal about me. And even, to Franklin: do not turn this place into a maudlin mausoleum.

Another message appears on Ruth's marker, for those who can read it. A Chinese character, signifying a combination of justice and righteousness, dominates the top third of the stone. The symbol calls forth Ruth's Chinese childhood, but also directly links her marker to those of her parents. The marble headstones for both Nelson and Virginia Bell — in Swannanoa's Piney Grove Cemetery, about twenty miles from Montreat — also feature Chinese characters. At the top of both is the Chinese character for "bell." The character meaning "come" adorns the lower third of Virginia's marker, perhaps a tribute to her evangelistic work in China and her generous hospitality to all comers in Montreat. The L-sound of the character's Chinese pronunciation may also allude to Virginia's maiden name, Leftwich.

But Ruth's marker bears an even more direct connection to Nelson's gravestone, which features the same character for justice and righteousness at its base. A firm commitment to divine justice and Christian righteousness animated Nelson's life and work as a missionary surgeon and a Presbyterian layman. As colleagues and associates would attest, these commitments made him either a valuable ally or a formidable adversary. They also made him a hero and a model to Ruth.

This reading of Ruth's grave marker suggests a kind of map or key to her public legacy. With her name and dates inscribed in the middle third of the stone slab, she appears literally between the justice and righteousness of her father and the mischievous wink to her elder son. Despite the early years of angularity in their father-daughter relationship, Ruth was Nelson Bell's daughter. And Franklin Graham — contrarian, outspoken, overtly political in contrast to his irenic, reserved, even evasive father — is definitely Nelson Bell's grandson. Franklin came by his self-righteousness honestly.

After Bill's death in early 2018, he was laid to rest at his namesake library, as per Franklin's plan, with a funeral attended by the powerful political and religious leaders of that moment. His grave marker, which now rests beside Ruth's, adds another dimension of meaning to hers. The two rough stones complement each other; the top edge of Ruth's smaller marker rises as if pointing toward Bill's larger one, as ever, directing attention toward Billy Graham and his evangelistic work. If viewed from overhead, the two stones seem to point up and away, heavenward.

The marker on Ruth's grave differs greatly from Bill's and may allow Ruth the last word. The upper half of Billy Graham's memorial stone features a cross. His name is etched in large letters below it, then his dates below that. At the bottom of the stone slab, roughly even with the jokey inscription on Ruth's marker, an efficient summary of Bill's life reads,

Preacher of the Gospel
of the Lord Jesus Christ

The final line of text carved on the stone is a Scripture citation, John 14:6, a verse in which Jesus claimed for himself a unique relationship to God: "I am the way, the truth, and the life; no one comes to the Father except through me." Even in eternal rest, Billy Graham witnesses to those who come near.

The contrast between the two markers complicates the picture of Ruth Graham as "the greatest Christian" Billy Graham ever knew. Nothing on her gravestone necessarily testifies to her Christian faith. Ruth Graham "followed" Bill, even to the point of agreeing to be laid to rest in this unfamiliar place. But she did get the last word, uniquely hers, a word about her beloved beginnings and her unique way of being in and seeing the world.

A Note on the Sources

—◇—

My interest in Ruth began with an invitation from Grant Wacker to present a paper on Ruth as part of a conference panel on Billy Graham. My claim in that paper, "Billy Graham: Man of God, 1949–1954," which I presented at the American Society of Church History winter meeting, January 8, 2010, in San Diego, was that one could not understand Billy without also understanding Ruth. This book magnifies that claim by asserting that we should give Ruth the attention she deserves as a significant woman participating in twentieth-century white evangelical American culture.

Subsequent conference presentations and invited lectures have contributed to this project: "'An Odd Kind of Cross to Bear': Mrs. Billy Graham in Image and Word" (presentation, Worlds of Billy Graham conference, Wheaton [IL] College, September 27, 2013, sponsored by the Institute for the Study of American Evangelicals at Wheaton with Lilly Endowment funds); "Ruth Graham: Her Story" (lecture, Great Awakenings: Evangelists & Their Impact on American Culture conference, Presbyterian Heritage Center, with the support of the Conference Center of the Mountain Retreat Association, Montreat, NC, May 29, 2015); "Unofficially Official: Telling Clergy-Wives' Stories; The Case of Ruth Bell Graham" (presidential address, Southeastern Commission for the Study of Religion annual meeting,

Atlanta, March 4, 2016); "Heroes, Women, Wives: Writing Other Lives" (lecture, American Society of Church History annual meeting, Denver, January 7, 2017; published under the same title in *Fides et Historia* 49, no. 2 [Summer/Fall 2017]: 48–51); "Ruth Bell Graham: In the Footprints of a Pilgrim" (lecture, A Centennial Symposium: Rev. Billy Graham, Institute for Studies of Religion, Baylor University, Waco, TX, November 7, 2018); "'Write or Develop an Ulcer': Ruth Bell Graham's Poetry" (lecture, The Beauty of Art, the Holiness of Saints: King Institute for Faith & Culture lecture series, Emmanuel Episcopal Church, Bristol, VA, February 24, 2020).

Preparing other published work on Ruth also advanced this project: "Ruth Bell Graham Was More Than Billy Graham's Wife," *Faith & Leadership: An Offering of Leadership Education at Duke University*, August 12, 2013; "Mama Was 'a Real Theologian,'" *Christian History: Special Bonus Issue* 111 (February 25, 2014): 24–28; and my chapter, "'An Odd Kind of Cross to Bear': The Work of Mrs. Billy Graham, from 'Pretty Wife' to 'End of Construction,'" in *American Pilgrim: Billy Graham in Religion, Politics, and Culture*, ed. Andrew Finstuen, Grant Wacker, and Anne Blue Wills (Oxford: Oxford University Press, 2017), part of the Lilly Endowment–funded Billy Graham project administered and hosted by the Institute for the Study of American Evangelicals at Wheaton College. An as-yet-unpublished article on Ruth's poetry and its exploration of Calvinist views of nature also contributed to my thinking here.

Although the story of clergy wives in the United States deserves a fresh telling, a literature on the subject does exist. The most recent contribution is Kate Bowler's *The Preacher's Wife: The Precarious Power of Evangelical Women Celebrities* (Princeton: Princeton University Press, 2019). Bowler focuses on women unlike Ruth who took more public, active roles alongside their famous preacher-husbands. But Ruth does appear at points. Bowler's book brings new attention to the particular negotiations of gender, power, and tradition that women married to male clergy have faced (and, especially in conservative evangelical traditions, still face). Older sources on clergy wives include Catherine L. Adams, *Daily Duties Inculcated in a Series of Letters, Addressed to the Wife of a Clergyman* (Boston: Crocker & Brewster, 1835); Wallace Denton, *The Role of the Minister's Wife* (Philadelphia: Westminster, 1962); William Douglas, *Ministers' Wives* (New York: Harper & Row, 1965); Marilyn Brown Oden, *The Minister's Wife: Person or Position?* (Nashville: Abingdon, 1966); Mary Schauffler Platt, *The Home with the Open Door: An Agency in Missionary Service* (New York: Student Volunteer Movement, 1920); Leonard Sweet, *The Minister's Wife: Her Role in Nineteenth-Century American Evangelicalism* (Philadelphia: Temple University Press, 1983); Margaret H. Watt, *The History of the Parson's Wife* (London: Faber & Faber, 1943).

Advice manuals for women married to (or desiring to marry) clergymen include but are certainly not limited to the following, whose titles and publication dates indicate that the vexations continue: Lorna Dobson, *I'm More Than the Pastor's Wife: Authentic Living in a Fishbowl World*, rev. ed. (Grand Rapids: Zondervan, 2003); Dr. Eddie Greene, "'And He Gave Some . . .' Minister's Wives, Too! A Minister's Wives Mini-Seminar" (unpublished typescript); Martha Hickman, *How to Marry a Minister* (Philadelphia: Lippincott, 1968); Lisa McKay, *You Can Still Wear Cute Shoes and Other Great Advice from an Unlikely Preacher's Wife* (Colorado Springs: David C. Cook, 2010); and Lora Lee Parrott, *How to Be a Preacher's Wife and Like It* (Grand Rapids: Zondervan, 1957), which includes a very brief introduction by Ruth.

Sources on particular women include biographies by Edythe Scott Bagley with Joe Hilley, *Desert Rose: The Life and Legacy of Coretta Scott King* (Tuscaloosa: University of Alabama Press, 2012), and Elisabeth D. Dodds, *Marriage to a Difficult Man: The Uncommon Union of Jonathan & Sarah Edwards* (Laurel, MS: Audubon, 1971); and memoirs by Mrs. Henry Ward [Eunice] Beecher, *From Dawn to Daylight; or, The Simple Story of a Western Home* (New York: Hurst & Co., 1859); Graham neighbor Betty Frist, *No Wings in the Manse: Life and Laughter under the Preacher's Roof* (Westwood, NJ: Revell, 1956); Rosalind Goforth, *Climbing: Memories of a Missionary's Wife*, 3rd ed. (Nappanee, IN: Evangel, 2008), which includes a brief introduction by Ruth Bell Graham; the classic by Catherine Marshall, *A Man Called Peter: The Story of Peter Marshall*, anniversary ed. (Grand Rapids, 2002; originally published by McGraw-Hill in 1951); Tammy Faye [Bakker] Messner, *Tammy: Telling It My Way* (New York: Villard, 1996); and Helen Smith Shoemaker, *I Stand by the Door: The Life of Sam Shoemaker* (Waco, TX: Word, 1967).

Two sociological studies also contributed to my understanding of clergy marriage: H. Papanek, "Men, Women, and Work: Reflections on the Two-Person Career," *American Journal of Sociology* 78 (January 1973): 852–72, and Mary G. Taylor and Shirley Foster Hartley, "The Two-Person Career: A Classic Example," *Sociology of Work and Occupations* 2, no. 4 (November 1975): 354–72.

Nelson Bell's letters (including Virginia Bell's occasional letters) from their twenty-five years in Tsingkiangpu were indispensable in introducing me to Ruth before she became Mrs. Billy Graham. See box 1, folders 1–10, collection 318, Papers of L. Nelson Bell, CN 318, Billy Graham Center Archives (hereinafter BGCA), Wheaton College, Wheaton, IL. See also Harold Lindsell, "L. Nelson Bell: In Memoriam," *Christianity Today*, August 31, 1973, and John C. Pollock, *A Foreign Devil in China: The Story of Dr. L. Nelson Bell, an American Surgeon in China* (Minneapolis: World Wide Publications, 1971). One hopes that someone will soon produce a new biography of Nelson that takes ample measure of Virginia's partnership with him. The Bells quietly shaped southern attitudes on race, religion, and gender in significant ways.

Because I had no access to her letters and diaries, which are held by the Graham family out of reach of researchers, Ruth Bell Graham's published works proved valuable sources. In order of publication, they are: *Our Christmas Story* (New York: Nelson, 1959), and a revised edition from World Wide Publications (Minneapolis, 1973); *Sitting by My Laughing Fire . . .* (Waco, TX: Word, 1977); *It's My Turn* (Minneapolis: World Wide Publications, 1982); *Legacy of a Pack Rat* (Nashville: Oliver Nelson, 1989); *Prodigals and Those Who Love Them* (Colorado Springs: Focus on the Family, 1991), and a revised edition that includes material by Gigi Graham Tchividjian, *Prodigals and Those Who Love Them: Words of Encouragement for Those Who Wait* (Grand Rapids: Baker Books, 1999); *Clouds Are the Dust of His Feet* (Wheaton, IL: Crossway, 1992); *One Wintry Night* (Grand Rapids: Baker Books, 1994); *Footprints of a Pilgrim: The Life and Loves of Ruth Bell Graham* (Nashville: Nelson, 2001); *Never Let It End: Poems of a Lifelong Love*, foreword by Jan Karon (Grand Rapids: Baker Books, 2001); and *Ruth Bell Graham's Collected Poems* (Grand Rapids: Baker Books, 2002). See also Sheri Toomb, "ECPA Honors David Koechel with Jordon Lifetime Achievement Award,"

ECPA.org (website of the Evangelical Christian Publishers Association), May 3, 2011, https://www.ecpa.org/news/64164/ECPA-Honors-David -Koechel-with-Jordon-Lifetime-Achievement-Award.htm. Koechel illustrated the 1973 edition of *Our Christmas Story*.

The 1953 copy of *Peace with God* that contains Ruth Graham's marginalia and handwritten notes, discussed in chapter 7 above, is at the BGCA, collection 15, box 2, folder 2. Archivist Bob Shuster made me aware of its existence, for which I am most grateful. Grant Wacker kindly shared an article about the authorship of the book's 1953 edition: George Burnham, "Graham Book, Peace with God, Puzzles Author Janet Baird," *Chattanooga News-Free Press*, March 28, 1953. A brief review of *It's My Turn*, discussed in chapter 7 above, is by Elise C. Dennis, "Graham, Ruth Bell. *It's My Turn*," *Library Journal* 107 (September 15, 1982): 1760.

Books and book chapters about Ruth Graham include: Patricia Daniels Cornwell, *A Time for Remembering: The Ruth Bell Graham Story* (New York: Harper & Row, 1983), reissued as *Ruth, a Portrait: The Story of Ruth Bell Graham* (New York: Doubleday, 1997); Julie Nixon Eisenhower, *Special People* (New York: Simon & Schuster, 1977), 47–85; Betty Frist, *My Neighbors, the Billy Grahams* (Nashville: Broadman, 1983); Hanspeter Nüesch, *Ruth & Billy Graham: The Legacy of a Couple* (Grand Rapids: Baker Books, 2014); Jhan Robbins, *Marriage Made in Heaven: The Story of Billy & Ruth Graham* (New York: Putnam, 1983); *Ruth Bell Graham: Celebrating an Extraordinary Life*, comp. Stephen Griffith (Nashville: Nelson, 2003); James Schaffer and Colleen Todd, *Christian Wives: Women behind the Evangelists Reveal Their Faith in Modern Marriage* (New York: Doubleday, 1987); and William Martin, *A Prophet with Honor: The Billy Graham Story* (New York: William Morrow, 1991), especially chapter 5, "Ruth."

My immersion in all things Ruth and Billy began at the BGCA at Wheaton College. Innumerable news and feature articles amassed by Graham's staff over the decades were held there until 2019, when Franklin Graham moved Billy Graham's archived materials to the Charlotte, North Carolina, BGEA headquarters (see Adelle M. Banks, "Billy Graham Archives to Move from Wheaton College to His North Carolina Library," Religion News Service, March 29, 2019, https://religionnews.com/2019/03/29/billy-graham

-archives-to-move-from-wheaton-college-to-his-north-carolina-library/; and Tim Funk for Religious News Service, "Billy Graham Archives Begin Move from Wheaton to Charlotte," *Christianity Today*, June 4, 2019, https://www.christianitytoday.com/news/2019/june/billy-graham-archives-frank lin-move-charlotte-library-wheat.html). Items that receive particular attention here are from the BGCA, collection 360 (clippings file), unless otherwise noted: Associated Press, "Movement Criticized: Graham's Wife No Libber Fan," *Victoria (TX) Advocate*, April 15, 1976, 6; Heather Burkey, "Mrs. Billy Graham Comes Home," *Sunday (Staunton, VA) News Leader*, May 3, 1998, A1; Hallie Burnett, "The Two Sides of Mrs. Billy Graham," *Woman's Day*, December 1969, 52–53, 88, 90, 92; Monica Dickens, "Would You Like to Have a Famous Husband?" *Woman's Own*, April 29, 1954, 16; Fern Rich, "My Life with Billy Graham," *Parade Magazine*, April 27, 1954, 8–11; Stanley High, "Mrs. Billy Graham Tells the Story," *Reader's Digest*, November 1954, 1–10; Lael Morgan, "Mrs. Billy Graham Speaks Out," *Washington Post*, September 28, 1969, 136; "Mrs. Billy Graham: Rears Family with Switch in One Hand, Bible in Other," *Christian Times for a Changing World*, 1969 (republished from *Grit*); Viviane Peter, "Rev. & Mrs. Billy Graham — How It Feels to Be a Crusader's Wife," *Parade Magazine*, March 9, 1970; Andrew Robin, "Living Legends," *Today's Health* 39 (1961): 77; "Women's World: The Woman behind Billy Graham," *Bible Speaks to Britain*, May 1954, 15; Wendy Murray Zoba, "Billy's Rib," *Christianity Today*, November 13, 1995, 28.

A chronology available through the BGCA website of Billy Graham's crusades and other major events frequently proved useful in constructing a timeline of Ruth's life: "Select Chronology," accessed October 29, 2021, https://www.wheaton.edu/media/billy-graham-center-archives/Chronolo gy-1934-2018.pdf.

Several news articles by reporter Laura Sessions Stepp describe the burial controversy: "A Family at Cross-Purposes; Billy Graham's Sons Argue over a Final Resting Place," *Washington Post*, December 13, 2006; "On Billy Graham," *Washington Post*, December 15, 2006; "Graham: Wife to Be Buried in Charlotte," *Washington Post*, June 14, 2007; "Ruth Graham; Evangelist's Wife Led Private Crusade," *Washington Post*, June 15, 2007. Tim Funk also covered the family's disagreement and public statements: "Feud Escalates with Siblings' Statements," *Charlotte Observer*, December 14, 2006, 13A.

For obituaries of Ruth, see Bob Paulson and Kristen Burke, "A Joyous Goodbye," *Decision Magazine*, special commemorative issue, July 2007, 26–27, https://decisionmagazine.com/a-joyous-goodbye/, and Richard Severo, "Wife of Rev. Billy Graham Dies at 87," *New York Times*, June 15, 2007, https://www.nytimes.com/2007/06/15/obituaries/15graham.html. The BGEA news release about Ruth's funeral service is available at https://ruthbellgrahammemorial.org/funeral-service/.

Excerpts of the "Production Notes" for the April 5, 1998, production in Asheville, North Carolina, of *Footprints of a Pilgrim* (discussed in chapter 8 above) are available at http://www.nph.com/vcmedia/2350/2350581.pdf. An article by Luis F. Amador, MD, explained the issues involved in the use of a feeding tube such as Ruth had in place at the end of her life: "To Tube or Not to Tube," *Hospitalist*, August 2006, https://www.the-hospitalist.org /hospitalist/article/123197/tube-or-not-tube.

Several interviews with Ruth by friends and family have provided insight. Dr. Lois Ferm conducted an interview with Ruth, the transcript of which is held at the BGCA, collection 141, box 4, folder 8, oral history 332. Available online are "Heart to Heart with Sheila Walsh," 1991, at https://www.youtube.com/watch?v=NJFJAVJ4T78&list=PLwsmP9-vcSYl44jsN hYnBqmCt_AWSmUGo&index=11; an interview, probably from 1991, with Canadian television host Moira Brown, "A Mother's Wisdom," at https://www.youtube.com/watch?v=g308T-N_-bU; and Anne Graham Lotz's "Conversation with Ruth Bell Graham," posted on Lotz's official YouTube channel at https://www.youtube.com/watch?v=pBS23WonTSc. A transcript of an interview with Ruth's college roommate Helen Stam was formerly located at Wheaton College in the BGCA at http://www2.wheaton .edu/bgc/archives/trans/074to78.htm, accessed August 29, 2014.

Works about L. Nelson Bell include context and information about Ruth: John C. Pollock, *A Foreign Devil in China: The Story of Dr. L. Nelson Bell, an American Surgeon in China* (Minneapolis: World Wide Publications, 1971); Harold Lindsell, "L. Nelson Bell: In Memoriam," *Christianity Today*,

August 31, 1973, at https://www.christianitytoday.com/ct/1973/august-31 /l-nelson-bell-in-memoriam.html.

Some of Billy Graham's autobiographical writing has provided perspectives on Ruth's character and her relationship with him: *Just as I Am: The Autobiography of Billy Graham* (New York: HarperCollins, 1997), and *Nearing Home: Life, Faith, and Finishing Well* (Nashville: Nelson, 2011).

Needless to say, much has been written about Billy Graham, not all of which helps us understand Ruth. But relevant material does appear in the following books or book chapters: David Aikman, *Billy Graham: His Life and Influence* (Nashville: Nelson, 2007); *America's Hour of Decision, Including a Life Story of Billy Graham* (Wheaton, IL: Van Kampen, 1951); Marshall Frady, *Billy Graham: A Parable of American Righteousness* (Boston: Little, Brown, 1979); Stanley High, *Billy Graham: The Personal Story of the Man, His Message, and His Mission* (New York: McGraw-Hill, 1956); David Poling, *Why Billy Graham?* (Santa Fe, NM: Sunstone, 2017), especially chapter 9, "The Gift of Tomorrow"; John Pollock, *Billy Graham: The Authorized Biography* (New York: McGraw-Hill, 1966); and two studies by Grant Wacker, *America's Pastor: Billy Graham and the Shaping of a Nation* (New York: Oxford, 2014), and *One Soul at a Time: The Story of Billy Graham* (Grand Rapids: Eerdmans, 2019). The above-mentioned volume that I coedited with Wacker and Andrew Finstuen, *Billy Graham: American Pilgrim* (New York: Oxford, 2017), contains a wealth of excellent original scholarship on Graham, notably Curtis Evans's chapter, "A Politics of Conversion: Billy Graham's Political and Social Vision," which provides tools for grappling with Ruth's politics as well.

Articles on Billy that include pertinent information about Ruth include the following: Associated Press, "Billy Graham Has Parkinson's Disease," *Tulsa World*, July 2, 1992, https://tulsaworld.com/archive/billy-graham -has-parkinson-s-disease/article_d93354fe-7adf-5f59-a832-f6dd87d62966. html; Tony Carnes, "Billy Graham and Johnny Cash: An Unlikely Friendship," *Christianity Today*, February 22, 2018, https://www.christianitytoday .com/ct/2018/february-web-only/billy-graham-and-johnny-cash-unlikely -friendship.html; and Frye Gaillard, "Billy at Home: Here, the Preacher Can Relax, Think and Speak More Freely," *Charlotte Observer*, Sunday, June 10, 1979, 1A, 11A.

The crowd-sourced website findagrave.com has provided me with some basic information about Ruth's sisters and brothers, and sometimes photographs and links to other sources: Rosa Bell Montgomery, at https://www .findagrave.com/memorial/121793643/rosa-wentenbaker-montgomery; her husband, Don, at https://www.findagrave.com/memorial/121793852/charles -donald-montgomery; Virginia Bell Somerville, at https://www.findagrave .com/memorial/45799181/virginia-somerville; and Clayton Bell, at https:// www.findagrave.com/memorial/45798874/benjamin-clayton-bell. Because of Clayton Bell's position as a leader of Highland Park Presbyterian Church in Dallas, during its divisive debate over denominational affiliation, coverage of that turmoil sheds light on his background and commitments: Jim Atkinson, "The Schism," *D Magazine*, May 1996, https://www.dmagazine.com /publications/d-magazine/1996/may/religion-the-schism/; Harold Myra, "Remembering Clayton Bell," *Christianity Today*, July 11, 2000, https://www .christianitytoday.com/ct/2000/julyweb-only/23.0a.html; Jerry L. Van Marter, "Obituary: Presbyterian Bell, 67, Dies," *Christianity Today*, July 11, 2000, https://www.christianitytoday.com/ct/2000/august7/14.28.html; and "Vote Splits Dallas Church," *Christianity Today*, June 24, 1991, 35. A later split of Highland Park is detailed in Leslie Scanlon, "PCUSA Continues to See Exodus of Churches," *Christian Century*, October 16, 2013, 17–18.

Several of the Grahams' five children have been prolific writers. Gigi and Ruth (nicknamed "Bunny") have written extensively about their childhood memories. See these books by Gigi Graham (some published as Gigi Graham Tchividjian): *Thank You, Lord, for My Home* (Milwaukee: Ideals, 1979); *Passing It On: Four Generations of Graham Traditions* (New York: McCracken, 1993); (with her mother) *Mothers Together* (Grand Rapids: Baker Books, 1998); and *Coffee and Conversation with Ruth Bell Graham and GiGi Graham Tchividjian* (Carmel, NY: Guideposts, 1997).

See these books by Ruth "Bunny" Graham with Stacy Mattingly: *In Every Pew Sits a Broken Heart: Hope for the Hurting* (Grand Rapids: Zondervan, 2004), and *A Legacy of Faith: Things I Learned from My Father, Billy Graham* (Grand Rapids: Zondervan, 2006).

For his part, Franklin Graham, in *Rebel with a Cause: Finally Comfortable Being Graham* (Nashville: Nelson, 1995), recounts some of his and his mother's best tussles. On Franklin, see also Tim Funk, "Did Billy Graham's Wife Shape Their Son Franklin More Than He Did?" *Charlotte Observer*, June 27, 2017.

Other materials have helped me understand details of the children's biographies, including occasional scandals involving them: Mark Barrett, "Overcoming Struggles, Billy Graham's Children Are Rooted in Ministry Today," *Asheville (NC) Citizen-Times*, February 25, 2018, https://www.citi zen-times.com/story/news/local/2018/02/25/overcoming-struggles-billy -grahams-children-rooted-ministry-today/360965002/; on Gigi's children, see Purvette A. Bryant, "Daughter of a Preacher Man," *South Florida Sun-Sentinel*, July 16, 2000, https://www.sun-sentinel.com/news/fl-xpm-2000 -07-16-0007180302-story.html; see also Purvette A. Bryant, "GiGi's Message," *Orlando Sentinel*, June 25, 2000, http://articles.orlandosentinel .com/2000-06-25/news/0006210061_1_tchividjian-family-heirloom -grandchildren/3. A rather florid account of Gigi's 2005 arrest for domestic violence appears at *Smoking Gun*, July 6, 2005, http://www.thesmokinggun .com/documents/crime/billy-grahams-daughter-arrested. A preacher in his own right, Gigi's son Tullian was also spotlighted by Timothy C. Morgan, "Tullian Tchividjian Files for Divorce," *Christianity Today*, August 22, 2015, https://www.christianitytoday.com/news/2015/august/tullian-tchividjian -files-for-divorce.html.

A video at https://www.youtube.com/watch?v=-_hcGnOCa68&list=PL yJvcaWGmvD1O7ZrdsqI3094csWRK8O29&index=15&t=0s shows Anne Graham Lotz describing how she met Danny Lotz. His account, "My Life with Anne Graham Lotz," is at Christian Headlines, September 6, 2002, https://www.christianheadlines.com/articles/my-life-with-anne-graham -lotz-1163200.html; part 2 of this feature focuses on Graham Lotz's evange-listic work and is entitled "Part 2: Anne Graham Lotz Begins Her Ministry," Christian Headlines, September 7, 2002, https://www.christianheadlines .com/news/part-2-anne-graham-lotz-begins-her-ministry-1163198.html.

The founding of Ned Graham's East Gates Ministries is described in an unsigned article titled "Ministerial Oversight?" *World Magazine*, Novem-ber 6, 1999, https://world.wng.org/1999/11/ministerial_oversight. Ned's 1999 divorce and admissions of substance abuse received coverage by Tony

Carnes and Art Moore, "Ned Graham's Woes Shake East Gates," *Christianity Today*, December 6, 1999, https://www.christianitytoday.com/ct/1999/december6/9te026.html.

An article by Billy Graham biographer William Martin and published after the evangelist's death explores the children's and grandchildren's various challenges: "Divorce, Drugs, Drinking: Billy Graham's Children and Their Absent Father," *Washington Post*, February 21, 2018, https://www.washingtonpost.com/news/acts-of-faith/wp/2018/02/21/divorce-drugs-drinking-billy-grahams-children-and-their-absent-father/.

China was where Ruth's story began. I drew on a multitude of sources to help me understand the American missionary experience of China in the early twentieth century, including John Bray, "Christian Missionary Enterprise and Tibetan Trade," *Tibet Journal Special Issue — Trade, Travel, and the Tibetan Border Worlds* 39, no. 1 (Spring-Summer 2014): 13–39, especially p. 20; G. Thompson Brown, *Earthen Vessels and Transcendent Power: American Presbyterians in China, 1837–1952* (New York: Orbis, 1997); Sophie Montgomery Crane, "A Century of PCUS Medical Mission, 1881–1983," *American Presbyterians* 65, no. 2 (Summer 1987): 135–46; Jane Hunter, *The Gospel of Gentility: American Women Missionaries in Turn-of-the-Century China* (New Haven: Yale University Press, 1984); Philip Jowett, *Chinese Warlord Armies, 1911–1930*, illustrated by Stephen Walsh (New York: Osprey, 2010); Larry S. Milner, *Hardness of Heart/Hardness of Life: The Stain of Human Infanticide* (Lanham, MD: University Press of America, 2000); Helen Barrett Montgomery, *Western Women in Eastern Lands: An Outline Study of Fifty Years of Woman's Work in Foreign Missions* (New York: Macmillan, 1910), available online at https://go-gale-com.ezproxy.lib.davidson.edu/ps/i.do?p=NCCO&id=GALE%7CAUXXAB973028742&v=2.1&it=r&sid=SERVICE_ID&userGroupName=nclivedc&u=nclivedc; D. E. Mungello, *Drowning Girls in China: Female Infanticide Since 1650* (Lanham, MD: Rowman & Littlefield, 2008); P. Frank Price, *Our China Investment: Sixty Years of the Southern Presbyterian Church in China with Biographies, Autobiographies, and Sketches of All Missionaries Since the Opening of the Work in 1867* (Nashville: Educational Department, Executive Committee of Foreign Missions, [1927?]); and Ann Waltner, "Infanticide and Dowry in Min and Early Qing

China," in *Chinese Views of Childhood*, ed. Anne Behnke Kinney (Honolulu: University of Hawaii Press, 1995). Ruth herself read Edgar Snow, *Red China Today*, rev. ed. (New York: Random House, 1970). Some information and photographs from Ruth's later travels to China can be found in Edward E. Plowman, *Billy Graham in China* (Minneapolis: BGEA, 1988).

Several resources helped me contextualize the Bell family's experiences in Tsingkiangpu and Shanghai, China, and Pyeng Yang, Korea: Donald N. Clark, *Living Dangerously in Korea: The Western Experience, 1900–1950* (Norwalk, CT: EastBridge, 2003); Clark includes Virginia Bell Somerville's own account of evacuating Pyeng Yang abruptly in November 1940; Li Ma, *Christian Women and Modern China: Recovering a Women's History of Chinese Protestantism* (Lanham, MD: Lexington Books, 2021), especially chapters 1–4. Some information about Ruth's years in Pyeng Yang appears in Will Ripley, "Billy Graham's North Korea Legacy: From 'Witch Doctor' to Honored Guest," CNN Wire Service, February 28, 2018. See also *Encyclopedia Britannica Online*, s.v. "Second Sino-Japanese War," accessed November 10, 2020, https://www.britannica.com/event/Second-Sino-Japanese-War; and maps showing territories controlled by various warlord factions, one from 1925, at Wikipedia, s.v. "Warlord Era," last edited September 19, 2021, https://en.wikipedia.org/wiki/Warlord_Era; and another from 1928 at "China History Map — Warlords 1928," Global Security, accessed October 29, 2021, https://www.globalsecurity.org/military/world/china/images/map-1928-warlords.jpg. The Moore Memorial Church in Shanghai is described at "Mu'en Church in Shanghai," China Culture, accessed October 29, 2021, http://en.chinaculture.org/library/2008-02/04/content_25619.htm.

Encyclopedia Britannica Online also helped me understand the Pinyin and Wade-Giles transcription systems for Chinese: s.v. "Pinyin Romanization," accessed July 6, 2020, https://www.britannica.com/topic/Pinyin-romanization, and s.v. "Wade-Giles Romanization," accessed July 6, 2020, https://www.britannica.com/topic/Wade-Giles-romanization. A helpful resource for identifying Chinese city names in both systems is "Romanisation of Chinese Names," Alpha History, accessed November 1, 2021, https://alphahistory.com/chineserevolution/romanisation/. A "Map of Korea Missions," dated 1984 but likely from the early twentieth century,

is available in the Pearl Digital Collections of the Presbyterian Historical Society, https://digital.history.pcusa.org/islandora/object/islandora
%3A136?solr_nav%5Bid%5D=705363e4ee51ff7fe224&solr_nav%5Bpage
%5D=0&solr_nav%5Boffset%5D=0.

Information on specific missionaries sent by the Presbyterian Church in
the United States is found at https://www.phcmontreat.org/bios/Bios-Mis
sionaries-China-1900-1920-PCUS.htm. See the online *Biographical Dictionary of Chinese Christianity* for an article on Virginia Bell: http://bdcconline
.net/en/stories/bell-virginia-leftwich.

General sources on Protestant missions include R. Pierce Beaver, *American Protestant Women in World Mission: A History of the First Feminist Movement in North America* (Grand Rapids: Eerdmans, 1968); Patricia R. Hill,
*The World Their Household: The American Woman's Foreign Mission Movement
and Cultural Transformation, 1870–1920* (Ann Arbor: University of Michigan
Press, 1985); and David A. Hollinger, *Protestants Abroad: How Missionaries
Tried to Change the World but Changed America* (Princeton: Princeton University Press, 2017).

Sources on Southern Presbyterians and their missions include Joel Alvis
Jr., *Religion and Race: Southern Presbyterians, 1946–1983* (Tuscaloosa: Uni-
versity of Alabama Press, 1994); *The Book of Church Order of the Presbyterian
Church in the United States*, rev. ed. (Richmond, VA: Presbyterian Committee
of Publication, 1933); Lois A. Boy and R. Douglas Brackenridge, *Presbyte-
rian Women in America: Two Centuries of a Quest for Status* (Westport, CT:
Greenwood, 1983), especially chapter 10, "Women in Missions: Entering
Church Professions"; Frederick J. Heuser Jr., "Culture, Feminism, and the
Gospel: American Presbyterian Women and Foreign Missions, 1870–1923"
(PhD diss., Temple University, 1991); Mary D. Irvine and Alice L. East-
wood, *Pioneer Women of the Presbyterian Church, United States* (Richmond,
VA: Presbyterian Committee of Publication, 1923); Lawrence D. Kessler,
*The Jiangyin Mission Station: An American Missionary Community in China,
1895–1951* (Chapel Hill: University of North Carolina Press, 1996), especially
chapter 5, "This Precocious Child: Response to Chinese Nationalism"; Bradley J. Longfield, *Presbyterians and American Culture: A History* (Louisville:
Westminster John Knox, 2013); *Our Church Faces Foreign Missions: A Compre-*

hensive Study by the Southern Presbyterian Church of Her Own Foreign Mission Problems and Responsibilities (Nashville: Executive Committee of Foreign Missions, Presbyterian Church in the U.S. [1931]); Dana Robert, *American Women in Mission: A Social History of Their Thought and Practice* (Macon, GA: Mercer University Press, 1996); T. Watson Street, *The Story of Southern Presbyterians* (Richmond, VA: John Knox, 1960), especially chapter 5, "Desolations Repaired, 1865–1887"; and two items edited by my cousin Julia S. Worth: a collection of letters titled *Far & Away: Worth Family Letters from the Mission Field* (Wilmington, NC, 2011) and her father (and my uncle) Charles W. Worth's *Recollections of a Happy Life* (Wilmington, NC, 2011). On the Presbyterian Historical Society website are many useful resources about missions, notably: Deana S., "Presbyterian Women: Then and Now," July 14, 2015; and a historical overview of medical missions in China in the "Western Medicine in China" online subject guide. "China: The Bell Clan Takes a Sentimental Journey," *Christianity Today*, June 27, 1980, 50, offers a report on the trip Ruth made with her sisters and brother to their childhood home.

Montreat's history is treated in several books: Robert Campbell Anderson, *The Story of Montreat from Its Beginning, 1897–1947* (Montreat, NC, 1949); Calvin Grier Davis, *Montreat: A Retreat for Renewal, 1947–1972* (Kingsport, TN: Arcata Graphics, 1986); Henrietta Wilkinson and Bluford B. Hestir, *The First Chapter: Early Montreat Homes, 1897–1917* (Montreat, NC, 1997); and "The Montreat Gateboys and Their Stories," ed. Mary McPhail Standaert (Montreat, NC, 2013). For the Grove Park Inn, where Ruth and Bill spent the first night of their honeymoon, see Elizabeth Scheld Glynn, "Grove Park Inn," in *Encyclopedia of North Carolina*, ed. William S. Powell (Chapel Hill: University of North Carolina Press, 2006). A history of school desegregation in Buncombe County, where Montreat is located, is "With All Deliberate Speed: School Desegregation in Buncombe County," Center for Diversity Education, October 31, 2005.

An outline of the history of the institution now known as Montreat College can be found online at https://www.montreat.edu/about/history/. Additional information includes a brief account of the dedication of the Montreat College library, named for L. Nelson Bell, at https://www.montreat.edu/mymontreat/library/digital-archive/buildings/; and the architectural information about the Chapel of the Prodigal on the college's campus, at McCulloch England Architects, http://www.mccullochengland.com /projects/montreat-chapel-of-the-prodigal-son/ (all accessed November 1, 2021). Regarding the 2015 renaming of Gaither Chapel for the Grahams, see "Montreat College Announces the Naming of Graham Chapel," Montreat College, October 21, 2015, https://www.montreat.edu/2015/10/mon treat-college-announces-the-naming-of-graham-chapel-2/. Two email exchanges with Hope Deifell, administrative assistant to the college's chief advancement officer and advancement communications manager, clarified the term and duties of Ruth's service on the Montreat College Board of Trustees. Billy's office in Montreat is featured in a story by Kristy Etheridge, "'It Was a Joy to Support Him': Billy Graham's Executive Assistant Reflects on Decades of Service in Montreat, N.C.," Billy Graham Evangelistic Association, April 25, 2018, at https://billygraham.org/story/it-was-a-joy-to -support-him-billy-grahams-executive-assistant-reflects-on-life-in-mon treat-north-carolina/. David Bruce, the source of that report, very kindly showed me through the Grahams' original Assembly Drive home and the BGEA's offices in Montreat.

Wheaton College in Wheaton, Illinois, figures large in Ruth's story. The *Tower* yearbooks from 1938 through 1944 as well as the *Bulletin* of Wheaton College for the academic years 1936–1937 through 1942–1943 provided essential information about Ruth's studies and her involvement in campus life and gave me a feel for the rapidly changing campus of that period. The history of the college and its environs can be found in Edith L. Blumhofer, *A History of College Church in Wheaton: The First 150 Years* (Carol Stream, IL: Tyndale House, 2010); accounts of revivals at Wheaton by J. Edwin Orr, *This Is the Victory: 10,000 Miles of Victory in America* (London: Marshall, Morgan & Scott, 1936) and *Full Surrender*, with an introduction by Billy Graham (London: Marshall, Morgan & Scott, 1951); and W. Wyeth Willard, *Fire on the Prairie: The Story of Wheaton College* (Wheaton, IL: Van Kampen, 1950). An account of the origins and history of the Rural Bible Crusade, in which Ruth participated while a Wheaton student, is located online at https://bibleimpact.org/history/. The papers of Katherine Shapleigh, a former missionary to China who served as Wheaton's dean of women while Rosa and Ruth were students, are held in Special Collections at Yale University Divinity School; relevant biographical information appears in the online finding aid at https://archives.yale.edu/repositories/4/resources /134?stylename=yul.ead2002.xhtml.xsl&pid=divinity:176&query=&clear -stylesheet-cache=yes&hlon=yes&big=&adv=&filter=&hitPageStart=&s ortFields=&view=c01_3. Edith Torrey's presence among Wheaton College faculty is mentioned in Kaitlin Liebling, "At Wheaton, Female Bible Profs Carry on a Long and Controversial Tradition," *Wheaton Record*, April 17, 2021, https://thewheatonrecord.com/2021/04/17/female-bith-profs-long -controversial-tradition/.

Although Ruth did not identify herself as a feminist — and indeed, was "no women's libber," according to one news report — the following sources have helped me understand the feminist movement she and others of her day rejected. Moreover, these sources have helped me, I hope, approach Ruth as one of a generation of white Protestant women in the South who was as educated and ambitious as any self-identified feminists, yet conse-crated that education and ambition to homemaking and child rearing. Fam-ily work was a Christian vocation for Ruth, although it is true that white patriarchal culture also expected that work of her. See Margaret Lamberts Bendroth, *Fundamentalism and Gender, 1875 to the Present* (New Haven: Yale University Press, 1996); Bendroth also wrote for *Religious Studies News* an excellent account and appreciation of Nancy A. Hardesty's life and work, "In Memoriam: Nancy A. Hardesty, 1941–April 8, 2011," http://rsnonline .org/indexab74.html?option=com_content; the Council on Biblical Man-hood and Womanhood website, including the 1987 Danvers Statement, at https://cbmw.org/; Donald T. Critchlow, *Phyllis Schlafly and Grassroots Con-servatism* (Princeton: Princeton University Press, 2005); Amy DeRogatis, "What Would Jesus Do? Sexuality and Salvation in Protestant Evangelical Sex Manuals, 1950s to the Present," *Church History* 74, no. 1 (March 2005): 97–137; Carol Felsenthal, *The Sweetheart of the Silent Majority: The Biography of Phyllis Schlafly* (New York: Doubleday, 1981); Betty Friedan, "The Prob-lem That Has No Name," in *The Feminine Mystique*, with an introduction by Anna Quindlen (New York: Norton, 2001), 15–32; R. Marie Griffith, *God's Daughters: Evangelical Women and the Power of Submission* (Berkeley:

University of California Press, 1997); Karen Halttunen, *Confidence Men and Painted Women: A Study of Middle-Class Culture in America, 1830–1870* (New Haven: Yale University Press, 1986); Carolyn Heilbrun, *Writing a Woman's Life* (New York: Norton, 1988); bell hooks, *Feminism Is for Everybody: Passionate Politics*, 2nd ed. (New York: Routledge, 2014); Emily Suzanne Johnson, *This Is Our Message: Women's Leadership in the New Christian Right* (New York: Oxford University Press, 2019); Amy Schrager Lang, *Anne Hutchinson and the Problem of Dissent in the Literature of New England* (Berkeley: University of California Press, 1987); Phyllis Mack, "Religion, Feminism, and the Problem of Agency: Reflections on Eighteenth-Century Quakerism," *Signs* 29, no. 1 (2003): 149–77; Marabel Morgan, *The Total Woman* (Old Tappan, NJ: Revell, 1973); Jeannette L. Nolen, "Learned Helplessness," in *Encyclopedia Britannica*, December 28, 2017, https://www.britannica.com/science /learned-helplessness; Phyllis Schlafly, *A Choice Not an Echo* (Alton, IL: Pere Marquette Press, n.d.); Quincy Newell, "Black History Month at the JI: Talking about Jane (Newell)," *Juvenile Instructor: Organ for Young Latter-day Scholars*, February 19, 2013; Letha Dawson Scanzoni and Nancy A. Hardesty, *All We're Meant to Be: A Biblical Approach to Women's Liberation* (Waco, TX: Word, 1975); Joan Scott, "Afterword: Feminism's History," in *The Feminist History Reader*, ed. Sue Morgan (New York: Routledge, 2006); Linda Wagner-Martin, *Telling Women's Lives: The New Biography* (New Brunswick, NJ: Rutgers University Press, 1994); and Rose Weitz, "Feminist Consciousness Raising, Self-Concept, and Depression," *Sex Roles* 8, no. 3 (1982): 231–41.

On marriage and family particularly, multiple sources provided background for situating the Grahams in the larger American landscape and the specific views of evangelicals: Stephanie Coontz, *Marriage, a History: How Love Conquered Marriage* (New York: Penguin, 2006) and *The Way We Never Were: American Families and the Nostalgia Trap* (New York: Basic Books, 1992); Nancy Cott, *Public Vows: A History of Marriage and the Nation* (Cambridge, MA: Harvard University Press, 2000); Seth Dowland, *Family Values and the Rise of the Christian Right* (Philadelphia: University of Pennsylvania Press, 2015); David Goodman, *A Parents' Guide to the Emotional Needs of Children* (New York: Hawthorn Books, 1959) and *What's Best for*

Your Child — and You (New York: YMCA Press, 1966); William J. Lederer and Don D. Jackson, MD, *The Mirages of Marriage* (New York: Norton, 1968); "Marriages: Trends and Characteristics, United States," Data from the National Vital Statistics System, ser. 21, no. 21 (Rockville, MD: National Center for Health Statistics, 1971; reprinted 1980), online at https://www.cdc.gov/nchs/data/series/sr_21/sr21_021.pdf; Elaine Tyler May, *Homeward Bound: American Families in the Cold War Era* (New York: Basic Books, 1988); Samira K. Mehta, "Family Planning Is a Christian Duty: Religion, Population Control, and the Pill in the 1960s," in *Devotions and Desires: Histories of Sexuality and Religion in the Twentieth-Century United States*, ed. Gillian Frank, Bethany Moreton, and Heather R. White (Chapel Hill: University of North Carolina Press, 2018), 152–69; Thomas G. Power, "Parenting Dimensions and Styles: A Brief History and Recommendations for Future Research," *Childhood Obesity* 9, supplement 1 (August 2013): S-14–S-21; John R. Rice, DD, *Rebellious Wives and Slacker Husbands: What's Wrong with the Modern Home?* (Wheaton, IL: Sword of the Lord, 1943); and Charlie W. Shedd, *The Stork Is Dead* (Waco, TX: Word, 1968). Information about median age at first marriage can be found online at https://www.infoplease.com/us/family-statistics/median-age-first-marriage-1890-2010.

For information about the towns of Zellwood and Mount Dora, Florida, and Hampden Dubose Academy, I consulted the current website for the school, admittedly a limited source of information since it serves as a recruitment tool for prospective students. See https://www.hampdendubose academy.com/history for brief background. Two books by Gilbert King explore the violent white supremacist history of Mount Dora: *Devil in the Grove: Thurgood Marshall, the Groveland Boys, and the Dawn of a New America* (New York: HarperPerennial, 2013) and *Beneath a Ruthless Sun: A True Story of Violence, Race, and Justice Lost and Found* (New York: Riverhead Books, 2018). See also Sharon Mcbreen, "Dubose School Determined to Pass Tests of Time," *Orlando Sentinel*, December 24, 1989, https://www.orlandosen tinel.com/news/os-xpm-1989-12-24-8912223324-story.html. To clarify for myself the Graham children's secondary educational histories, I consulted years 1959–1962 of *Esse*, the yearbook of Hampden Dubose Academy; the 1965 edition of the *Black Swan* from Charles D. Owen High School in Asheville; and years 1968–1969 and 1977 of *Res Gestae*, yearbook of the Stony Brook (NY) School, all on the Classmates.com website.

Exploring the history of log cabins and how Ruth's house, Little Piney Cove, differed from what millions of Americans inhabited in the mid-twentieth century led me to a variety of sources: Dale L. Anderson, *The Log House in America: And the History and Preservation of the Lewis Anderson Homestead, Pleasant Ridge, Wasco County, Oregon* (Ft. Washington, MD: Silesia Companies, 2001); Clifford Edward Clark Jr., *The American Family Home, 1800–1960* (Chapel Hill: University of North Carolina Press, 1986); Andres Duany, Elizabeth Plater-Zyberk, and Jeff Speck, *Suburban Nation: The Rise of Sprawl and the Decline of the American Dream*, tenth anniversary ed. (New York: Farrar, Straus & Giroux, 2010); Emily J. Followill with Lisa Frederick, *The Southern Rustic Cabin* (Layton, UT: Gibbs Smith, 2015); Elizabeth Fraterrigo, "The Answer to Suburbia: *Playboy*'s Urban Lifestyle," *Journal of Urban History* 34, no. 5 (July 2008): 747–74; Steven Gelber, "Do-It-Yourself: Constructing, Repairing, and Maintaining Domestic Masculinity," *American Quarterly* 49 (March 1997): 66–112; Henry H. Glassie, "Southern Mountain Houses: A Study in American Folk Culture" (master's thesis, State University of New York College at Oneonta, 1965); Lesley Jackson, *Contemporary: Architecture and Interiors of the 1950s* (New York: Phaidon, 1998); David B. Kaufman, "Log Cabins — Their History and Description," *Tulpehocken Settlement Historical Society* 16 (November 1984); Barbara M. Kelly, *Expanding the American Dream: Building and Rebuilding Levittown* (Albany: State University of New York Press, 1993); *Log Cabins of the Blue Ridge Parkway* (Belcher, KY: Belcher Foundation, 2005); Henry C. Mercer, *The Origin of Log Houses in the United States* (Doylestown, PA: Bucks County Historical Society, 1976); Sarah Smith Nester, "The History & Intrigue of the Appalachian Log Home," *Smoky Mountain Living*, December 1, 2011; Joel Sanders, ed., *Stud: Architectures of Masculinity* (New York: Princeton Architectural Press, 1996); and C. A. Weslager, *The Log Cabin in America: From Pioneer Days to the Present* (New Brunswick, NJ: Rutgers University Press, 1969).

On background for the National Prayer Breakfast, see Gregory Korte, "How Presidents Pray: The Prayer Breakfast from Eisenhower to Obama,"

USA Today, February 4, 2016, https://www.usatoday.com/story/news/poli
tics/theoval/2016/02/04/how-presidents-pray-prayer-breakfast-eisenhower
-obama/79786384/; Kevin Kruse, *One Nation under God: How Corporate
America Invented Christian America* (New York: Basic Books, 2015); and
Diane Winston, "The History of the National Prayer Breakfast," *Smithsonian*, February 2, 2017, https://www.smithsonianmag.com/history/national
-prayer-breakfast-what-does-its-history-reveal-180962017/. The agreement
that Ruth refused to sign at the first Lausanne meeting can be found at "The
Lausanne Covenant," Lausanne Movement website, accessed November 1,
2021, https://lausanne.org/content/covenant/lausanne-covenant#cov; the
offending passage about "a simple life-style" appears in section 9, "The Urgency of the Evangelistic Task."

Billy Graham famously cultivated US presidents, or at least tried to.
Ruth participated in these relationships to varying degrees. The literature
on Billy Graham and the presidents and certain world leaders is sizable. In
keeping my focus on Ruth, I have drawn on only a portion of these sources.
Indispensable for accounts of the Grahams' relationship with Presidents
Truman, Johnson, Nixon, and Carter is Nancy Gibbs and Michael Duffy,
The Preacher and the Presidents: Billy Graham in the White House (New York:
Center Street, 2007), especially chapters 2–3; 6; 12; and 24–25. On Harry S.
Truman, see also Chuck Raasch, "When Harry Met Billy: The Beginning
of the Rev. Graham's Presidential Relationships," *St. Louis Post-Dispatch*,
February 28, 2018, https://www.stltoday.com/news/local/govt-and
-politics/when-harry-met-billy-the-beginning-of-the-rev-graham/article
_d35fd86b-4989-54b9-a0e3-fc407ff57d67.html.

Video of Nixon's first and second inauguration ceremonies is available
on C-SPAN.org. Billy offered one of the prayers at Nixon's 1969 inauguration; the Reverend E. V. Hill, a Graham surrogate, prayed the invocation in
1973, and Hill's obituary provides a useful portrait: see Larry B. Stammer,
"E. V. Hill, 69; Longtime L.A. Pastor Was National Civil Rights, Religious
Leader," *Los Angeles Times*, February 26, 2003. On the Grahams' friendship
with the Nixons, see R. W. Apple Jr., "Nixon Inaugurated. For His Second
Term; Sees World on Threshold of a Peace Era," *New York Times*, January 21,
1973, https://www.nytimes.com/1973/01/21/archives/nixon-inaugura-ted

-for-his-second-term-sees-world-on-threshold-of-a.html. I used captions from several news images on the Getty website to understand the timeline of Richard Nixon's hospitalizations in the fall of 1974; see https://www.getty images.com/detail/news-photo/long-beach-ca-former-president-richard -nixon-still-in-a-news-photo/515354444 and https://www.gettyimages.com /detail/news-photo/file-photo-dated-of-dr-eldon-hickman-left-and-dr -john-news-photo/569110017. I also referred to Nixon's own account of the Graham relationship: *In the Arena: A Memoir of Victory, Defeat, and Renewal* (New York: Simon & Schuster, 1990).

Gerald Ford's appearance at the 1975 Meck Dec celebration received coverage in "Ford's Visit: A Spirited Picnic of a Day," *Charlotte Observer,* May 21, 1975, 1A, 10A; Ruth's actions toward the protestor are reported by Fran Schumer, "Mrs. Billy Graham Grabs, Keeps Demonstrator's Sign," *Charlotte Observer,* May 21, 1975, 1A, 10A.

Some information about Carter and disarmament is in a memoir written by Carter's secretary of defense: Harold Brown with Joyce Winslow, *Star Spangled Security: Applying Lessons Learned over Six Decades Safeguarding America* (Washington, DC: Brookings, 2012), 104–7. On the Grahams and disarmament, see also "A Change of Heart: Billy Graham on the Nuclear Arms Race," *Sojourners,* August 1979, https://sojo.net/magazine/august-1979/change -heart. For background on the nuclear strategy of mutually assured destruction, see *Encyclopedia Britannica Online,* s.v. "Strategy in the Age of Nuclear Weapons," accessed November 1, 2021, https://www.britannica.com/topic /strategy-military/Strategy-in-the-age-of-nuclear-weapons#ref968731; and s.v. "Anti-Ballistic Missile Treaty," accessed November 1, 2021, https://www .britannica.com/event/Anti-Ballistic-Missile-Treaty#ref940546.

Some background and information on other international issues the Grahams addressed are found in "Billy Graham in South Africa," *Charlotte Observer,* March 23, 1973, 18A; John S. Bowman, *The Vietnam War: An Almanac* (New York: World Almanac Publications, 1985); Bethany Moreton, *To Serve God and Wal-Mart: The Making of Christian Free Enterprise* (Cambridge, MA: Harvard University Press, 2009); and Jennifer Robison, "Decades of Drug Use: Data from the '60s and '70s," Gallup, July 2, 2002, https://news .gallup.com/poll/6331/decades-drug-use-data-from-60s-70s.aspx.

Sources that have helped me characterize Ruth's opinions of or relationships with people of note not already listed above include the four chapters by Aleksandr Solzhenitsyn included in *From under the Rubble*, with an introduction by Max Hayward, trans. under the direction of Michael Scammell (Boston: Little, Brown, 1975) and Solzhenitsyn's *The Gulag Archipelago, 1918–1956: An Experiment in Literary Investigation*, trans. Thomas P. Whitney, vols. 3–4 (New York: Harper & Row, 1975). On Johnny Cash, see Leigh Edwards, *Johnny Cash and the Paradox of American Identity* (Bloomington: Indiana University Press, 2009), especially chapter 4, "Race and Identity Politics."

Ruth befriended many incarcerated people. For information on her friendship with Velma Barfield, see Velma Barfield, *Woman on Death Row* (Minneapolis: Worldwide Publications, 1985); Jerry Bledsoe, *Death Sentence: The True Story of Velma Barfield's Life, Crimes, and Execution* (New York: Diversion Books, 1998); "Mourners Recall Executed Woman's Faith in the Lord," *Asheville (NC) Citizen-Times*, November 4, 1984, 32; and William E. Schmidt, "First Woman Is Executed in U.S. Since 1962," *New York Times*, November 3, 1984, https://timesmachine.nytimes.com/timesmachine/1984/11/03/057375.html?action=click&contentCollection=Archives&module=LedeAsset&region=ArchiveBody&pgtype=article&pageNumber=46.

For Ruth's friendship with Edgar Smith, see "Death Row Author Confesses Slaying after 20 Years," *Asheville (NC) Citizen*, March 30, 1977, 12; David Stout, "Edgar Smith, Killer Who Duped William F. Buckley, Dies at 83," *New York Times*, September 24, 2017, https://www.nytimes.com/2017/09/24/nyregion/edgar-smith-killer-who-duped-william-f-buckley-dies-at-83.html.

On Ruth's friendship with Jim Vaus Jr., see Lois Ferm's interview with Vaus, May 26, 1976, formerly located at https://www2.wheaton.edu/bgc/archives/exhibits/LA49/09memories11.html.

Context for Ruth's views on the death penalty and criminal justice comes from Sarah Pulliam Bailey, "The National Association of Evangelicals Has Changed Its Position on the Death Penalty," *Washington Post*, October 19, 2015, https://www.washingtonpost.com/news/acts-of-faith/wp/2015/10/19/the-national-association-of-evangelicals-has-changed-its-position-on-the-death-penalty/; Aaron Griffith, *God's Law and Order: The Politics of Punishment in Evangelical America* (Cambridge, MA: Harvard

University Press, 2020); and National Association of Evangelicals, "Capital Punishment 1972," National Association of Evangelicals, accessed November 1, 2021, https://www.nae.net/capital-punishment-1972/. See also resources on the website of the Death Penalty Information Center: "Countries That Have Abolished the Death Penalty Since 1976" and "Abolitionist and Retentionist Countries." For context on Ruth's views about pornography, including the legal background of the Supreme Court case regarding Fanny Hill's memoirs, see *Book Named "John Cleland's Memoirs of a Woman of Pleasure" v. Attorney General of Mass.*, 383 U.S. 413 (1966); Ruth Graham (no relation), "How 'Fanny Hill' Stopped the Literary Censors," *Boston Globe*, July 7, 2013, https://www.bostonglobe.com/ideas/2013/07/06/how-fanny -hill-stopped-literary-censors/YEx9KPuHMv5O5avhB87MeI/story.html; and Simon Stern, s.v. "Fanny Hill," *The First Amendment Encyclopedia*, 2009, https://www.mtsu.edu/first-amendment/article/808/fanny-hill.

On details large and small at the Cove, see "About Us," Chatlos Foundation Inc. website, https://chatlos.org/about-us/; and Daniel A. Gross, "The Lazy Susan, the Classic Centerpiece of Chinese Restaurants, Is Neither Classic Nor Chinese," *Smithsonian Magazine*, February 21, 2014, https://www .smithsonianmag.com/arts-culture/lazy-susan-classic-centerpiece-chinese -restaurants-neither-classic-nor-chinese-180949844/. Coverage on the 2016 dedication of "Ruth's Prayer Garden" at the Cove is at https://www.wcnc .com/article/life/ruth-graham-legacy-lives-on-at-the-cove/239743959 and https://mountainx.com/blogwire/newly-installed-prayer-garden-in-honor -of-ruth-bell-graham-dedicated-at-the-cove/, both accessed June 17, 2020. See also "Saturday Snapshot — Ruth's Prayer Garden Dedication," Billy Graham Training Center at the Cove website, accessed July 1, 2021, https:// thecove.org/blog/saturday-snapshot-ruths-prayer-garden-dedication/.

Tracking the books and authors that influenced Ruth led me to these sources: R. Bruce Bickley, "Joel Chandler Harris (1845–1908)," *New Georgia Encyclopedia*, December 2, 2019; Amy Carmichael, *Rose from Briar: Letters Written to the Dohnavur Fellowship Invalids' League* (London: n.p., 1950) and *Gold by Moonlight: A Dohnavur Book* (London: Society for Promoting Christian Knowledge, 1952); Robert Cochran, "Black Father: The Subversive Achievement of Joel Chandler Harris," *African American Review* 38, no. 1 (2004): 21–34; Thomas Dixon Jr., *The Clansman: An Historical Romance of the*

Ku Klux Klan (New York: Doubleday, Page & Co., 1905); Elsie E. Egermeier, *Stories of Great Men and Women: Stories for Boys and Girls*, rev. ed. (Anderson, IN: Warner, 1961) and *Bible Story Book: A Complete Narration from Genesis to Revelation for Young and Old*, new and rev. ed. (Anderson, IN: Warner, 1947); Elisabeth Elliot, *A Chance to Die: The Life and Legacy of Amy Carmichael* (Grand Rapids: Revell, 1987); Armistead Lemon, "Summary of Uncle Remus, His Songs and His Sayings: The Folk-Lore of the Old Plantation. By Joel Chandler Harris. With Illustrations by Frederick S. Church and James H. Moser. New York: D. Appleton and Company, 1881," Documenting the American South, accessed November 1, 2021, https://docsouth.unc.edu/southlit/harris /summary.html; *George MacDonald: An Anthology*, ed. C. S. Lewis (New York: Macmillan, 1947); George MacDonald, *The Princess and the Goblin* (New York: Dutton, 1949); Jane Merchant, *In Green Pastures* (Nashville: Abingdon, 1959) and *Think about These Things* (Nashville: Abingdon, 1956); G. H. Morling, *The Quest for Serenity*, with notes and commentary by Ruth Bell Graham (Dallas: Word, 1989); Sarah Jorunn Oftedal, *A Window on Eternity: The Life and Poetry of Jane Hess Merchant* (Nashville: Abingdon, 1989); William Raeper, *George MacDonald* (Batavia, IL: Lion, 1987); Richard Reis, *George MacDonald* (New York: Twayne, 1972); and John William Tebbel, *A History of Book Publishing in the United States*, vol. 4 (New York: R. R. Bowker, 1972).

The ceremony during which Ruth and Billy Graham received the Congressional Gold Medal on May 2, 1996, can be viewed on the C-SPAN.org website. The reading offered by North Carolina senator Lauch Faircloth differs slightly from the text of the act awarding the medal, HR 2657 (104th Congress), available on the Congress.gov website.

Many generous people — family, friends, or associates of Ruth — were kind enough to share with me their knowledge and memories about her, through in-person interviews, telephone conversations, email exchanges, or a combination of all three: Andy Basinger, Peggy (Mrs. Clayton) Bell, David Bruce, Leighton and Jean Ford, Evelyn Freeland, Chris Garborg, Jill Gottenstrater, Gigi Graham, Ruth ("Bunny") Graham, Stephen Griffith, David Jarzyna, Jerry and Dee Miller, Marilee Melvin, Robert Montgomery, Maury Scobee, Walter Somerville, John Stoll, Dorothy Thielman, Erin Somerville Thielman, Richard Jesse Watson, and Alexander W. Whitaker IV.

Index

Fletcher, Lucy
  abandoned baby incident, 33
  mentioned in correspondence, 26
  at Ruth's Pyeng Yang enrollment, 41
  Tsingkiangpu teaching assignment,
    28–29, 38–39, 40, 192
Footprints of a Pilgrim (play), 67, 69, 220
Ford, Gerald, 173, 174–75
Ford, Leighton, 216
Foreign Missions Fellowship (FMF), 62
Foreman, Chad, 123
Foster Hartley, Shirley, 5, 6
Frady, Marshall, 186
Freeland, Evelyn, 196, 211
Friedan, Betty, 96, 180–81
Frist, Betty, 105–6, 108, 111–12, 119
From under the Rubble (Solzhenitsyn
  et al.), 199

Gaillard, Frye, 185–86, 187, 197
Garborg, Chris, 207
Geiser, Ken, 58
gender roles, midcentury American
  views on
  Bill's opposition to, 69, 72, 79, 148
  education and careers, 125
  expectations of pastors' wives, 5–6, 138
  feminist movement and (*see* femi-
    nism, second-wave)
  learned helplessness and, 142
  missionary contexts and, 11–12,
    17–18, 21, 36, 68
  modesty and femininity in, 94–95
  Ruth's navigation of (*see* Graham,
    Ruth Bell, perspective on Chris-
    tian womanhood)
  "sexual containment," 125
  stay-at-home motherhood, 92–93
  two-person careers, 82

Gibbs, Nancy, 162, 198
"Gift" (Ruth Bell Graham), 47
Gingrich, Newt, 217
Glassie, Henry, 108, 111
Glendinning, Victoria, 4
Good Earth, The (Buck), 141
Goodman, David, 124–25, 126
"good sense," 151
Gore, Al, 217
Graham, Anne McCue. *See* Lotz,
  Anne Graham (daughter)
Graham, Billy
  aesthetic preferences, 113
  Jim Bakker encouraged by, 214, 215
  burial site and grave marker, 224,
    225, 226, 229–30
  college relationships, 68–69
  Congressional Medal of Honor
    awarded to, 216–19
  courtship and early tensions with
    Ruth, 69–71, 72, 73, 74
  death, 229
  denominational affiliation, 83
  Edith Torrey's prayers for, 58
  faith and practice, 142, 229–30
  fatherhood, 94, 114, 131, 137, 150
  health, 86–87, 222
  "Man of the South" award, 175
  marriage to Ruth, 12, 74, 80 (*see
    also* Graham, Ruth and Bill, life
    together)
  Wheaton enrollment, 64
Graham, Billy, ministry career of
  absence from family, 81, 87–88, 94,
    169–70
  army chaplain post, 86
  criticized for Ruth's Presbyterian
    affiliation, 85, 98

Titles published in the

LIBRARY OF RELIGIOUS BIOGRAPHY SERIES

A Heart Lost in Wonder: The Life and Faith of Gerard Manley Hopkins
by Catharine Randall

Sworn on the Altar of God: A Religious Biography of Thomas Jefferson
by Edwin S. Gaustad

*The Miracle Lady: Katherine Kuhlman and
the Transformation of Charismatic Christianity*
by Amy Collier Artman

Abraham Kuyper: Modern Calvinist, Christian Democrat
by James D. Bratt

The Religious Life of Robert E. Lee
by R. David Cox

Abraham Lincoln: Redeemer President
by Allen C. Guelzo

*Charles Lindbergh:
A Religious Biography of America's Most Infamous Pilot*
by Christopher Gehrz

The First American Evangelical: A Short Life of Cotton Mather
by Rick Kennedy

Aimee Semple McPherson: Everybody's Sister
by Edith L. Blumhofer

*Mother of Modern Evangelicalism:
The Life and Legacy of Henrietta Mears*
by Arlin Migliazzo

Damning Words: The Life and Religious Times of H. L. Mencken
by D. G. Hart

Thomas Merton and the Monastic Vision
by Lawrence S. Cunningham

God's Strange Work: William Miller and the End of the World
by David L. Rowe

Blaise Pascal: Reasons of the Heart
by Marvin R. O'Connell

Occupy Until I Come: A. T. Pierson and the Evangelization of the World
by Dana L. Robert